The Emperor
of
Ice-Cream

Gary M. Almeter

The Emperor
of
Ice-Cream

Gary M. Almeter

Attention schools and businesses: for discounted copies on large orders, please contact the publisher directly.

For information contact:
Unsolicited Press
Portland, Oregon
www.unsolicitedpress.com
orders@unsolicitedpress.com
619-354-8005

Cover Design: Andrew Almeter
Author Photo: Rachel Rock Palermo
Editor: Chandler S. White

ISBN: 978-1-947021-82-2

"For Grandpa A., whose memory, sweet tooth gene, and genuine goodness all live on."

Contents

Tell me what did you learn
From the Tillamook burn?
Or the Fourth of July?
We're all gonna die.

—Sufjan Stevens, from *Fourth of July*

Tell me:
Which is the way I take;
Out of what door do I go,
Where and to whom?

A lively understandable spirit
Once entertained you.
It will come again.
Be still.
Wait.

—Theodore Roethke, from *The lost son.*

And so the days pass
and so we drift and dawdle.
Bright stood the mountains
brighter loomed the sea
And so the nights go
And so we flash and fade.
Green lay the hills,
greener a river evening.
Stones wore gray lichen
and trees a morn mist.
And so the bold be gone
and so the harm be ashes.
First moved the moonrise.
Later dropped the moondown.
Handy showed the dawn.
Handydandy shown the sun

—Carl Sandburg, Harmonica Humdrums

Introduction

In Toni Cade Bambara's short story, "The Lesson," Miss Moore, the self-appointed advocate and teacher, asks the inner-city children she has commandeered and taken to F.A.O. Schwartz if they believe that "where we are is who we are." As a boy on a small dairy farm upstate, I often asked myself, albeit in different phrasings, the same thing. In endeavoring to answer the question, I often looked to my paternal grandfather (hereinafter "Grandpa") for answers. He was a perpetually happy man and I wondered why this was so with some frequency, as if I could not believe it, in light of the nature of farm work: the corrosive effect it has on a body, the malodorousness of it, the Sisyphusean nature of the endeavor, the arbitrariness of the diseases and bugs and locusts, the unreliability of the sun and the rain; in light of some of the hardships Grandpa endured, in light of the way he and Grandma were chronically frugal.

When you get to a point in your life when you want a more authentic understanding of who your grandparents are, you are likely at a point when you have lost them. Or are on the cusp of losing them. It takes a while—a couple decades really—to realize your grandparents are people too. It's astonishing and sad and ironic in so many ways. When you take your thumbnail and scratch a little beneath the surface—beneath the myth that surrounds a child's understanding of that myth as it takes hold of a family—you can see that grandparents are actual human beings. Complex, mercurial, whimsical, capricious, flawed, dynamic, interesting, and if you are lucky, genuinely likable people.

A ubiquitous anthem, upon which we frequently rely to justify whimsy or a splurge or humor or irresponsibility, is that life is short[1]. But life is actually quite long too. We are so many people in the course of a life - in all of our guises and circumstances and standings and conditions. Grandpa was a son, a brother, a husband, a father, a farmer, a grandfather, an executioner, a planter, a nurturer, a mechanic, a widow, a worker, a patient, a doctor (bovine obstetrics a specialty), a trucker, a Catholic, a tourist. I too have been a son, a brother, a husband, a father, a planter, a doctor, and a worker, though a thoroughly reluctant one. Never a mechanic or a widower or a trucker. My experience with bovine obstetrics has been minimal. But some part of both of Grandpa and me is the same at various junctures.

But there are also fundamental differences between Grandpa and me. There are two types of people in the world, those who leave home and those who don't, and we fell into separate camps.[2] Grandpa never left his home and, as far as I could tell, never got to reinvent himself. Reinvention was important to me. There came a time when the streets and the sounds and the cadence and every single thing about my hometown started to feel oppressive. When I thought that if I have to navigate these roads one more time or have to wait at this traffic light or wait to turn left onto Route 20A or wait in line at the gas station convenience store while the cashier chatted inanely with the customer ahead of me about the Buffalo Bills or their heating bills or any other Bills like Clinton and Ray Cyrus, that I would just go fucking bonkers. I wondered if Grandpa ever felt that same way. How does one live on the same road for nearly eight decades and not go bonkers?

---

[1] "Life is short" originates from the *Aphorismi* by the ancient Greek physician Hippocrates. The first line of which reads: "Life is short, and Art long; the crisis fleeting; experience perilous, and decision difficult."
[2] Obviously each of those groups is further subdivided into those who drink Miller Lite because it tastes great and those who drink Miller Lite because it is less filling.

I was determined to not stay in the town where Grandpa and I lived. But then the day came when I was set to leave the hometown and I felt guilty for ever finding it oppressive and found myself wondering what life would be like if I stayed. It was Grandpa's town too and we both grew up in it, though separated by five and a half decades, and he had stayed and turned out great. So after college I moved to Boston and then to New York City and then to Baltimore. I had a Bachelor's Degree and got a Master's Degree and a Law Degree.

But even if where we are is not necessarily who we are, the where-we-have-been remains a part of us. And to be authentic a person has to learn how to embrace this. If *embracing* isn't your thing that's okay; but you must at least need to get some sort of grip on it.

This book is a memoir insofar as it tells the story of a man, or men, in the context of how their lives intersected. It is the culmination of decades of me writing stuff down in the various notebooks that I have carried with me since graduating from college. You know those notebooks – filled with lists of things to get at Target and my wife's dress size and the kids shoe sizes and movies I wanted to see and song lyrics I heard on the radio which I would later Google to learn who sang them comingled with things I didn't want to forget about Grandpa and quotes from my children I wanted to remember and general lists of chores and things to do this year like clean the chimney and the names of electricians and painters. Then I smelled Grandpa's house when I ran the Boston Marathon in 2013 and wanted to write more substantively about that and so I did and 86,000 words later, here we are. Each chapter is its own reflection of how Grandpa's life is still affecting mine, of what I wish I could know for certain, and of how many truths I accepted as such are simultaneously less than absolute and somehow still etched in stone.

These are stories of things he and I did or of things he and I shared when I was little, and the lens through which I view those things today. It is the story of how Grandpa wrested happiness from often bleak circumstances. And then it is the story of me wondering whether or not he was really happy, ruminating on how unanswerable that question is, ruminating on how and how much where we are determines who we are. And how, if at all, that determines our happiness. Sometimes I just ruminate. It'll probably get annoying. But in telling and recalling and writing down these stories, I have learned (and learned to accept) how unexceptional they all are. But that is what might make them most useful. That in fact, it is their lack of remarkableness that makes them worth sharing.

Part I

Invincible

Quadripoint

"Theory"

I am what is around me.

Women understand this.
One is not a duchess
A hundred yards from a carriage.

These, then, are portraits:
A black vestibule;
A high bed sheltered by curtains.

These are merely instances.

—Wallace Stevens

When a person dies, the loved ones left behind cling to the tactile remains of who they were. Grandpa and Grandma loved stuff. They loved things. Not in a profane, materialistic way, but in a hybrid of the way that people who grew up with nothing tend to value objects, mixed with the way people who focus on their own legacies tend to value the things they leave behind. The things they valued were simple. They valued the stories which accompanied every vase, every candy dish, every utensil, every garden tool, every seashell, every shellacked pine cone, every throw pillow, every brooch and earring and wristwatch, every afghan, every figurine, every book, every tree and bush and plant, every cufflink, photograph, scarf, book, earring, vase, gun, quilt.[3]

During the last decade or so of their lives, they began giving away their things to their five children and eight grandchildren. The process was always very diplomatic and fair, and the protocols were always strictly adhered to, and the importance of the story was always paramount. These touchable things emerge as those things that define the dead; become who they were.

There's this photo of Grandpa. It's a square photo with rounded corners and 1970s colors with that 1970s tint which makes everyone look sallow and muted, as though they should be working the games at a traveling carnival or working the phones of a telethon behind the telethon emcee. In it, Grandpa is squatting at the Four Corners Monument, the *quadripoint* of Arizona, Colorado, New Mexico, and Utah.[4] Grandpa poses with at least one limb in each state where they converge.

He looks at the camera with an expression evincing something between pride and mirth. He is wearing beige shoes that appear to be some sort of dress- and tennis-shoe hybrid, a pair of light blue, almost white pants; a light blue spread collar shirt; and some sort of beige polyester jacket made of fabric that kind of puckers, that has some sort of seersuckerish hint to it. The jacket has four exterior pockets with exterior flaps that close with big white buttons. It also has a built-in belt with

---

[3] This is not an exhaustive list. I am a trusts and estates attorney, one of the best in the greater Baltimore area, and I see this phenomenon every day. First, in talking with the individual who is preparing her last will and testament and seeing what and who are important to her, but then also in seeing those she loved on the post-demise front, seeing what is important to them with respect to remembering the person. Often the two are incongruous.

[4] A quadripoint is a point at which four borders meet. The point where these four states meet is the only single point in the whole United States shared by four states! This book is going to be interesting and educational!

a large white buckle. The jacket is something that Kate Jackson, the demure angel, might have worn while starring in the television version of *Charlie's Angels;* or something Angie Dickinson might have worn in her groundbreaking series *Police Woman;* or maybe even something Cagney and/or Lacey might have worn as they fought crime and sexism in *Cagney & Lacey.* More succinctly, it looks like something a lady police officer would wear in the 1970s or 1980s. Or Gene Rayburn, the host of TV's *Match Game* with his extra-long microphone; or the person that would happen if Diane Keaton and Robert E. Lee had a baby; or if Bea Arthur in her *Maude* days and Rodney Dangerfield had a baby. You could stare at and analyze the jacket for hours and still not be able to wrap your mind around it. The jacket is a chocolate-mocha polyester brown—a color perfectly suited for the photograph processing techniques of the seventies. Grandpa's ensemble is not the almost-white pants and light blue shirt and beige jacket of those who summer in Nantucket. Grandpa's ensemble—and Grandpa himself—is simpler and more modest than that. Anyone looking at the photo can tell by his expression, posture, smile, and overarching gestalt knows this. They convey modesty and humility; and maybe the look of someone who doesn't give a hoot about what other people think really think of his jacket because it's a perfectly fine jacket.

It's a photo that surely exists in countless photo albums belonging to countless Americans.[5] I first saw the photo when I was about five or six. Maybe seven. Likely sitting at Grandpa and Grandma's kitchen table amidst the rocks and shells and

---

[5] The Navajo Nation owns the parts of Utah, New Mexico and Arizona which come together at the monument; the Ute tribe owns the Colorado portion. Despite its remote location, the monument gets thousands of visitors every year. The Visitor Center is open year-round, and features a Demonstration Center with Navajo artisans. Navajo vendors sell handmade jewelry, crafts, and traditional Navajo foods nearby.

plant specimens and hotel shampoos they triumphantly brought back to rural Western New York. This was back in the day when people sent their plastic film cartridge via the United States Mail for development at a secret processing plant which would return the photographs three or four weeks later. Grandpa and Grandma would have been home from their months-long excursion out west, home to their ranch house adjacent to their old dairy farm and our current home,[6] for weeks by the time the photos came back, time enough for them to give my siblings and I all of our treats—oddly shaped rocks and pieces of petrified wood and enormous pine cones from redwoods and brightly colored sedimentary rock and napkins and menus and notepads from restaurants and diners and hotels -- from states we knew only because Grandma had quizzed us with some frequency about the states. And when they visited the west, the states were large and square and easy to put in our United States puzzle.

Looking at pictures with Grandma was painful; it was drudgery.[7] Typically, one had to sit at Grandpa and Grandma's

---

[6] This was a farm and a style of farming rooted in familial legacy and responsibility. Once when I told someone that I grew up on a farm they asked me if it was "like our CSA [Community Supported Agriculture]." It was nothing like that. There was no youthful enthusiasm and no naiveté and no social responsibility and no smoking marijuana and frolicking in the carrots. If there was smoking of marijuana and frolicking in the carrots, then I was neither aware of nor ever informed of it. This farm was about obligation. More specifically, obligation to the past and obligation to existing expectations. This book is about how—in lieu of frolicking—we find and form ourselves when not tethered to the obligation.

[7] While this is an accurate assessment of my thoughts as a boy, I almost instantly regretted typing it as soon as I did so today. It feels mean-spirited. But it's honest. I think you can still love someone while also disliking some of the things they do. I wonder if there is a special place in hell for people who say they did not always love it when they looked at photos with their Grandma. It really wasn't that bad. Wouldn't that be ironic if I do go to hell for complaining about looking at photos with Grandma, and the punishment is that I must look at Grandma's vacation pictures for eternity.

kitchen table, in close enough proximity to the refrigerator to keep us rapt, lest Grandma decide to go open the refrigerator, where the perpetual threat of pickled cauliflower dwelled. She meticulously drew each photo forward along the plastic floral table cloth and presented it to me, then identified the scene, the setting, the historical significance of where they were, where they had eaten that morning, what they had eaten, the quality of what they had eaten, something funny Grandpa had said about a sub-average crop or tree they passed, whether the waitress's fingernails were too long, whether there was too much smoke in the diner or restaurant, whether the waitress's hairnet was too snug, her lipstick too pink, her fingernails too red or her rouge too robust, too *rougey*. She identified the plants in each picture; when they flowered, if they flowered; how much water they liked; if there was another person in the photo, she would identify that person, delve into an oral history of that person's family tree, and identify how that person was inevitably related to us; how hard-working that person was; whether or not they took good care of his or her automobile; the quality of their cursive; she would tell us that she didn't like to gossip then proceed to tell us something juicy about the third party in the photo—juicy by Grandma's standards—like how Grandma saw them bring what they had identified as a five-bean salad to a church potluck dinner but when Grandma ate it there were only four beans in it and that person should be ashamed for lying about the bean quantities in their church salads. That sort of juicy.[8]

Though since Grandma is likely in heaven, I will sit with her evil doppelganger and look at the evil doppelganger's vacation photos. Though, frankly, as I write this, sitting at Grandpa and Grandma's kitchen table looking at their vacation photos sounds like the very most comforting and wonderful thing I could ever do. I wish I could do it now. Today. And I am not just saying that to avoid eternal damnation.

[8] Later, in the 1990s, when three residents of the valley in which she had been born and raised and lived in her whole life succumbed to temptations of the flesh and the

The photo of Grandpa standing at the Four Corners Monument was different. It was uncharacteristically frivolous and boyishly silly. It was also majestic. There was an element of triumph to it. He might as well have been Superman—standing in four states simultaneously like that.[9]

I went home that afternoon, upended my United States puzzle, and located for myself the spot where the corners of Arizona, Colorado, New Mexico, and Utah melded into one finite point; put the puzzle up to my eyeball so I could look at those coordinates closely. Such resourcefulness Grandpa had; such unmitigated audacity; such derring-do—to stand at the fucking *quadripoint* of four fucking states. I could see it on the map. Grandpa was there.

In that photo, you can see other people, other tourists, milling about in the background. You can see their cars parked in the background. There is a dearth of foreign-made automobiles. The cars are very American and very large. The cars—like Grandpa's *Police Woman* jacket and the photo itself—have colors that belong exclusively to that decade: 1970s Pontiac muscle-car colors like Verdoro Green, Palomino Copper, Bermuda Blue, Coronado Gold, Castilian Bronze, and Palladium Silver.

A decade after that photo was developed, when I was forced to go to my grandparents' house and resorted to looking at photo albums to avoid talking to people and would see the photo at the Four Corners monument, my attention wandered

---

one wife had an affair with her across-the-road neighbor, Grandma was surprisingly neither shocked nor overly histrionic about their liaison or the subsequent misbehaviors, which included a highly dramatic and highly destructive corn-chopper sabotaging. She merely said, with almost a snicker, "those three are turning my hollow into a regular Peyton Place!" *Grandma*, circa 1998.

[9] This was decades before Leonardo DiCaprio stood at the helm of the Titanic and proclaimed, "I'm the king of the world," thereby setting a new standard – perhaps *the* standard – for triumphant posturing.

from my mythical Grandpa to the other tourists. I wondered what the other tourists—other Americans with families and grandchildren and grandparents—thought, or if they thought at all, about Grandpa as he was squatting at the Four Corners. I wondered if they mocked his jacket, his leisure shoes, his leisurely pace. My focus was enduringly on how others—any others—perceived me. Naturally, I was concerned about how others—any others—perceived Grandpa as he meandered about the country. If folks from more refined parts of the country—places with universities like Ann Arbor or Burlington or Cambridge or New Haven or Columbus or places with mansions with gates and convertibles and skyscrapers with elevators that have elevator operators who get their butts pinched by business men in grey flannel suits and briefcases and ocean views and stores with tweed jackets—could see the corn stalks in his complexion or the alfalfa in his irises. Or if folks from more refined parts of the country—places like the Ann Arbor or Burlington or Cambridge or New Haven or Columbus—even visited places like the Four Corners Monument; they likely avoided such destinations to circumvent interfacing with the hoi polloi. If sophisticated people did go to the quadripoint, I suspected that they laughed at Grandpa. And I think for a time I was probably okay with that.

As a young adult, I was beginning to understand what sort of people drove hundreds of miles out of their way to stand on the Four Corners Monument: people who luxuriated in the complimentary breakfasts of cereals in cylindrical plasticine tubs offered at motels with no stars; who avoided the hullabaloo and dangers of metropolitan areas at all costs; who drove through nature and to destinations of natural wonder and liked them; who wanted the government to stay off their everything; who kept loaded shotguns "secured" and "hidden" in the pantry off the kitchen; people who preferred Clint Eastwood and *Dirty Harry* to Woody Allen and *Annie Hall*. I began to wonder if Grandpa and Grandma were those sorts of people. I began to wonder if I was that sort of person too.[10] I began to fear that I was that sort of person—a simple person; one who celebrated complimentary cereal and manipulative if not altogether manufactured tourist destinations.

A couple decades later, as I was courting the woman who would become my wife, she and I would spend hours at Grandpa and Grandma's whenever possible when we came home from Boston to visit. I wanted Elizabeth to know them. She loved Grandma. They were both into flowers and knitting and crafts and fabrics and plants. And Elizabeth may or may not have had a little geriatric crush on Grandpa, especially when he nicknamed her "Old Lib" after his mean grade school teacher. One afternoon we were again looking at photo albums, and Grandma was doing the thing she did with me—explaining the migration patterns of whatever bird was in each photo and discussing the species of plants native to whatever land mass on which the picture was taken and discussing the McDonald's they had been to the morning the picture was taken and whether or not the fries were too salty—and we came across the photo of Grandpa standing at the Four Corners Monument.

Because children see the world one way and adults see the world another way and adolescents are basically just assholes, I saw him and photos of him with a new reverence. Grandpa seemed to stand there with a new poise; a new confidence; something almost resembling defiance. But he brandishes his stature not as a weapon so much as contentment. I was perplexed.[11]

---

[10] Can you keep a secret? Sometimes I still wonder if I am still that sort of person, that while you can't go home again, you also can't escape where you come from. That no matter how hard you try to extricate yourself from your origins, be they genetic or geographical or a nice potpourri of both, such extrication is ultimately futile.

[11] The Monument has similarly evolved. In 1875, a marker was placed at the intersection of the 37th parallel north the 32nd meridian west of Washington to

But I also looked at it and him with something resembling suspicion. No, something more innocuous than suspicion—maybe just disbelief. I began to wonder how a man could so ferociously love his origins and yet so ferociously yearn to extricate himself from them. Grandpa loved taking these months-long excursions. He loved exploring and took great pride in having been to forty-eight states.[12] Yet when he was home, he was also clearly a happy man.

But was he?

I start to picture Grandpa and Grandma driving around the country—en route to the Four Corners Monument or Mount Rushmore or the Hoover Dam or Petrified Forest National Park or the Everglades or the Grand Canyon—and I can't help but feel sad because a) I know so much of the trip was spent calculating gas mileage and eating at McDonald's, and when they splurged they splurged at places like Perkins and Howard Johnson's, and they did not eat meat on Fridays during Lent, and you wonder if they ever had to forego eating BBQ ribs somewhere like a famous rib joint because it was a Friday during Lent; and b) I wonder if Grandpa secretly yearned to visit cities.[13] My sadness is somewhat assuaged when I realize

---

mark these borders. The stone broke and was replaced numerous times until a surveyor placed a brass disc at the spot in 1931. In 1962, the Bureau of Land Management and the Bureau of Indian Affairs poured an elevated cement pad around the 1931 brass marker. The monument was completely rebuilt in 1992, and the 1931 brass marker was replaced with a disc-shaped aluminum-bronze plate set in granite.

[12] And Alaska was one of them! I will reveal the two states he never went to later in the text.

[13] I picture Grandpa and Grandma doing their best to circumvent cities. It's funny—they always said they hated cities and I understand why, on an intellectual level, but I can never *fully* understand it, given their otherwise startling propensity for adventure. On the eve of me moving there, Grandpa told me that he hated Boston. It was because he used to deliver maple syrup to Boston, and once a load of maple

14

that to some degree they enjoyed economizing and relished their frugality. They were adept at economizing. Wore it like a badge of honor. And I recall stories they told you of how they sacrificed in World War II and did so proudly. They enjoyed driving around looking for a Catholic mass in lieu of doing fun stuff; enjoyed the triumph of Triple A discounts; enjoyed saving ketchup packets and packing apples and generic granola bars for the trip.

The photograph has evolved. At the outset, it depicted Grandpa as conqueror, an almighty sojourner, sojourning for truth and justice. He was omnipotent in every way, as evinced by how he could stand at the very quadripoint of four states! Later, it depicted Grandpa the ordinary man, who never learned to live and got suckered into things like driving fourteen hours out of his way to stand at the one point in the United States where four states come together and buy a few postcards and maybe an ornamental keepsake from the gift shop. It was around this time that I began to look at Grandpa as more of an enigmatic figure. The myth in our family (and it is funny how myths take hold of people and families and become the adhesive by which truths adhere) is that Grandpa was a hard worker who loved the farm and sacrificed deeply and proudly. That he loved the small town in which he was born and raised and where he raised his own family. That he yearned not for the sinful pleasures of the secular world and was perfectly content with the simple joys of nature. How accurate was that perception? At some point in my own search for a place in which to dwell and a place to love, I started to wonder if that Grandpa myth was true. And then if it wasn't true, how did Grandpa find contentment—was it a manufactured thing? Did he create it

---

syrup cans spilled off his truck and all over the street and no one helped him pick them up and that story has made me laugh and cry at the same time for decades. Every now and again, when I was walking around Boston, I would try to identify precisely where the spill happened and wondered where he delivered the syrup cans.

15

himself? What did he do to enjoy life in the face of such austerity? To be fulfilled? To have fun?

The photo evolved into what it is now: a depiction of a man who was inexplicably happy. I think about the things he did to wring out joy and satisfaction. Because I saw it too late to really ask him about it.

Now, when I think about that picture, I also think about how annoyed I get when people take too long to go when the light turns green or drive too slowly in the fast lane. I love to honk at slow drivers, but when I pass them and discover they are old, I feel bad (sometimes). Yet I keep honking nonetheless. Did people honk at Grandpa and Grandma? I sort of have to assume they did. I wonder what they said to each other if they ever saw someone give them the bird. I suspect that Grandma was positively aghast, and I suspect that Grandpa laughed.

When I look at photographs of him now—from any decade—I tend to examine them more than merely look at them. I look for—and generally find—a poise he had that I had theretofore not recognized; a new stature, evincing a new confidence; a certain stance—something that doesn't quite rise to the level of bluster but is certainly more than mere self-assurance. And I wonder if that was there all along. But there is also the bad posture—the perpetual slouch that was so inexplicable and inevitable, simultaneously. He was statuesque and constantly cautious. He was just a man doing the best he could.

Grandpa and Grandma are now gone. I will never get another postcard from them.[14] Or another napkin from some odd-sounding diner; or a receipt from a far-away McDonald's;

---

[14] And even though Grandma never seemed to quite get me, she always picked out postcards that were perfectly suited to me. My favorite one was the vintage-looking one from Florida with a map of the state on a light blue background and a sun with sunglasses in the upper right corner. Though it always sort of pissed me off that the sun was wearing sunglasses.

or a shell that looks like a bird or a horse or Mother Teresa; or rocks shaped like birds or horses or Mother Teresa. All photographs of them are now, quite necessarily, old ones. And fading. Increasingly, I find myself wishing I had listened more attentively to Grandma telling me about the desert vegetation surrounding the Four Corners Monument; about where they ate that day; about where they went to church the Sunday before and even the Sunday after. Because I could have asked questions. Which would have led to more significant questions: why didn't Grandma get her picture taken at the Four Corners Monument? Did she want to have her picture taken, and Grandpa didn't know how to work the camera? Or did she want her picture taken, but not at the cost of making other people wait an extra few seconds while she did so? Grandpa, did you walk with enthusiasm to the bronze disc marking the quadripoint? Or was it a reluctant shuffle? Where did you eat that day, Grandpa and Grandma? Was the waitress kind to you? Did she wear too much rouge? Were her finger nails too shiny? Did you splurge and get dessert? Did it cost anything to get your picture taken at the Four Corners Monument? Did you worry about money all the time?

I wonder if I can get all CSI on the photo and blow up the license plates and cross-check them with DMV databases and identify the owners of the cars in the background and talk to them about the intervening four decades. Are you still alive? How have you spent the past four decades? Were you loved? Were you loved too much? Were you loved not enough? What sort of losses have you endured? What sort of joys have you had? Where are the pictures of your loved ones standing at the Four Corners monument? Is my Grandpa in your background? Was he happy? Did Grandpa and Grandma hold hands when they walked from the car to the medallion? Did they talk to each other as they walked? Were they eating apples they brought from home or had they splurged on something? Was there an admission fee or was it a suggested donation? What

17

day were they there?

I want some assurance that the moment in which Grandpa was standing at the Four Corners was his. That he was, to use today's parlance, *living in the moment.* And the moment belonged to him. That he was basking in it. That he was happy.

Were I still at the kitchen table and were the square photos with rounded edges and 1970s tints still fresh—I could have asked so many more questions. I wish I had. I wish I still could.

Because there are still so many questions to ask him. Because there are still so many things to learn. Because he was and is a bigger part of me than I thought. And a bigger man than I understood.

Gary M. Almeter

Rain on the Scarecrow

"Study of Two Pears"

I
Opusculum paedagogum.
The pears are not viols,
nudes or bottles.
They resemble nothing else.

II
They are yellow forms
Composed of curves
Bulging toward the base.
They are touched red.

III
They are not flat surfaces
Having curved outlines.
They are round
tapering toward the top.

IV
In the way they are modelled
There are bits of blue.
A hard dry leaf hangs
From the stem.

V
The yellow glistens.
It glistens with various yellows,
Citrons, oranges and greens
Flowering over the skin.

VI
The shadows of the pears
Are blobs on the green cloth.

The Emperor of Ice-Cream

The pears are not seen
As the observer wills.

—Wallace Stevens

Grandpa and I were very different. He liked nature; I hate nature. He hated cities; I love cities. He liked tranquility; I thrive in chaos. He was kind; I fancy myself an unkind person, prone to mischief and mean-spiritedness, but only because it's warranted. There was a period of approximately a decade—that certain ten years between my first memory of him and that time when I was an adolescent—when I thought, or rather *knew,* that he was perfect. I relished[15] those things we had in common and was bewildered by the things we did not.

I. The Farm

I grew up on the farm Grandpa had bought from his father-in-law. It was the farm on which he raised his five children, and he sold it to my father the year before I was born. He and Grandma erected a prefabricated ranch house exactly one hayfield away, where they lived until Grandma died in 2004. When I was seven, it typically took me between 300 and 400 steps to walk there. I know this because I counted them. As I got older, both the number of steps and the frequency of the visits diminished. Grandpa visited the farm every day—it took him no more than eight seconds to get to our house on his Yamaha three-wheeler. He helped milk cows, brought meat scraps for our dogs, drove tractors, fixed things, held ladders, entertained us. From our house, we could see Grandpa hang his

---

[15] Interestingly, and as you will learn in greater detail later, I loathe relish. So the use of the word "relish" to refer to something I enjoy greatly always strikes me as displaced. I loathe all condiments. This is addressed in a later chapter. And fortunately there is no double meaning to the word mayonnaise.

20

Christmas lights and hear him mow his lawn and see when he was leaving to come take us somewhere, so we would be ready.

Our farm, with its big red gambrel-roofed barn, rolling hills, white farm house, large yard besotted by centuries-old trees looked just like any other dairy farm in upstate New York on which a young family was being raised in the 1970s. And just like any other dairy farm, it had supported generations of a family. The barn, filled with hay and grain on the top ground level and with cows and a complex system of milking equipment on the bottom level, was separated from the big white farmhouse by a circular driveway. It's tough to say what was the epicenter of activity; the barn was home to about seventy-five cows, a bunch of pigs, and dozens of cats. The big white farmhouse was home to me and my parents and my three siblings and a slew of dogs. There was also a machinery shed, a garden house, a two-car garage, a bath house adjacent to an in-ground swimming pool, two silos, multiple flower beds, centuries-old trees and, depending on where we were in the season cycle, bicycles strewn across the lawn, a homemade baseball diamond, baby pools, outdoor playpens, a swing set, various cars, vans and pickup trucks, sandboxes, tractor-tire bouncy things, three-wheelers, hockey rinks, snow forts and who the fuck even knows what else— towels and bathing suits hanging on railings and fences and tree branches. Of course there was also a ton of farm equipment: big tractors, little tractors, later we had a giant green tractor with an air-conditioned cab and a radio, hay wagons, corn wagons, hay balers, hay rakers, hay twirlers, hay mowers, hay elevators, planters, choppers, manure spreaders, dump trucks, garden hoses, garden equipment, and lawn mowers. Home.

Grandpa kept a big cement block on his lawn. The cement block made the worms crawl to the surface and frolic underneath. Whenever it was time to go fishing—which is what rural kids did in the 1970s when they weren't *book learnin'*— my siblings and I would walk to his house and he would lift up

21

the block and there would be about fourteen-trillion fat juicy bulbous worms slithering about. He had an old Planters Peanuts jar filled with dirt in his garage and he would invite us to put a few worms in the jar for easy transport to the creek behind the farm where we would fish. I found the whole thing revolting. I liked fishing with Grandpa, but there was no way in fucking hell I was ever going to pick up a worm, fold it in half, put a hook through its fat stupid head such that the hook punctured the worm thrice, and then just go on about my day as if that was normal behavior. We went fishing with some frequency—from as early as I can remember until high school. And in all that time I don't think I ever touched a worm. I'm proud of that now. But, at the time, the fact that I didn't touch worms (and in fact made my little sister do it) led me to suspect that Grandpa thought I was a coward; that maybe he found my cowardice as revolting as I found the worms. He never indicated that he thought I was revolting. But that's just how a kid thinks. I think. It's how I thought, at least. I, as the center of the universe, knew that surely everyone was thinking about me, analyzing what I did (or in this case didn't fucking do because it was gross) and then formulating an opinion about it/me.

(This is the extent of the fishing stories, by the way. Typically, stories such as these culminate in a catfish the size of a fucking horse jumping onto the raft or the bridge or the ledge and the grandpa and the wussy child drop kick the big ugly catfish into submission and then they carry it home and fry it and feed the family. No such story here.)

Grandpa never said, "put the worm on the hook, you little wussy" or anything of the sort. He never said, "Lawd have mercy, but you is as worthless as a horsefly on shit" or anything like that, though that would have been sort of awesome if he had. He never raised an eyebrow or gave a demeaning look or ever suggested in any way that I was any less lovable because I wouldn't touch a worm.

Grandpa and I shared a connection. Though generations

apart, we drank the same water and breathed the same air and harvested the same crops from the same fields and caught the same fish from the same creek and picked berries form the same blackberry bushes and had adventures in the same apple orchard and hayloft and woods.

But it wasn't a perfect connection. I hated fishing. I hated the wilderness. I liked blackberries but hated picking them. I hate the smell of cow shit. I hate nature. I hate its arbitrariness (*why did that tree or that house or that whatever the fuck it is have to get hit by lightning?*). I hate its relentlessness (*really? another day of rain? another tornado? another foot of snow?*). I hate its parasitism (*do I really need to get bitten by another fucking horsefly today?*). I hate its indomitability coupled with precariousness (*really? If nature is so grand, then why do we have to keep taking care of it?*). I hated the frogs we used to find swimming in our swimming pool. I hated the mosquitos and the flies and the wasps. When we saw a snake on the steps of our barn, I hated that snake, too. I hated the bajillion maggots that would magically appear on a woodchuck carcass after our dog killed a woodchuck. I hated the woodchucks— alive or as carcasses.[16]

2. The Town

Grandpa and I also grew up in the same town. Or village. Or hamlet. Or municipality. Or whatever the fuck it was. And is.

According to the *Billboard* archives, John Cougar Mellencamp's "Small Town" was the seventy-second most

---

[16] I also loathe fates, furies, gods, muses, nymphs, fairies, dragons, and cryptozoological creatures of any kind. I despise any sort of mythological creature, supernatural things, deities, talking beasts, silent beasts, gargoyles, gnomes, hobbits, anything that dwells in some sort of subterranean habitat or anything that does sorcery. But these things were few and far between on the farm.

popular song in 1986.[17] In 1986, I turned sixteen when the prefrontal lobe of my cerebral cortex was still developing, and I was still trying to figure out who I was.[18] As I was asking myself who I was, John Cougar Mellencamp was telling me that I should be thankful that I, like him, was born in a small town.[19] With all due respect to John Cougar Mellencamp, he's full of shit. People in small towns do not let you be just what you want to be. Mellencamp's song, which glorifies life in a small town, was ubiquitous at all school functions and parties and neighborhood functions. I did not like growing up in a small town. I had not seen it all in a small town nor did I have myself a ball in a small town. Additionally, I could not be "myself here in that small town." And while my bed was in a small town, it was not good enough for me. This was confusing. We grew up reading all sorts of variations of Aesop's "The Town Mouse and the Country Mouse" wherein the country mouse learns that

---

[17] The Top 10 songs of 1986 were: "That's What Friends Are For" by Dionne & Friends; "Say You, Say Me" by Lionel Richie; "I Miss You" by Klymaxx; "On My Own" by Patti Labelle and Michael McDonald; "Broken Wings" by Mr. Mister; "How Will I Know" by Whitney Houston; "Party All The Time" by Eddie Murphy; "Burning Heart" by Survivor; "Kyrie" by Mr. Mister; and "Addicted to Love" by Robert Palmer. Archetypal 1986 songs on this list include "Sledgehammer" by Peter Gabriel at no. 23; "Rock Me Amadeus" by Falco at 28; "Papa Don't Preach" by Madonna at 29; "Your Love" by the Outfield at 62; "Take Me Home" by Phil Collins at 88; and "King for a Day" by Thompson Twins.

[18] The rational part of a teen's brain isn't fully developed and won't be until age twenty-five or so. In fact, recent research has found that adult and teen brains work differently. Adults think with the prefrontal cortex, the brain's rational part. This is the part of the brain that responds to situations with good judgment and an awareness of long-term consequences. Teens process information with the amygdala. This is the emotional part. In teen's brains, the connections between the emotional part of the brain and the decision-making center are still developing— and not necessarily at the same rate. That's why when teens experience overwhelming emotional input, they can't explain later what they were thinking. They weren't thinking as much as they were feeling.

[19] Teens get their concepts of who they are and who they should be from innumerable sources.

he would much rather sacrifice opulence to live in a place that is safe and secure than live in a place which affords him the finer things but forces him to live in perpetual fear. I hated safety and security and simplicity, along with worms and bugs and plants and thorns and feces and snakes and salamanders and smells.

The town has garnered some attention of late. Nowhere in New York did Donald Trump fare better than the rural areas between Buffalo and Rochester, with seventy-two percent of Wyoming County[20] voters backing the Republican presidential candidate. It's simultaneously baffling and completely rational. They're rural. They're aging. They've slowly lost population over the past twenty years. Their unemployment rates are higher than the state average. Their residents are more than ninety percent white. They love guns and rebels who are rebellious but not overly so—rebels like The Charlie Daniels Band and Toby Keith. They are independent-minded and hardworking. They are fed up with giveaways and entitlements.[21]

For the most part, this means that there is simply a great deal of gun-toting, independent-minded, get-the-government-

---

[20] That's the county in which I was raised!

[21] This is as far as I will delve into trying to understand the *why* of this man's election as president. I would have thought that these people loathe sexually assaulting women, engaging in corrupt business dealings around the world, firing the FBI director for investigating yourself, sharing classified information with Russia, eliminating healthcare, campaigning on racism, juvenile name-calling and generally lying about everything, almost as much as they love their land and their guns. But no. This footnote, written on June 15, 2017, will conclude with me saying: "What the fuck?! How much worse does it need to get? Have we gone insane? What is happening? I miss the days when Facebook was filled with pictures of entrées and people getting water dumped on their heads. And, speaking of, surely the release of the president's pee-pee tapes is imminent." But hey. Copyediting the book in November 2018. He gets stupider, greedier, more brazen, more dishonest, more dangerous every week. Fuck him.

out-of-my-life-and-off-my-property, quasi-Libertarian types of people who live there. They are farmers who loathe the EPA and the IRS and anyone else who sets forth anything resembling a regulation. Wyoming County has more than 207,000 acres of farmland and is the state's biggest producer of milk, with its cows producing about one billion pounds a year, according to the Wyoming County Business Center.

The county's tourism bureau proudly boasts that Wyoming County is home to more cows (about 53,000) than people (about 42,000). Trump's campaign message resonated among county residents, particularly among farmers who favor small government. But clearly did not resonate with the folks in NYC who know him. Neither faction—the farmers nor the people who live in the five boroughs and Long Island, Westchester—can comprehend the life the other lives. I know that the farmers want nothing to do with the life downstate, with its taxicabs and immigrants and pollution and crime and graffiti subways.

In the town, everyone looked the same. They were white farmers of German origin who were perpetually tired—tired of shoveling snow and plowing earth and chopping wood and harvesting corn and tossing hay bales and pulling on cows' teats to make milk come out of them. They were perpetually worried—worried that it would rain too much and that it would rain too little and that the cows would all get sick and die and that the snow and ice would knock down power lines and that the tractors wouldn't start and that the hay wouldn't dry. They were always fighting—the snow and the sun and the stubborn cow and the muddy fields and the overflowing creeks and the companies that sent them the too-small checks for the delicious milk. As such, they looked perpetually crushed—perpetually vanquished.

In the rural area outside of Buffalo, there are no breaks. Summer meant baling hay and planting corn. Autumn meant harvesting corn. Winter meant spending hours and hours every day removing the four to eighteen feet of snow in your driveway so the milk truck could come to take the milk to the factory where they bottled the milk so they could get money, so you could eventually receive your too-small check. And spring meant plowing fields and planting corn.

3. John Francis Almeter

Grandpa did not look perpetually vanquished. Maybe a little tired from time to time, and sometimes contemplative to the point of momentarily withdrawn. But never vanquished. Outwardly, he had a pride and attention to appearances that prohibited such a dismal guise. He possessed an interest in things like grooming and clothes but no matter how much attention to paid to either, the interest read not as boastfulness, but as transcendence. He had monogrammed brushes and put product in his hair before it was called product; he wore cufflinks and tie clips and clothes that indicated an attention to detail. He wore red pants and a green blazer at Christmas—but not in a Nantucket-like sort of way; more like a "I'm jolly and it's Christmas" sort of way.

The town was not like him and as such didn't seem to suit him. He was an insider, to be sure, but he was also a little more refined, a little more sophisticated, a little too eager to leave and explore than his neighbors and friends seemed to be. One of his defining characteristics seemed to be "striving." This was a town where people seemed to kill themselves in gruesomely rural ways—out of control Camaros crashing into utility poles at two o'clock in the morning; a snowmobile ride ending in decapitation via barbed wire fence; a suicide in a cornfield with the rifle your dad used to scare away woodchucks; drownings; a visit to the silo ending in death from the inhalation of toxic corn fumes. Clearly some of these were problems born of country living. But citizenry of anywhere with an excess of time and boredom and access to recreational vehicles surely suffers similar—though slightly modified—fates. No one in our town,

27

for example, has ever suffered from the bite of a great white shark. Or fallen out of a hot air balloon.

John Francis Almeter was born in 1914, one of 37,948 Johns born in the United States that year.[22] He was born on March 29, the 391st day of Woodrow Wilson's presidency, and died on January 26, 2009, the 7th day of Barack Obama's.[23] He was alive for 34,637 days. He was the second oldest child and first son born to John Sylvester and Elizabeth Schwab Almeter.

He was born on a farm like any farm in rural upstate New York in 1914. They had horses and cows and a home heated by burning wood, and they ate things they caught themselves and grew themselves. It snowed a lot. They worked hard. They rejoiced in simple things like hearty apple crops and frolicking

---

[22] John was the most popular name for boys born in the United States in 1914. The next most popular name for boys, William, was given to 29,755 boys born that year. John would be the most popular boys' name until 1923, when it fell to number two. It bounced around the top five most popular names until 1973 when it fell to number six. It first fell out of the top ten in 1986. In 2015, it was the twenty-sixth most popular name given to boys in the United States. This, of course, does not include variations thereof: Johan, Johnny, Jon, Jonah, Jonas, Juan, Jonathan, Jonathon, etc. How sobering to think very few if any of these 37,948 Class of 1914 Johns are still alive. What sort of lives did they lead? Did they get polio? Survive the wars? Were they loved? Did they have children? There is a photograph hanging in a third-floor bedroom of my friend Dave's parents' summer home, a panoramic portrait of Yale University's Class of 1922 that prompts the same thoughts. Who were these men? Did they go on to achieve great things? Was one of them the founder of some great thing? Where did they summer? My wife and I also recently located my father in law's Eighth-grade class picture from Our Lady of Lourdes parochial school in Paterson, NJ. These people, clearly all either Polish or Italian, are either deceased or eighty or eighty-one years old.

[23] In between them were Warren Harding, Calvin Coolidge, Herbert Hoover, Franklin Roosevelt, Harry Truman, Dwight Eisenhower, John F. Kennedy, Lyndon Johnson, Richard Nixon, Gerald Ford, James Carter, Ronald Reagan, George H.W. Bush, William Clinton, and George W. Bush.

in the creek on summer afternoons.

I'm surmising here; I have to surmise, because I never asked him things, never asked him, "What sort of life did your parents want for you?" partially because I never thought to ask him that, never thought it would be pertinent or valuable or interesting, and partially because I sort of knew what answer he would have given; he would have been self-deprecating and said that he wasn't important and that he just wants to work on the farm and be good. But I can fairly safely surmise that his parents wanted a simple life for him, a life of good friends and good crops and good comradeship with his country and his countrymen.

Grandpa's father, John Sylvester Almeter, died of pneumonia in 1932, when Grandpa was sixteen. Grandpa and his dad both had asthma, and I am certain that caused Grandpa to consider the idea that he too would expire early. After his dad died, a Navy recruiter visited his hometown, and Grandpa expressed interest in joining the Navy, but a neighbor convinced him that his mother needed him on the farm. So, as if following a script reminiscent of Frank Capra's *It's a Wonderful Life*, he stayed. Whether Grandpa asked the neighbor for his opinion or whether the neighbor volunteered his opinion and his judgment, I do not know. From that point, Grandpa worked on the farm to support his mother and three siblings. He gave his older sister Ethel away at her wedding and stayed on the farm until he married Grandma in 1942 and moved to her parents' farm about half a mile away.

Despite all this, I recall Grandpa being content, if not ebullient, wherever he was. Grandpa was all country: he played the harmonica and enjoyed chewing on long blades of grass or pieces of alfalfa, and he liked Mel Tillis and pancake dinners in the basements of volunteer fire departments. He loved to square dance.[24] I did not like those things.

---

[24] Once, when I was in high school, I went with Grandpa and Grandma to one of their

Grandpa was neither a redneck nor a hillbilly. He never said anything like "I done spilled the durn beans" or anything like that. He would refer to facts as facts and not beans. He was smart. He maintained a perfect balance of valuing education while not appearing too uppity or showy. He maintained a perfect balance of inclusion in the town while staying above its less enchanting elements.[25]

When Grandma died, Grandpa moved in with Aunt Janet for a while. He took a few photo albums with him. When I went to visit him in March 2006, I saw the photos in these albums for the first time. Many of the couple dozen or so photos that there were of Grandpa chronicled his life between when he was a baby to when he was twenty-eight and married Grandma—years I had thought of infrequently, if ever. In this one photo, Grandpa is a boy, probably about fifteen or sixteen, but he is really probably just twelve or thirteen; in those days people looked older than they were, since they always dressed

---

square dance groups in Sardinia, NY. They wore their matching square dance outfits that Grandma had made. Grandpa's had black pants and a white shirt, the cuffs and shoulders made of the same black fabric with orange and blue flowers as Grandma's outfit. I hated square dance music and square dancing in general and anything connoted a simpler time, but I was sufficiently intrigued with Grandpa and Grandma's newfound love for square dancing. And they loved it. There was a whole community of square dancers who met once a week in this town called Sardinia. They had a professional caller and everything. I sat on one of the folding chairs that lined the old church hall and just watched. Every so often they would smile at me when they were being swung or dosey-doed in such a manner that we were eye to eye. They took such pride in all their moves, their knowledge of the steps. A few years later, this group started traveling to nearby towns and performing at local fairs and old timer festivals. I could feel that then—much like Civil War re-enactors or Grateful Dead followers or marathon runners—that the camaraderie that blossoms from doing things with people just like you must be pretty intense. Like the Bee Girl in the Blind Melon video for "No Rain," I had never really felt such camaraderie.

[25] "Less enchanting elements" is a euphemism for "abundant and abject depravity."

up, and the responsibility they had seemed to make them mature faster. I question the wisdom of wearing dress pants and a freshly pressed white shirt to do farm chores in light of how difficult it must have been to make and wash such clothing. I attribute it to the pride they took in their work, pride now missing from modern discourse about work. I wonder what Grandpa and his friends talked about in the absence of *Madden Football* and *The Dukes of Hazzard* and *Space Invaders* and *SpongeBob SquarePants* and things I talked about at that age and things I hear my own son talk about now.

In the photo Grandpa is smiling, and I hope—no, I instinctively ~~know~~—that Grandpa was a happy boy. I know that in a few years his dad will die, and I wonder what losing a parent is like. I am thankful to have seen Grandpa cry as an adult because I suspect—though I do not know—that when he was a boy, Grandpa had to go to the woods to cry.

In another photo, he is standing next to a water wheel. Grandpa told me that he made that water wheel and installed it in the stream and used what it generated to power the farm. I asked him, "How did you know how to make a water wheel?" and he replied, "I just did." I am rather certain that I never would've been able to conceptualize, design, and build a water wheel when I was boy. But this is not about me[26].

Who took these pictures? With what sort of camera were they taken? What is Grandpa thinking? Is he thinking? His expressions: always a smile, sometimes a smile belying pride. Sometimes just an expression of genuine mirth. This smiling man—my grandfather to be.

The people in these photos were farmers. But in pictures they look like the sort of folk from Newport, Rhode Island of whom Edith Wharton might have written. There were no pitchforks or dungarees or long pieces of grass between their teeth. Grandpa explained that the only time people took

---

[26] Nonetheless, how the fuck does a boy build a water wheel?

pictures was when people were dressed up; but then he scratched his head and said, "Or maybe they dressed up when they saw the camera being wheeled out."

When looking at pictures, Grandpa always knew with alarming precision and detail the circumstances and ancillary details of the photo. If there was a dog in the photo, he knew the dog's name, its origins, breed, and date of death. I always liked this because in most other respects, his memory was poor.

There are a few photographs, though, in which the subjects are depicted in more authentic ways. There's a picture of Grandpa using a pitchfork to toss hay onto a flatbed wagon; one of a group of people laughing and drinking beers on a wagon in what appears to be some sort of post-harvest indulgence. I asked him who these people were, and he told me. Despite the fact that he couldn't recall what he had for breakfast a few hours earlier, he could have told me the high and low temperatures of that day, the brand of beer they were drinking, who bought the beer, and since the caps were inevitably not twist-off, who brought the bottle opener. He could have told me what he liked most about each of the people with whom he worked and laughed, what he was hoping for that day, what he was afraid of that day, what he had been hoping for, generally. Had I asked.

I think I never asked him anything more probing because I had already made the presumption that the people in the photo spoke only of impending storms and poisonous berries and mischievous possums and corn and fish, or the rate at which butter churning churned the best butter, or what windowsill was most effective at cooling apple pies. Certainly, they never discussed hopes and dreams and feelings; that was the purview of a more enlightened people, like myself. None of these photo people had any hopes or dreams, or guilty pleasures; they were never naughty; they didn't taunt each other or make fun of each other's moms or girlfriends; nobody ever confessed they actually sort of liked whatever was that decade's equivalent of

Duran Duran or Britney Spears; they didn't binge-listen radio shows or eat a dozen packs of licorice or get wasted on sarsaparilla or search for Asian lesbian gangbangs on Pornhub. No. I was sure he did none of those things.

Or did they? Did they even have guilty pleasures in the first half of the twentieth century?[27] Did they eat big slabs of gooey cake while lamenting the caloric intake? Was there a 1920-something equivalent to Hanson's "Mmm Bop"? *Melrose Place? Scandal?* Did bridesmaids eat Yoplait yogurt at the tail end of wedding receptions? Did he retreat to his room when he was angry at his parents—if not to play *World of Warcraft,* then maybe to just hate-whittle some sort of corn cob pipe?

Now when I look at these pictures, I wonder beyond the journalistic 5Ws; I want to know what Grandpa is thinking. What did he think—about things, people, the future? His expression in each photo, always a smile, sometimes a smile belying pride but more often just a smile that expressed genuine mirth.

4. Gary Michael Almeter

I recall an interview John F. Kennedy, Jr. did with Larry King in September 1995. King asked Kennedy if it was hard being JFK, Jr. JFK, Jr. replied succinctly, "Well, I really don't have anything to compare it to, do I, Larry?" This is one of the

---

[27] "Guilty pleasures" refers to cultural artifacts with mass appeal—genre novels, catchy pop songs, action movies, TV shows—that bring with them an easy enjoyment without any pretense to edification. These so-called "guilty pleasures" never involve actual wrongdoing and people are generally eager to talk about their guilty pleasures. The term exudes a false note, a mix of self-consciousness and self-congratulation. If you felt really, truly ashamed of or guilty about it, you probably wouldn't announce it to the world, would you? The guilt signals that you prefer the élite precincts of high art, but you're not so much of a snob that you can't be at one with the people. So, you confess your remorse whenever you deign to watch *The Bachelor,* implying that the rest of your time is spent reading Albert Camus.

most succinct and most thorough and most insightful comment about growing up I have ever heard. I, like JFK, Jr., have nothing else to which I can compare my upbringing.[28] Of course, it's hard growing up; it is hard for everyone. It's supposed to be hard.

I was born on October 20, 1970, the 638th day of Richard Nixon's presidency. I am writing this paragraph on the twenty-fifth day of Donald Trump's. I was one of 10,732 Garys born in the United States in 1970, making it the thirty-fifth most popular name for boys that year, just shy of the 10,952 Shawns and a few more than the 10,417 Douglases born with me. The apex of Gary's popularity was a couple decades prior, in 1954, the year Gary Cooper won his Best Actor Academy Award for his role in *High Noon*, when 37,898 of us were born, making ours the ninth most popular name in the United States.

I generally fancied myself an unlovable if not repulsive kid.[29] It seemed like I was always doing something wrong. Or was just generally wrong. I recall being unhappy much of the time, always wishing I were elsewhere. I recall throwing a tantrum one Christmas when I was about five or six. My mother wanted to take our picture in front of the Christmas tree holding our favorite gift. I screamed and cried because I didn't "have a favorite gift. I hate[d] all my gifts." The resultant picture shows me holding a stuffed raccoon (that I really did like) with swollen and bloodshot eyes. (My eyes, I mean; not the raccoon's.)

When I was in sixth grade, Michael Kaizer and I smoked

---

[28] This is just one of an astounding number—almost an infinite number—of things I have in common with JFK, Jr.

[29] Using the JFK Jr. analysis, I sort of always figured that everyone felt this way. That it was developmentally appropriate to loathe yourself. I have nothing to which to compare the feelings; I never asked any of my peers if they loathed themselves.

cigarettes and looked at naughty magazines at his house.[30] I recall coming home from that overnight stay to find Grandpa petting our new dog (a dog who loved him more than it loved me, and I was her favorite in our house), and thinking to myself that if Grandpa knew about Michael and me smoking and looking at naughty magazines he would be really disappointed in me, and I sort of knew he smelled the smoke in my hair and on my clothes. Later, when I was in high school, mom used to work Bingo on Friday nights to get some tuition remission from the Catholic school I attended. On nights I had tennis practice, I had to stay for Bingo, and I would stealthily meander through the parking lot and steal cigarettes from the dashboards of unlocked cars and smoke them.[31] As a teenager, I was the world's most insecure narcissist. So, naturally, I assumed Grandpa thought about nothing but me all day every day and that when he did, he instinctively knew that I stole cigarettes from the dashboards of hardworking Bingo-playing Catholics and smoked them. Like a naughty-naughty smoking thief boy.

As a teenager, I also sometimes skipped dinners at his house to go to my own friends' houses and parties. Or if I did go to his house, I did so begrudgingly. I was a brash unpopular child who succumbed to the hostility of high school and withdrew almost completely.[32] As soon as I turned sixteen, I got

---

[30] Michael and I are still friends. (Hi Michael!) In today's parlance, I think this is what they call "throwing someone under the bus." I hope I do not get Michael in trouble.

[31] Interestingly, scientists have determined that a Venn diagram of "people who smoked in 1986" and "people who played Bingo in 1986" would be one solitary shaded circle.

[32] High school is an awful time for everyone. It's developmentally appropriate. It was really awful for me. Out of obligation, I went to a Catholic high school about thirty miles away from my house. In winter, the bus ride could be two hours long. The high school's curriculum was aimed at curbing abortion. In history, we learned about the history of abortions; in math, we did word problems involving adding and subtracting fetuses; in English class, we wrote abortion haikus and read stories about abortion;

a job at an amusement park near our house and worked there during the summers, instead of on the farm with Dad and my brother and Grandpa. Now I look back and ask myself, "How could he not have deemed this a rejection—of both him and the life he had lived?" But then I ask myself, "Why do I still think I am the epicenter of the universe? He probably didn't even notice I wasn't there."[33]

When, as a kid, you are told that you dwell in utopia, you begin to wonder if there's something wrong with you when you are unhappy.[34] I was a skinny kid who liked to read amidst a town full of burly illiterate folks.

As such, I felt like an outsider in my own town. And sometimes in my own family.[35] Which wasn't fun. I hated farming; I hated the idea of it, so Sisyphean yet even more nefarious. I wanted everything to do with the urban ills eschewed by the town folk. Always did. Always will. My dad

---

and in religion class—well, let me just say that you don't even want to know what we did in religion class.

[33] This to emphasize my futility more than Grandpa's powers of observation.

[34] Though, to be certain, for lots of years the place *was* utopia for me. It was perfect. But then you get older, and each new place you see also serves to create a chink in the armor of where you grew up. Of course a small town is utopia when you have never seen the townhouses of the Upper East Side lit up at Christmastime, or walked Newport, Rhode Island's Cliff Walk and seen how those people lived, and the list goes on and on. There was a time when our neighbor bought a new Trans Am with a painted eagle on the hood. I thought, "It doesn't get any cooler than this place."

[35] Luckily, though unbeknownst to me at the time, my family and our farm fostered far more sophisticated thinking. I recently told my parents, both being the rare Wyoming County-born HRC voters in 2016, how lucky we children are—how rare it is—that they are free thinkers. Statistically speaking, mom and dad should be deplorables. But they aren't. They encourage and engage in free-thinking and intelligence.

seemed to love the farm. Grandpa seemed to love it. I think I knew at an early age that I could never perform the nonstop tasks farming required. You feed the cows a ton of food, so they make a lot of milk. And they do. They also make a ton of shit. So you milk the cows every morning and the cows are shitting all over the place. When you are done milking the cows you spend hours cleaning up their shit and disposing of their shit. If it is spring, summer, or fall, you will spend the rest of the day planting or raking or mowing or baling or harvesting. You plant the crops every spring and you pray for rain and fertilize them and, in some cases, harvest the crops all summer; and then in the fall you chop the corn.

You do all these tasks with tractors. You know how you have a car? It might be a Honda Accord or a Volvo XC90 or a Honda Pilot or some sort of Toyota. And you know how you have to do all the routine maintenance on the car like oil changes and gas fill-ups and all that shit and every once in a while something goes wrong and it is such a huge pain in the ass to take the car to the shop and get it fixed and you sit there and wait for the mechanic to tell you what's wrong and whether you *have to* get it fixed (like will it explode if I don't? will people die?) and then you get it fixed because you have to? Imagine doing that for dozens of tractors and sophisticated machines and farming vehicles with complex hydraulics and chains and functions; think of when you were a kid and you went on a field trip to watch potato chips being made or Oreo cookies or books or newspapers or whatever fucked up shit they made in your town and how nuts the machines were that made them—think of that married with a Pontiac Grand Am, and that's what farmers have to rely on and fix.

Then you milk the cows again and go to bed and wake up the next day to do it all over again. All the while praying it rains enough but not too much and that it's sunny but not too sunny and that the cows don't get meningitis or small pox or mad cow disease or any of the other fucked up diseases bovines can get.

Every fucking day feeding the cows wholesome grains and nutrients and milking them and cleaning up their shit. Twice. No weekends off. Every fucking year plowing the fields and planting shit and praying and fertilizing and harvesting and tending.

While it might not sound like it, I am very thankful for my childhood and the way I was raised.[36] Equally thankful that I made it to college with all my limbs. Growing up sucks. My parents went through it and my grandparents went through it and my kids are going through it. Sometimes I watch my son as he puts on his humongous backpack and walks out the door to meet his friends, and one of his friends will say something mean about his hair or his hat or his too-short jeans, and my heart will break. It's taken me a long time to be able to say I hated growing up. It will always feel so unreasonably lavish and self-indulgent; there were other kids who had it a lot worse off than me. But extending that logic, then, the only person who has a right to complain is the person who is the very worst-off person in the whole wide world. Who is that? Some guy crawling through the Sahara on his hands and knees while vultures gnaw at his eyeballs and maggots crawl out of his ears?

My only measure or understanding of popularity came

---

[36] I have only been really very hungry one time. In December 1992, after graduating from college, I had a job as an intern in the sales department of a radio station for which I received no money. And I worked at the Gap in Eastern Hills Mall. One Friday, just before Christmas, I worked at the radio station, then met a friend who was still at University of Buffalo. We got wasted at a bar downtown and I threw up, slept at his house, overslept for the promotion I was to attend at a Tops grocery store for the radio station the next morning, went to the promotion hungover, then went to my job at the Gap where I worked without a break because Christmas was nigh until about 8:00 p.m. when I went on break and ate at the Woolworth's counter. I ordered a turkey platter with double the meat. I literally said, "Please double the meat." That was really the only time I was ever hungry, and I knew that food was imminent. So it feels indulgent and self-important to say I was ever unhappy. But I was. And as indulgent as it may feel, writing about it is how to heal.

from the town where I lived. Grandpa always had lots of people with whom he could talk after church and at pancake lunches; people swarmed to him. But he wasn't all mean-girlish about it. He was modest. Using kid logic, if Grandpa is lovable and lovable people put worms on hooks, then the fact that I do not put worms on hooks makes me unlovable.[37] I, on the other hand, did lots of rotten things. It's funny how shame starts and then builds and builds and builds until you have to let it out. It's not like a snowball in that regard —snow melts eventually. Shame is more like a pearl, which forms when an irritant or parasite walks into an oyster or a clam. The oyster or clam, eager to defend itself, starts coating the irritant with a fluid coating which hardens, and then the oyster or clam continues to emit the coating, and layer upon layer of coating covers the irritant and a pearl is formed. Shame functions this same way, resulting in an impenetrable rock. But shame is not shiny and lustrous. Maybe this is a bad metaphor, as a pearl tends to be valued while shame is just corrosive.

It took me a while to think of Grandpa as a person. For me, that time came when I realized that the reinvention upon which I had been heretofore relying was no longer possible. I prided myself on reinvention. At seventeen, I left my small town and went to college and befriended actual folks with similar interests. I told a friend recently—talking about a U2

---

[37] The fear of worms is called *scoleciphobia*. I think I have that disease. My name is Gary, and I am a scoleciphobe. While I know that nothing a worm can do could ever harm me, the thought of its little worm face looking at me and breathing on me and leaving its worm residue on me as I kill it with a fish hook drives me bonkers. I understand that they are an essential part of our ecosystem. I also know the threat of being afflicted with intestinal worms is a perpetual one, and worms evoke a disgust response owing to their ability to spread infectious diseases. And once I saw worms wriggling around in my dog's feces. I also think that worms evoke the movement and appearance of poisonous snakes, something of which man has always been appropriately fearful. More succinctly, worms are fucking stupid. I hate them.

concert—how ashamed I still was with regard to the first time I saw U2 in concert. It was October 1987, and I was a senior in high school, and they were touring for *The Joshua Tree*. No one I knew wanted to go with me. No one. I bought four tickets and literally had to give them away—though with the caveat that Rudy T. would drive, Karen O. would bring the weed, and Sue M. would bring some wine coolers. For thirty years, I thought that no one liked me. The friend with whom I was speaking to recently told me two things, he said, "first the kids in your high school didn't like U2." Which is true. They liked Black Sabbath and Led Zeppelin and the whatnot. Then he told me that I should stop feeling ashamed, that I was like the P. Diddy of my high school—getting people to do what I wanted to accomplish my goals. It was a transformative conversation.

Anyway, in college in 1988, *everyone* liked U2. It was mind-boggling to realize that I was not an anomaly, that I could be fun and well liked and appreciated. After college, I moved to Boston and worked for a publisher and subsequently devised a whole new me—more confident and maybe even a little more laid back. Then I moved to New York City and worked as a high school English teacher. Then I moved to Baltimore and started law school.

Reinvention while conceptualizing and executing new identities was always the magic elixir for me to assuage this shame. I was able to rationalize past defeats by saying that I had never really been invested in that endeavor anyway; I could look forward to new sets of people and new challenges rather than repairing or focusing on the current ones.

Law school ended; my son was born; I got a job at a big law firm. And it was suddenly and jarringly apparent that freedom and opportunities for self-reflection would be kept to a minimum. No more whimsy or occupational metamorphosis or personality mutations or geographical relocations or social transmogrifications. This was it. And since this was the me I was going to be stuck with, I had best try to figure out who that me was.[38] And from whence he originated.

It's astonishing in many ways and sad, really. That you have to get married first to see what an amazing accomplishment being married for sixty years can be. You have to worry about paying a mortgage now and again before you realize the strength of character it must have taken to survive the Great Depression. You have to be a parent first before you can even begin to understand how you could never understand what it must be like to lose a child. You have to hit forty and get your own aches and pains before you realize what an act of love it was for Grandpa to get down on the floor and play games with me. And by the time we learn that, there's not much time left. I wish I would have thanked him for doing this and while we were being human, asked him questions to embarrass him, to make him recall what it was like for him as a kid, to have engaged him more and more authentically.

5. Grandpa and Gary

Grandpa never had a chance to reinvent himself. He was okay with that (at least I think he was). I wasn't. When you live on the same rural road your entire life, you forget that you are capable of bold things. That boldness might bubble inside of you, but it doesn't go anywhere. How could you not be angry that the very assets which kept you here—loyalty, commitment, devotion—are now the very things that prevented you from seeking more? How do you not feel double-crossed and betrayed? If so much of what you believe about yourself when

---

[38] I have since learned that this is not the case; reinvention is possible at all stages of life and even at all levels. I have changed jobs several times since then; I have been pretty good at making new friends and keeping old ones; I have lots of bad habits and begun assessing the reasons for those bad habits in the first place. I have been writing and have been published. Reinvention is a perpetual prerogative. And right. And in many cases, necessity.

you are twenty turns out to be wrong, then how does one re-right the ship when you discover the smaller, truer part much later in life? Are you ever free of that weight? Are you ever authentically yourself?

Grandpa and I were no closer or less close than any one of his other seven grandchildren. Frankly, I don't think he really liked me all that much. This assessment comes not from anything he said or did or did not say or did not do. This assessment is derived from cogent analysis and the basic tenets of human nature. More succinctly, how could a hardworking, proud, gentle man actually *like* a kid such as me? It just seems—looking back armed with the cognizance I have now—metaphysically impossible. I don't see how could he have. I was such a silly and unfocused kid; I lacked the work ethic to which he adhered and which I think he thought was to be expected of boys, especially boys on a farm. I had skinny arms, and I was always reading books and frolicking about, and I rarely if ever did anything to help anyone else. I recall as a young boy taking a nap on a lawn chair next to where these construction people were building us a new barn. What did Grandpa think of this? I suspect he was annoyed; perhaps embarrassed; likely astounded. Obviously, tenets of genetics and self-perpetuation demanded that he loved me. But there is no such law regarding *liking*. I don't think I was an *integral* part of his life.

I am certain that by the time I was ten or twelve, he—if speaking truthfully—found me so obstinate as to be intolerable. But he never exhibited behaviors to suggest so, so maybe he genuinely liked me? Maybe it wasn't an act? Maybe giving someone your name creates a tolerance for the stupid shit they do. And fosters forgiveness. There was this one time when my brother and I—we were about five and four, respectively—painted his Arctic Cat snowmobile with motor oil. I do not recall the genesis of this idea or who initiated it or why; I recall being in what we called the "old" section of our shed, where Grandpa stored his snowmobile. We must have been playing

42

there amid the antique scythes and sickles and machetes and hay-cutting tools of yesteryear and for some reason decided his snowmobile was too white. Dad had a barrel filled with motor oil that had a cool pump attached. Pumping motor oil is one of the most gratifying feelings: the pump provides a sufficient amount of resistance but there is also an odd fluidity and ease to the whole process. From the spout, the oil emerges shimmering, and dances as it falls into the container—in our case, an old Cool Whip container.

Painting a snowmobile with oil is about the stupidest fucking thing a person can do. We even painted the seat. And yet Grandpa didn't get mad. He didn't even raise his voice. He just looked at us with a mix of disgust and bewilderment and sorrow and pity—but there was no anger. He just gave us some rags and told us to clean it up.

The transgressions were not always so horrible. In fact, the little things were often worse. Little things I did or expected that could not have been understandable to a man who had lived through the Great Depression. There was this one time, when I was about five, Grandpa and Grandma had to take my brother and me to the dentist. (Mom was the choir director at St. Cecilia's, our parish, and was frequently required to attend liturgical music ministry workshops and seminars. It was only later that I learned that "liturgical music ministry workshop" was a euphemism for "two for one whiskey sour night at a nightclub in Niagara Falls")[39]. After the dentist, we stopped at Red Barn,[40] a fast food restaurant in East Aurora, New York.

---

[39] Just kidding. Mom really did go to the liturgical music ministry workshops. She is faith and goodness and harmony incarnate

[40] The Red Barn restaurant was a fast-food restaurant chain founded in 1961 in Springfield, Ohio by Don Six, Martin Levine, and Jim Kirsch. In the late 1960s, Servomation bought the company. Motel 6 bought the new parent company itself in the late 1970s. The Red Barn in East Aurora, NY, where our dentist was, became a Burger King in the mid-1980s.

Grandma did not know to order my burgers plain—without ketchup and mustard and pickles and all that other revolting shit they slathered on burgers—so when my burger arrived, I took one bite and tasted the ketchup and mustard and shit, put the burger down, and started to cry. It took a while for Grandma to notice me crying. When she did, she said, "Oh, for heaven's sakes. What is wrong with you now?" Unable to make words, I merely pointed to my burger. My big brother told her that I only ate my burgers plain. She reluctantly and very aggressively scraped the condiments off my burger and said, "Here. Now it's plain." This made me cry harder because I knew the ketchup and mustard and shit were, despite Grandma's best efforts, all still there, nefariously soaked into the bun like toxic chemicals discharged from a chemical plant seeping into a neighborhood's drinking water. Grandma then asked if I was okay just eating fries, and I said, "Yes." Throughout this horrific event, Grandpa said nothing; he just looked at me, eating his own burger, with a look that I had never seen before and have not seen since. I now know it to be a look that of a mix of disdain, amusement, astonishment, disgust, sadness, and the knowledge that whatever glorious future he had envisioned for his descendants was quickly and irrevocably eroding. Here was a man who during the Depression likely would've walked for miles to get some ketchup. How could he not have found me despicable? How could a man who, as a boy, walked to school early to start the fire in the schoolhouse stove, built his own water wheels, and shot and killed and harvested his own hamburger meat ever like or have faith in me? A condiment-hating, worm-fearing, book-reading, asking-for-books-for-Christmas instead of a BB gun, dashboard-cigarette-stealing worthless boy-child like me? Had I no idea of his sacrifice? Had I no idea of the pain he'd been through?

I realize that I am forgiving myself when I write this. I have felt guilt for decades over asking Grandpa and Grandma—

people who during the Depression would have surely licked condiments off the floor—to wipe the condiments off my burger.[41]

Growing up in close proximity to Grandpa forced me to look at all of my transgressions through the lens of a grandparent with some frequency. Most of the time I was certain they were aghast and ashamed.

Were I to create a Venn diagram with one sphere representing things in which I was interested and the other representing things in which Grandpa took interest, there would be very little, though some, overlap. He liked engines and motors and automobiles and wheels and helping others and *Murder, She Wrote* and movies with John Wayne and Jack Lemmon and square dancing and *Popular Mechanics* and *The Old Farmers' Almanac* and chassis.[42] I liked Judy Blume books and Pac-Man and Centipede and *Raiders of the Lost Ark* and Van Halen and Duran Duran.

There were days when we would wait for the bus and Grandpa, finished with helping Dad do farm chores and ready to drive home on his three-wheeler, would wait with us. In grade school, this was fun. In high school, it was less so. He would ask us what we were doing and learning, and I would mumble something condescendingly. After one such incident, having gotten on the bus, I wondered if Grandpa had ever read any of the books we had to read. I thought to myself that I had never seen his handwriting; that I had never even seen him write. It made me wonder if he could read. And I felt really guilty for wondering this. My inner dialogue went something like, "Of

---

[41] I still loathe condiments. All of them.

[42] Chassis, the supporting frame upon which the moving parts of an automobile are constructed, is one of those words—like moose, deer, sheep, scissors, cattle, pants, doldrums, smithereens—where the singular and plural forms are the same!

The Emperor of Ice-Cream

course he can read, he reads *Popular Mechanics* magazines all the time." But then, "Maybe he just looks at the pictures and diagrams."

Yet intermittently throughout our relationship there would have been a shaded area on the Venn diagram where our interests aligned. He was into Stompers, and once asked me if I would be interested in going to a Stomper Pull.[43] There was also the time that he got the Kenny Rogers's *Twenty Greatest Hits* album for Christmas; an album also on my Christmas list. I was actually jealous of an album that Grandpa had. And there was a time when we were both really into roller-skating. As disorienting as it was to hear people talk about what a great man Grandpa was while simultaneously realizing I had nothing in common with him, the alignment of likes and interests was equally disorienting. I had always thought of Grandpa as belonging to another time.

I recall one day becoming aware that he didn't like pizza. The fact that Grandpa didn't like pizza also revolutionized how I thought of him. He was no longer omnipotent; no longer flawless; he was no longer that guy who "ate everything" when he was a boy. He, like me, also had likes and dislikes, and made it known when he disliked something. We never had pizza when he came over. I, too, didn't like pizza. The sauce was too much like ketchup, apparently. I loved sharing this mutual anomaly with Grandpa. We were renegades—because what contributing member of society didn't like pizza? It's odd being told you're weird by your friends' parents when you don't like something. Or when a hostess huffs and puffs because she has

---

[43] Stompers were little toy trucks that were popular in the early 1980s. They ran on a single AA battery and featured four-wheel drive. As Stompers grew in popularity, Moose Lodges, taverns, and places of general civic gatherings hosted Stomper Pulls. Stomper owners could modify and augment their Stompers and enter them in contests of strength, pitting them against other Stompers owners.

to make a sandwich in addition to pizza because you inexplicably don't like pizza. One night when I was staying at his house, my friend Jeremy's sister Susan brought home a pizza from Nino's in Attica. She was all happy because dinner was done. I told her I didn't like pizza. She made me a bologna sandwich and put mustard on it. I told her I didn't like mustard and she said, "What do you like?" And I said, "Peanut butter" and she said, "Let me guess, you don't like jelly?" and I said, "That's right," and she said, "For crying out loud, kid." She stormed back into the kitchen while Jeremy and I played Stompers. She said I was weird. It wasn't my fault I didn't like pizza, mustard, or jelly. "You wanna know who doesn't like pizza, bitch?" I wanted to say. "Me and my Grandpa. That's who."

It also made the fact that I never touched worms a little more digestible. To me anyway. Grandpa and I *were* similar. This is not an abuse memoir. This is something of my own manufacturing; but it does make the epiphany that Grandpa and I were more alike than I ever thought that much more gratifying. Even joyous. In one of the scrapbooks they made for me, my parents said that of my four grandparents, the one of which I reminded them most was Grandpa. This made me happy.

When I was in sixth grade, I tried pizza at my friend Paul's house.[44] And—to my very great surprise—I found I really liked the pizza. No, I *loved* it. This presented a problem. I really loved pizza, and being able to enjoy what everyone else was having felt great. But there was a little bit of guilt and sadness at no longer having this thing in common with Grandpa. This paradox is something that has stayed with me my whole life. "I have enjoyed not liking pizza with you, Grandpa, but now I like

---

[44] Sixth grade was really a transformative year for me. I tried cigarettes, *Penthouse,* and pizza in the span of just a few months.

pizza and I am enjoying the new freedom it brings" becomes "I have enjoyed spending time with you Grandpa as I grew up on this farm but now I want to move to Boston and be an urban dweller." It's hard trying to discern when differences between my forebears and I are liabilities and when differences between my forebears and I are assets. Loving to read—good thing. Independence—good thing. Lack of work ethic—not such a good thing (but I'm learning to make it work for me). An eagerness to get up and explore new cities—good thing. No matter what, though, there is always guilt attached to the leaving—whether you are leaving a relationship built on loathing pizza or leaving the farm for the city.

I also loved the fact that Grandpa never really liked sports. If the Buffalo Bills were on TV, he would watch them. But he didn't obsess over sports or follow any particular team religiously. This was anomalous in Buffalo, as the people there really really like their sports. I admired this about him. He made it okay for me to not like sports.

Even as an adult, I cannot opine to a reasonable degree of certainty that he would like me today. I curse. I publish things on the internet that have cursing in it and in which I share too much information. I don't save money. During the summer months, I do not prepare for winter; rather, I enjoy the summer. I make fun of people. I troll conservative legislators on Twitter. I curse at the conservative legislators. I don't garden. I still don't touch worms. My pleasure-reading-to-home-improvement-project ratio is still way out of whack.

This analysis is not borne from a low self-esteem, just facts. Though I think Grandpa would sort of like Quentin Tarantino movies, and maybe some of REM's more twangy songs. I know that he would love me. And I know that he always loved me. Because I just know. It takes a while to learn that liking and loving are two very different things. I know that he loved me. I could feel it and see it and hear it. As the authority on love M. Scott Peck states, love is not a feeling but rather an

48

activity or investment. He defined love as "The will to extend one's self for the purpose of nurturing one's own or another's personal growth." He was always nurturing, and always teaching. I know that he was proud of what he saw me accomplish. He and Grandma called me the day before the bar exam and told me that they would be praying the rosary "all day" so that I would do well.[45] When I passed, I thanked him, and he told me he was proud of me. I took the bar exam in July 2004 and learned the results in November 2004.[46] In October 2004, Grandma died. So I knew I was going to pass. Not because I harbor any latent legal genius; but because I knew Grandma would see to it that I did.

A year or so later, on my thirty-fifth birthday, a birthday on which I was sullen to the point of melancholy, I called him and told him that I was old enough to be president, and he said, "Yeah," and I said (through tears), "Though I probably never will be," and he said, "Now why in the hell would you even want to be. You're doing a great job right where you are."

---

[45] If there are any non-Catholics reading this book, the rosary is a prayer that Catholics say when they really want shit to go down. It consists of three sets of mysteries, each containing five mysteries related to the birth and death and resurrection of Jesus. Each mystery begins with an "Our Father" and then you say ten "Hail Mary's" and then one "Glory Be" while contemplating the mystery. Typically, you employ a rosary, which resembles a beaded necklace with a crucifix appended to it. Rosaries range from plastic glow-in-the-dark ones to ones beaded with precious gems. Rosaries also increase in value by getting blessed by priests, having threads of old sacred garments sewn into them, being made with rock from holy places, etc.

[46] Interestingly, the first day of the bar exam was Tuesday, July 27. It was that evening that then-Illinois State Senator Barack Obama gave the keynote address at the Democratic National Convention in Boston. I met my friend J. for coffee the next morning, the second day of the bar exam, and he told me that he saw an amazing speaker at the DNC the previous evening. I hadn't watched it. But I remember him trying to recall the name.

The Emperor of Ice-Cream

Were I to create a Venn diagram today with one sphere representing salient characteristics of me and the other sphere representing salient characteristics of Grandpa, there would be a great deal of overlap. This is something of which I am very proud. And surprised.[47] It makes me feel guilty at the pride I felt for fancying myself such an independent man. Being a parent makes me realize how much it hurts when we are the ones from whom our offspring wish to extricate themselves. I love being independent. But I hate it when my son demonstrates the same joy at his own independence. Which he does with ever-increasing frequency now that he is thirteen. But then I tell myself that he will always be more like me than he might care to acknowledge. Which leads me to think that I have always been and will always be more like my dad and my mom and my grandparents than I might wish to acknowledge.

I wonder if we would have been friends had we been contemporaries. My gestalt comes from somewhere. Isn't it fair to assume that at least 25 percent of that gestalt comes from him? That we would have at least 25 percent in common? Maybe even more—there is no genetic black-letter law that says each grandparent contributes 25 percent to your gestalt.

He would like my humor, I think. My irreverence. But it would be a fine line, as he would hate my propensity for cursing. He would find my propensity for excess way too excessive. And deem my lack of interest in gas mileage way too frivolous. Of all my characteristics, my propensity for self-indulgence is the one I think Grandpa would loathe the most. I am always buying shit. Even if he didn't notice it, I am certain that he did and

---

[47] There are ten years—between when Grandpa was sixteen and his father died and when Grandpa was twenty-eight and he married Grandma and their story began—about which I know nothing, except for the fact that he wanted to join the Navy, and in 1937 Grandpa gave away his sister Ethel when she got married. These are the ten years I found to be most formative, the most edifying, in my own life. I do not know if Grandpa was ever lonely during this time, or whether he worried about getting married; what he worried about, what frightened him, what made him happy.

certain that he—austerity incarnate—found it revolting. When I was in law school and my wife and I were struggling to put food on the table, I bought three bow ties: $120 on the credit card. $120 that could have gone for meals or for our house fund or for something besides silky things to adorn my neck. But even this propensity (I don't think it's a flaw; it's probably not an asset, but it's not as much of a liability as I had always thought) came from somewhere.

On the other hand, though, we never clicked. I realized this when I was about twelve or thirteen. My sister and I were swimming in the pool Grandpa had built. Next to the pool was the cow pasture where a cow was giving birth. Grandpa emerged from the barn to assist. My sister and I watched. Grandpa said, "Gary, why don't you get in here and help me." So I did. There was no fear that Grandpa would yell at me, but I was afraid of doing something wrong. I stood by Grandpa as he coaxed the baby calf out of the cow's big sweaty floppy vagina. He actually put his hand in the cow's big sweaty floppy vagina. We had to pull the calf out; we had our hands on the calf—our hands on each other's hands—and pulled it out of its mother's big flippety-flappety throbbing vagina. The calf was born. Grandpa put his hand back in the big sweaty vagina and pulled the giant pulsing placenta out where it flopped and jiggled on the ground like a giant veiny Jell-O mold. Then Grandpa thanked me and smiled and said, "We did it!" and clicked his tongue against the roof of his mouth.

Typically, following events like these, the young boy learns a lesson or hears his calling or feels a oneness with the universe. If there was some sort of historic, elemental, fundamental, universal component to this endeavor—like Mufasa teaching Simba about his kingdom in *The Lion King* or an ancient mariner teaching his offspring about the laws of the sea and how to harvest quahogs—I did not feel it. I felt nothing but disgust. And I recall walking back to the pool feeling disgusted with myself that I felt nothing but disgust.

What sort of monster was I that I could have this experience with my grandfather and feel nothing? Nothing except for disgust. The only wonder I felt was when I wondered whether the afterbirth juice would stain my new flip-flops. That was the only wonder I felt. There was no connection, no tears, no feeling of oneness with Nature or the universe or any identifiable celestial body; no feelings of pride or unity with my ancestors who had come before me. I just wanted to go back to making merry in the swimming pool.

I figured Grandpa sensed this. And that he was equally disgusted by it. Another characteristic I lacked was the impulse to help. Knowing this made me feel guilty too.

This all contributed to the weight of the guilt I felt when he died. I realized then I had no idea who he was, and I suddenly wanted to know more. In the legal profession we call what we use to do this "evidence." And the best evidence is firsthand testimony. I had lots of answers and artifacts, but I would have loved to ask him questions that I had never asked; questions that I was just learning how to ask. Questions as innocuous as what is your favorite birthday memory? Or did you date anyone before Grandma? Along with questions a bit more incisive, like what did you love most about Grandma? Do you feel sad sometimes? I had lots of memories. Could recall lots of conversations and interactions and memories. But sadly, there seemed to be scant substantive evidence to determine who Grandpa—as a man—was, whether he would like me now, whether he was happy. I never asked him, "Grandpa, who are you?" or "Grandpa, do you like me?" or "Grandpa, what stands in the way between you and complete happiness?" These are odd, nearly unanswerable questions, and Grandpa would have likely lightly ridiculed each. I would have had to have done it more subtly, with more nuance than such direct questions allow.

So much of our relationship was based on assumptions—specifically *mine*: me assuming Grandpa had no authentic thoughts or fears when he was growing up, me assuming he wouldn't know or care about what was going on with me—either because he genuinely wouldn't know what to think about Van Halen or Duran Duran or *The Catcher in the Rye,* or because my problems were too small. Me assuming that he and Grandma never fought, or that he never wondered if he was happy. Me assuming that he was always happy, that he never yearned to be elsewhere, that he never grew tired of the status quo, of the smallness of the town, of the chicken BBQs sponsored by volunteer fire departments and the pancake breakfasts in church basements.

To gather some evidence, I looked to the things he owned. Those things we clung to possessed a new sort of magic when Grandpa was gone just by virtue of the fact that he touched them. These include intangible things like the hopes they had of who you were going to be one day. But it also includes the tangible – the stuff.

These lessons are easy to learn but hard to put into practice. Despite the regret that simmers around Grandpa, I have never asked my parents what sort of life they wanted for me. It'd be weird. I suspect they might also say, "a simple one." But they would pepper it with something about me being happy. They are both people who have been able to identify and commit to the things they love, meaning: they are people who understand the importance of self-actualization and of doing what you love to live a happy life. That said, I recall them being very sad when they dropped me off in Boston for what was clearly the last time they would drop me off anywhere.[48] I

---

[48] Though it was clearly understood by all parties that it would not be the last time I would ask them to do something for me—things like send me an emergency check via FedEx so we could close on a house after I fucked up the numbers, buy me stuff, help me move, help me pack, help me watch kids, help me just generally and then help me some more. They also voluntarily did stuff. They bought a "Learn the Polka" CD and learned the polka in their garage before Elizabeth's and my wedding. When they got good enough, they set up sawhorses and other garagey obstacles to mimic

think they always suspected, if not outright *knew*, that I would move away someday, and that such a move, despite the chronic love-hate relationship that country folk seem to have with cities, was necessary and would prove fruitful.

It has only been in the last decade or so—certainly later than Erik Erikson's psychoanalytic theory[49] might suggest—that I have begun to wonder whether Grandpa and Dad actually did enjoy farming, or found it gratifying, or if they actually ever wondered if they were doing the thing they were meant to do. People did not quit farming to go to law school or write books or find themselves or follow the Dead. But maybe they did not equate their identity with their means of subsistence so much back then either?

Theoretically, I could still ask my father if he enjoyed farming. I could ask if he liked it, if it satisfied him intellectually, or, if given the choice again, would he still choose it as a profession. But I don't think I ever could since I don't think I could handle it if he responded in the negative to any of those queries. Writing how much I disliked worms and feces and plants and rivers feels so indulgent; it is precisely these plants and rivers (not so much the worms) that paid for me to go to a Jesuit college and then move to Boston with nary a

---

the obstacles found on a wedding dance floor, so they could learn how to polka around people.

[49] Erikson's stages of psychosocial development, as articulated by Erik Erikson, in collaboration with Joan Erikson, is a comprehensive psychoanalytic theory that identifies a series of eight stages in which a healthy developing individual should pass through from infancy to late adulthood. All stages are present at birth but only begin to unfold according to both a natural scheme and one's ecological and cultural upbringing. In each stage, the person confronts, and hopefully masters, new challenges. Each stage builds upon the successful completion of earlier stages. The challenges of stages not successfully completed may be expected to reappear as problems in the future.

concern that my bills would somehow get paid.

With respect to likability, it's important to remember that people are just different. There are certain fundamental traits that people possess that determine their compatibility with others. Prior to algorithms employed by online dating sites and, prior to that, dating services, people presumably just asked themselves, "Do I like that person?" It's interesting to see my son—in sixth grade as I write this—in his first year at middle school. Six elementary schools feed into his middle school, so for the first time he has been able to choose friends without it being based on geography or who his parents are friends with or what team he is on. It's interesting to gauge how he sees himself and what he sees as valuable characteristics in people. In college, I recall meeting my best friend the first weeks of freshman year and seeing that we had the same backpack, shoes, belt, sense of humor, and targets of disdain. You often hear how people are wired differently. When Grandpa began one of the trips that meant so much to him, his priorities were in maximizing gas mileage and making sure he would be in a town with a Catholic Church wherever he would be on any given Sunday. The first and only things I think about prior to a trip is making an appropriate playlist for the drive and determining which route passes the most Starbucks. And then, since bingeing is more acceptable on trips, thinking about all the Frappuccinos I can get.[50] Two people with such disparate priorities probably should not take a road trip together. They can love each other, and there will surely be times when they will like each other, but a road trip will inevitably net more strife than mirth.

---

[50] In the summer of 2010, to celebrate my imminent fortieth birthday, my wife planned a trip to Cape Cod. That playlist was a work of art, employing kid-friendly songs, songs with references to Cape Cod, songs of our courtship, and general vacation songs. And we got so many Frappuccinos.

The Emperor of Ice-Cream

Of course, sometimes such a road trip is inevitable. You can't always travel with your soulmate. There are lots of road trips in life. Deciding on which ones to go on depends on one's tolerance for another's idiosyncrasies, one's tolerance for the risk involved with an inaccurate assessment of the cost-benefit analysis of going on a trip, one's tolerance for tolerance, most succinctly.

I recall a road trip I took my junior year in college. Four friends and I climbed into Jay Quimby's Dodge Omni to travel from Syracuse to Pittsburgh to see the Replacements at the Metropol. I really wanted to see the Replacements. The friends with whom I traveled were part of the faction of friends I had who were more into flannel and rugby and camping than the J. Crew and Nantuckety friends with whom I most closely associated. So we are driving to Pittsburgh. We have a beer-ball in the back of the Dodge Omni, and because we are running late for the concert, we can't stop, so we have to pee in a giant Mini Mart cup and toss the pee out the window. Because Jason is tinier than me, he sits in the middle, and whenever he tosses pee out the window it splashes on me. Additionally, Jason chews chewing tobacco and it fucking stinks. Soon I'm thinking to myself, "Why am I going on this road trip with these heathens?" But in the end, it was fun.

On a trip with someone, be it in a car or a van or in a barn or through life, you learn about them, what's important to them. The longer you are on a trip with them, the more prone to argument you might be. But also, the more commonalities you discover.

Once, after Grandma died, Grandpa and I drove around for about an hour. It was fun. I wonder what a road trip with him would have been like. I suspect it would have been rather easy to cajole him into indulgence and lavishness. I suspect I would be astonished by his insight.

Gary M. Almeter

Boston

"Metamorphosis"

Yillow, yillow, yillow,
Old worm, my pretty quirk,
How the wind spells out
Sep – tem – ber. . . .

Summer is in bones.
Cock-robin's at Caracas.
Make o, make o, make o,
Oto – otu – bre.

And the rude leaves fall.
The rain falls. The sky
Falls and lies with worms.
The street lamps

Are those that have been hanged.
Dangling in an illogical
To and to and fro
Fro Niz – nil – imbo.

—Wallace Stevens

After college, when I was thinking of moving to Boston with a friend, Grandpa told me not to. This was unusual for him—for him to be so outspoken and direct. He told me he hated the city, above and beyond his characteristic disdain for all things urban. When I asked him why, he told me how he used to transport maple syrup cans there in the 40s and 50s. The chaotic, unnavigable roads had angered him; the rude and boisterous people had embarrassed him. He said that once he was delivering a truckload of maple syrup cans somewhere in

57

Boston and a driver cut him off, and all the maple syrup cans, hundreds if not thousands of them, spilled off the truck. Traffic stopped while he reloaded the ones he could salvage. This incident had indelibly convinced him the entire city was a godforsaken place.

I had never heard that story before. But my enthusiasm for getting out of the rural town was unassailable, and I moved there anyway. I was a twenty-two-year-old, single, jobless college graduate who had never been to Boston—indeed, had never lived in any sort of major metropolitan area; never been to a city long enough to gauge its cadence, hear its unique cacophony, taste its cuisine, see its renditions of things, meet its personalities.

On October 10, 1993, my parents drove me along with all my possessions to Boston in their sedan. The seventeen months I had spent living in the small town where I had grown up and getting rejection letters from every job[51] to which I had applied had had a corrosive effect on my self-esteem. It was eighteen months filled with rejection letters, the third consecutive Bills' Super Bowl loss, an unpaid internship at a radio station in Buffalo, a fuckload of snow, and serving drinks to my former high school physical education teacher at the sports bar where I worked.

My friend and I moved to Allston, Massachusetts. Just

---

[51] It wasn't all bleak. did get a job doing "marketing" for a Fortune 500 company called Philip Morris. This provided me with the opportunity to drive a souped-up red Marlboro van from gas station to gas station and set up a kiosk where I gave people who purchased cartons of cigarettes valuable Marlboro merchandise. For example, if a person with limited means bought three cartons of any Marlboro brand cigarettes, he or she would get a beach towel. I did this for one week. There were some actual bright spots. The summer of 1992, I interviewed twice for an editorial assistant position at *Field & Stream* magazine. Interviewing at a big media company located at 2 Park Avenue in New York was awesome. My friend's sister worked there and said the final decision came down to two people, me, and someone else. The someone else got it.

off the Green Line's B-Line and just south of Harvard Ave. and north of Boston University. It was good to feel like I was at the heart of everything—but I spent the first few days crying. I was going to miss my dog, Brandy, for one. Also, the first night in our new apartment, I spotted the helium balloon that my colleagues at the sports bar had given me as a going-away gift start to violently bob up and down. I was on my cot, loaned to me by Uncle Tom and Aunt Rosemary, and this balloon was just bopping up and down. I got up, turned on the light, and six to eight mice that had been chewing on the butterscotch candy tied to the ribbon of the balloon scurried away. Rather than try to exterminate the mice, I just wept. This freedom to which I had been looking forward for years was anything but utopia.

Then I started exploring the city. People in Boston talked differently. They walked differently, as though they knew they were always in the midst of something extraordinary. It did not take long for me to learn that by the associative property, I too was in the midst of something extraordinary. That fall, I got lost on the Green Lines, the Red Lines, the Orange Line, and the Blue Line. I walked through the North End, the South End, Charlestown, Cambridge, Boston Common; walked up and down the Freedom Trail, Newbury Street, Commonwealth Avenue, and Harvard Square. I got to see Jacqueline Onassis rededicate the JFK library. I ate clam chowder at the Union Oyster House. I bought my own Brooks Brothers tennis sweater. I drank beer at the Sunset Grill. I had a job interview at Little, Brown and Company's 34 Beacon Street headquarters. I raked leaves for a lady in Wellesley for extra cash. I spent a day with a friend in Marblehead. I tailgated at a Boston College football game. I got a library card.

It was in those early months that I decided to become who I was supposed to be. As a result, my life changed. I changed.

I got a job doing customer service for a cellular phone

company. I worked the three to eleven o' clock shift and walked every afternoon through streets crowded with Ivy League-pedigreed financial people. Everyone marched with rigor in freshly polished, cordovan-shell leather shoes built to withstand such rigor. Everyone looked astute, refined, adept, and at their best. Everyone not only wore Brooks Brothers; everyone exuded Brooks Brothers. Everyone, it was clear, was ambition incarnate. Everyone, I was certain, was on their way to achievement. Everyone was in a place where I was not. Everyone reinforced the inveterate nature of the universe. Then, when my shift was done at eleven, I scurried through the same—though by then barren and spookily empty—cavernous financial district streets back to the Government Center T-Stop to catch the last Green Line train home. It would take me home, under a desolate Boston Common, under a quiet Newbury Street, and under Kenmore Square. It surfaced near Fenway Park and then rambled up and along Commonwealth Avenue to my Harvard Avenue stop, which by then was filled with drunk Boston College students, reminding me that my college days were over.

As hard as it was to be (or feel) poor while others were flourishing, to walk with my head up to my customer service job through the envy-inducing world of finance, to eat alone and commute home on a near-empty train, to digest the negative effects that came with the social comparisons for which I had a propensity, and to be away from my family at Thanksgiving, the resultant pride that came from existing in my new arena was incalculable.

I realize now that I should have been extremely lonely during these inaugural weeks in a big city by myself, surrounded by people who were going places—people who effortlessly looked and talked like Kennedys, more refined people than the Buffalonians to whom I was accustomed—I really wasn't. I never even thought I was and would have never identified myself as such. I realize now that I was learning to distinguish loneliness from solitude, and that the rush of self-awareness, the deluge of self-confidence, and the newfound eagerness for self-actualization far outweighed and diluted any threat of loneliness.

It turns out that self-reliance is far more buoyant, and far less elusive, than we think it is. And I was more confident than I'd believed myself to be.

I got that job at Little, Brown & Co. and was officially a publisher. I hung out with publishing colleagues, many of whom had gone to Ivy League schools, and they thought I was funny and smart, and eventually we became friends. In those days, you could smoke in bars, and we did. I watched the Big Dig[52] get dug. I watched my very first marathon ever from the rooftop of a building on Commonwealth Avenue. I took a class at Harvard. I saw Bob Lobel get teary when he announced that Jacqueline Kennedy Onassis had passed before the May 19, 1994, sportscast on WBZ. I met Ted Kennedy and saw him annihilate then-candidate for Senate Mitt Romney at a debate in Faneuil Hall. I went to the Cape for my very first time. The world of music changed as I saw indie bands at the Paradise, saw big bands at the Boston Garden, and saw the *Boston Pops* at the Hatch Shell. I moved to Brookline, a more refined neighborhood, with friends from college. I went to Fenway. I bought new CDs at midnight at Tower Records on Newbury Street, made friends. I passed out on the T and strangers drove me home. I went to Rose Kennedy's funeral. I played softball

---

[52] The Big Dig was Boston infrastructure project that rerouted the Central Artery of Interstate 93, the chief highway which ran right through the heart of the city, into the Thomas P. O'Neill, Jr. Tunnel. The project also included the construction of the Ted Williams Tunnel (extending Interstate 90 to Logan International Airport), Bunker Hill Memorial Bridge over the Charles River, and the Rose Kennedy Greenway in the space vacated by the previous I-93 elevated roadway. The project infamously took a great deal longer and cost a great deal more than initially proposed or expected. Planning began in 1982; the construction work was carried out between 1991 and 2006; and the project concluded on December 31, 2007.

in Boston Common. I got a Master's degree at Boston College. Sometimes flying home from a wedding on a Sunday night, the shuttle from Logan Airport to the Blue Line would pull up just as I was leaving baggage claim, and I just fucking loved the city as I knew it had done that just for me; if we were driving home, the butterscotch streetlamps of the Mass Pike lighted our path.

Boston gave me confidence—the confidence for which I had always yearned growing up. A confidence I equate with being happy with who and where you are. I learned it was okay to wear cool glasses in Boston, and to generally be yourself; that it was cool to be smart. That my wit was unparalleled. Each day I got to feel like a little kid jumping in a pile of leaves. In Boston I met the woman who would become my wife. Our first date was to a Red Sox game at Fenway. We smoked and drank beers at El Phoenix in Brighton. Soon we were taking weekend trips to the North Shore. We fell in love in Boston. We both preferred Dunkin' Donuts over the new and ubiquitous Starbucks. We loved lobster.

I was a man in my twenties, and inevitably I hurt people: the artsy girlfriend I dumped when my college friends moved to town; the girls from work who I rejected; the people to whom I was rude because I was hungover or just annoyed. I stole from people's coats when I did not feel like taking the train home. I puked on people. I quit jobs with no notice.[53] I offended people at sales conferences. This is what twenty-somethings do, I know, but it still made me feel "bad," for lack of a better word. Bad and shitty and ashamed. I feared I was confidently becoming an asshole.

Boston was a punctuation mark—though not the final

---

[53] The Little, Brown & Co. job lasted about two years and was wonderful. When my editor left for a larger publisher, she took me with her. Which led to me meeting my now wife, quitting publishing, and getting a Master's in Education at Boston College. The jobs I quit with no notice were the twelve or so jobs I had during the first twelve months I lived in Boston.

one; more like a semicolon—on the feelings of inadequacy I felt growing up. But it meant a geographical distance from growing up and a philosophical one too. Reinvention was so awesome.

And Grandpa, this man who had never done it, was missing out. I missed him during this time. I cannot say with any great certainty that I thought about him every day; or that I did not think about him every day. I believe that his influence simultaneously diminished and increased during this time as I did things on my own—in this city he loathed—while also learning that the tenets of manhood do not change, no matter where you are.

Every now and again—while walking amid the Brooks Brothered Bostonians who moved with such purpose—I would wonder precisely where Grandpa's truck loaded with maple syrup cans had overturned. There was no maple syrup district in the city, no pancake section per se, no epicenter of breakfast within the city limits. Grandpa didn't recall the street upon which all the maple syrup had toppled. It was easy to envision him on any one of Boston's serpentine streets, working patiently to reload the maple syrup cans alone, bemoaning the apathy of nonplussed passersby; easy to imagine the fury with which inconvenienced Bostonians surely treated him. I wondered if he had had his kerchief to wipe sweat off his forehead, or the syrup off his hands so he wouldn't get it on the steering wheel.

How was it for him, driving to Boston alone? Was there even a radio in the old truck? Was there even heat? What is the decibel level of a truckload of maple syrup cans at fifty-five miles per hour? Could that old truck even go fifty-five miles per hour? Where did he eat? Did Grandma pack him a lunch? Of course she did. Where did he sleep—in the truck? Certainly not in a hotel. But what if there was no heat in the truck?

The Emperor of Ice-Cream

In Boston I met the woman who would become my wife. I proposed to her in front of JFK's birthplace, and we celebrated by drinking with Samuel Adams. But we both had a New York City itch that needed to be scratched, and in time we scratched it, and through our tears my fiancée and I left Brookline, Massachusetts for New York City on August 22, 1998. I was older, more confident, had a Master's Degree in Education and was profoundly grateful to the city I was leaving for the ways it had taken care of me. I still frequently reflect on those years. Still get surges of jealousy when I think of the twenty-somethings pulling up to their apartments in Allston each September 1. The years were transformative in every sense of that word, changing me from a callow selfish youth to a man closer to what I wanted to become.

We moved to New York City, and I taught high school at public high school in Manhattan. After teaching for three years and getting restless, I wanted to go to law school. I was rejected by both Harvard and Boston College, so we moved further south to Baltimore where the Starbucks far outnumber the Dunkin' Donuts and Orioles fans far outnumber Red Sox fans. But I returned to Boston as often as possible, jumping at the chance when I needed something for work, or when friends got married or had babies christened. My wife and kids took me to the Cape for a week when I was on the cusp of turning forty.

Decades later, after he was gone, my aunts cleaned out Grandpa and Grandma's house. They gave my wife all of Grandma's old fabric: florals and brocades and laces and upholstery that were all familiar to me though I had only known them as chairs and pajamas and shirts and square dancing outfits. The fabrics still held the smell of my grandparents— the smell that returned me to their house, to the basement in which those fabrics lay stacked for decades.[54] These bags of

---

[54] Why do smells trigger such strong emotions and memories? Scientists believe

Gary M. Almeter

fabric included all of Grandpa's hankies. The smell of those hankies remained for their next trip to Boston.

---

the answer is due to brain anatomy. Incoming smells are first processed by the olfactory bulb, which starts inside the nose and runs along the bottom of the brain. The olfactory bulb has direct connections to two brain areas that are strongly implicated in emotion and memory: the amygdala and hippocampus. Interestingly, visual, auditory, and tactile information do not pass through these brain areas. This may be why olfaction, more than any other sense, is so successful at triggering emotions and memories. There is a whole potpourri of scents that accompany a person; some of them emanating naturally from the body, and some the result of chemical accouterments, or where the person has been, or what the person has eaten.

The Red Turban of the Boatman

"The Load of Sugar-Cane"

The going of the glade-boat
Is like water flowing;

Like water flowing
Through the green saw-grass
Under the rainbows;

Under the rainbows
That are like birds,
Turning, bedizened,

While the wind still whistles
As kildeer do,

When they rise
At the red turban
Of the boatman.

—Wallace Stevens

It started, as most things did back then, with Arthur Fonzarelli. He, known as "Fonzie" or "The Fonz," was so ubiquitous as to be inescapable in the late 1970s. The Fonz, usually depicted in worn dungarees, a white T-shirt and black leather jacket and sitting atop a motorcycle with two thumbs up at the end of arms outsplayed,[55] appeared on lunch boxes,

---

[55] Until recently, Fonzie's leather jacket was in the Smithsonian Institution's National Museum of American History, along with Kermit the Frog, Eddie Van Halen's guitar, Archie Bunker's chair, and Bob Dylan's jacket—black leather like Fonzie's, but his worn July 25, 1965 at the Newport Folk Festival when he treasonously plugged in his

T-shirts, magazine covers, coffee mugs, board games, fast food keepsake cups, posters, and he even had his own pinball machine. His anomalous patois insinuated itself into America's vernacular; for the eleven seasons it aired between 1974 and 1984, *Happy Days,* the show in which the Fonz was featured, was consistently ranked as one of the top ten television shows in terms of viewership. Every Wednesday morning, I discussed the previous Tuesday night's episode with my classmates, this being the era when everyone got just three channels and watched the same programs at the same time. So the appearance of Fonzie's cousin Chachi Arcola was an event. It happened in a *Happy Days* episode that aired October 4, 1977, called "My Cousin the Cheat" during the show's fifth season.[56] Fonzie had a cousin? I don't recall the circumstances of how and where we first met Chachi, played by Scott Baio.[57] Fonzie may have dragged him into the Cunningham's' living room, or maybe he walked into Arnold's on his own accord, or maybe it was something else entirely. I do recall that Chachi typically wore faded dungarees, around which he tied a red bandana just above his right knee.

It was the same sort of bandana that Grandpa always kept readily at hand—though Grandpa called it his "hanky" or his

---

electric guitar. Fonzie's jacket is, as of this writing, in storage and has been replaced by the bathing suit Farrah Fawcett wore in her famous poster from the mid-70s.

[56] *Happy Days* was the second-highest-rated television show that year, just behind a show that had spun off of it called *Laverne & Shirley. Happy Days* had an estimated weekly audience of 22,890,600 households that year. It is estimated that there were 72,900,000 American households with a television that year. Thus, on any given Tuesday in 1977–78, nearly one-third of American households were watching *Happy Days.*

[57] This being well before Scott Baio was hand-selected by then-Republican Presidential nominee Donald Trump to speak at his D-List convention in 2016.

"kerchief."[58] Grandpa's kerchief was neither a fashion nor a personal statement. It was simply what he used to blow his nose or wipe his mouth or wipe his glasses. He, like Chachi, used that standard cotton paisley-patterned bandana—though he had both blue and red—typically associated with cowboys and cattle-rustling and the covered faces of bank robbers robbing the banks of old western towns and causing frontier mayhem in general.[59]

The versatility of Grandpa's kerchiefs was most notable at the end of a day baling hay, which is one of the worst, most foul and exhausting jobs a human being could ever do. Out of necessity, the baling happened on the hottest and sunniest days of July such that the sun served to simultaneously dry the hay and to act as a hot compress on your scalp and shoulders for ten-plus hours. The hay bales weighed about sixty pounds apiece, and my scrawny little arms had to fling them where they needed to be, and when I did, my arms got scratched and bled and I breathed in all the stifling hay dust and these days never seemed to end and the entire enterprise was just miserable and grueling. Grandpa loved every minute of it. Typically, Grandpa drove the tractor to which the hay baler and the hay wagon were attached. The baler swept up the cut hay, reformed it into bales, and flung the bales into the wagon. While Grandpa baled, my brother, sister, and I unloaded the previous wagon's bales onto an elevator. The elevator carried the bales up to the barn's hayloft, where Dad stacked them. When the hayfield was swept clean of its cut hay, Grandpa drove the last wagonload to the barn and helped us unload, his smile a nice punctuation mark to the day's rigor. He stood at the foot of the elevator and

---

[58] I use bandana, kerchief, and hanky interchangeably.

[59] In her iconic poster, Rosie the Riveter wears a red cloth that could be a bandana around her head. I'm not certain that hers and Chachi's and Grandpa's are all the same.

helped secure the bales, strings up so that Dad could grip them easily. When he was done, he pulled out his handkerchief, gave it an authoritative snap, and blew the hay dust out of his nose, wiped the sweat off his forehead, swished the hayseeds out of his arm hairs. His big arms, more muscular than one would expect for a man his age, were tan, making the hairs on his arms extra white and extra splendorous—whiter than the hair on his head, which maintained a rumor of yellow throughout. Despite the disparity in our approaches to these haymaking days, I could understand—on a cognitive level—how it felt to extract the sort of pride that Grandpa took in his work.

There are times in a life when a significant event occurs and we are completely unaware of it—the last time you pick up a son before he's too heavy or too mature to lift, say, or the last time you ride a city's subway car before moving to another city, or the last time a daughter lets you kiss her goodbye at the school entrance; the view of a landscape you'll never see again.

There are many such significant events I am unable to recall. I cannot recall my last beer (though I do remember my last drink); my last blackout; my last days of school; my last time at favorite movie theaters. I also can't recall the last time I unloaded a wagonload of hay bales with Grandpa. You might think I would remember that final release from such miserable work with great precision or satisfaction, but in truth I can't even faintly recall it.

Days on which we unloaded hay bales were simultaneously awful and spectacular. Despite the arduousness of the task, it was always one of my favorite things because of the camaraderie. When Grandpa arrived, it meant the end of the day was nigh; it meant Grandpa swimming with us was nigh; it meant lemonade and ice cream sandwiches and beer in the backyard under the giant maple were nigh. Grandpa chatted with us on the last hay wagon of the day; he laughed; he was interested in us; I loved to see how the hayseeds got stuck in his arm hair. Whatever load came last, there was no warning that this load—this bale, this beer, this Popsicle, this dive into the pool—was going to be the final one. He sauntered up to the wagon and asked us how we were; he smiled; he called the bales things like "son-of-a-gun" when they proved too obstinate for us to move; he encouraged and cajoled us. Then, once that last bale was in the barn, he joined us for lemonade and a dip in the pool, and we were exhausted and free. Free from those bales for another week or so.

The bandana has its origins in India, where the climate is perfect for growing cotton and where methods of fabric dyeing and printmaking also originate. The iconic paisley pattern, too, has its origins in India. Bandanas wended their way to England in the late 1700s, where they became fashionable as a means of flirtation. A woman could daintily though intentionally drop a square of patterned fabric to give a favored man a chance to pick it up and thus have an excuse to speak to her as he returned it. Bandanas were sometimes scented to be used as a nosegay, a way of protecting those who could afford them from the obnoxious scents in the street. Eventually they made their way to America. The bandana used by *real* cowboys and ranch hands was never about flirtation. Bandanas—in the approximately twelve-by-twelve-inch form as we see them today—wiped the sweat off a cowboy's face and protected him from sunburn during a long day wrangling cattle. It served as a backup stirrup, or a makeshift bandage if a branch sliced his arm as he rode through the woods. It was used for protection from nature's elements or whatever threatened to bite, burn, or scratch him. A cowboy could use one to cover his face so as not to inhale the swirling dust from empty tumbleweed-ridden ghost town streets. On the trail, he could tie one around the horse's legs to hobble him while he fixed his equipment with another. As a strap or lace, it could mend a rein or create a makeshift stirrup. Around the campfire, it came in handy to grab a skillet's handle, or if his coffee was strong enough to float a pistol, he could use it to strain the grinds as he poured himself a cup. In an emergency, he could whip up a tourniquet, cover a wound, set a splint, or make a sling. A warm, damp bandana soothed a sore neck or served as a sweatband. And, if properly snapped approximately one inch from the "behind," it made a great motivator for either man or horse. And yes, if he planned on robbing a bank or a stagecoach, the bandana served as his disguise.

A few years after Chachi debuted his bandana on *Happy Days*, Mike Reno of the band Loverboy wore one on *Solid Gold* to sing "Turn Me Loose." Bruce Springsteen, Mark Knopfler, and a few of the guys in Def Leppard followed suit.[60] It was during this time—thanks to the technological advances in boom box manufacturing—that the boys who rode my bus, boys with monosyllabic names like Steve and Dale and Keith, would bring their boom boxes on the bus and play their rock tapes. These Steves and Dales and Keiths played Bob Seger and Charlie Daniels Band and Styx and Bad Company.[61] These

---

[60] This is not an exhaustive list, just the names of some individuals who inspired me. Obviously, Willie Nelson has been wearing a bandana since the dawn of time. And Tupac Shakur, Axl Rose, and Johnny Depp all did it later.

[61] One of my worst memories is this one time in fifth grade. I was on the school bus. Living in a rural area meant that we had an oppressively long bus ride to and from school; it was over an hour each way. I know that this incident was on the bus ride home because it was hot, and I was reading *Island of the Blue Dolphins* by Scott O'Dell (a book about a Native American girl abandoned on an island in the Pacific). I really discovered reading that year and blasted through all of Judy Blume's books. Anyway, one of the bandana boom box boys was playing "Feel Like Making Love" by Bad Company. He was playing it so loudly that I couldn't concentrate on *Island of the Blue Dolphins*. So I looked up and looked to the bus driver—her name was Sharon and she smoked cigarettes while she drove—for some relief or, at the very least, some solace. Surely, she couldn't properly drive the bus with the loud blaring rock music. To my chagrin, Sharon was bopping her head up and down to the song and singing along with enthusiasm. I looked around the bus and everyone was entranced

71

Steves and Dales and Keiths were bold and brazen enough to play boom boxes so loud that everyone on the bus had to listen, and they were also bold and brazen enough to wear bandanas as a fashion statement—across their foreheads, around their arms, over their heads as a scarf covering. A few people in the Steve/Dale/Keith crowd even wore them around their necks, like an ascot; I suspect now that this was less a fashion statement than it was an effort to conceal hickeys.

I was neither a Dale, nor a Keith, nor even a Steve, and I knew it. But I flirted with the idea of wearing a bandana around my head. I bought one on a Saturday morning after a visit to the doctor's office. It was just like those that Grandpa had, but its newness was both a blessing and a curse. It was new and mine; but it was new and too-red, too-square, and too-stiff. I folded it into a triangle the long way and then, beginning at the triangle's apex, folded it so that it was about an inch or two wide and long enough to tie around my head. I practiced in my bedroom mirror. Played air guitar while listening to my Loverboy tape on my mom's tape recorder. But I never had the courage to wear it out in public. I know I looked cool in the bandana, but I guess I was also afraid of being labeled a phony. My name had two syllables, I loathed Bob Seger and his Silver Bullet Band, and I did not have a switch blade. This really bothered me. I was aware of this lack of courage and even at the age of twelve knew it was a character flaw. Like most adolescents, I simultaneously yearned for and eschewed

---

and bopping their heads up and down to Bad Company's "Feel Like Making Love." Everyone. The bleary-eyed high school motor heads; the dweebs; the jocks; the geeks; the sluts; the wastoids; the five children in one family who could all solve the Rubik's Cube in less than two minutes; even the Mickey Mouse backpacks on the innocent kindergarteners were moving to and fro to Bad Company's "Feel Like Making Love," perfectly synchronized the bombastic ode to vigorous love making. It was horrifying. To learn that I was a *Blue Dolphin* boy in a Bad Company world and would continue to be for the foreseeable future—that was one of the very worst days.

attention. It had to be the right kind of attention; preferably adulatory. My inability to don a bandana belied a lack of confidence of which I was acutely aware. I was unconfident.

One day, around this time, my sister and I saw Grandpa's stack of "kerchiefs" in our grandparents' basement. We had probably seen them a million times without ever really noticing. They were two dozen or so, stacked as haphazardly as Grandma could metaphysically allow—blue and red alternating in no discernible pattern. We deduced that Grandpa would grab one on his way out the door. I was astonished by his apparent indifference to the bandana. What beguiled me so was of no consequence to him. So it was with Christmas and birthday presents, as he always let us open those intended for him. He thought so little of the ritual. And I thought him so strange not to care—about a bandana; or about a present.

In a few years, I was into more sophisticated sartorial choices—like skinny leather ties and parachute pants and my prom tuxedo from After Six's *Miami Vice* line—and I no longer flirted with the idea of wearing a bandana around my head. Before long, college happened, and I no longer even thought about Grandpa's kerchiefs. And I no longer saw Grandpa every day. These are the kinds of absences we don't notice until later, as we're so swept up in our own lives, so busy with the immediate at hand—it's only after a long time has passed, days or weeks or months, when the sudden realization hits that we haven't seen someone we love in a long time. Someone we used to see every day.

Later, after we moved to New York and I started teaching high school, I noticed the kids wore bandanas, and it set me to musing over how fashion is cyclical, or maybe in this case the bandana never went out of style; only later did I understand the kids wore them to identify to which gang they belonged: red like Chachi for Bloods, yellow for Latin Kings.

The Emperor of Ice-Cream

In 2012, I decided to run the 2013 Boston Marathon. It was always something I wanted to do, and I could raise money for a charity and not have to qualify. I had run two Baltimore marathons before, and this seemed like a natural progression. This was different. This was *Boston*. This would be a homecoming, a triumphant homecoming tinged with contrition, a chance to make amends of sorts, to show the city my thanks. I asked my wife to make a special marathon sweatband for me to wear. She sewed four of Grandpa's old kerchiefs together to make one giant bandana: two red and two navy blue ones in a checkerboard pattern.

My son and I flew to Logan, where my college friend Kevin picked us up in his Land Rover,[62] and we played all day Sunday, my son and Kevin's kids; his wife made a pasta dinner, so I could load up on carbohydrates and have the fuel to run super-fast the next day.

We made the drive to Hopkinton on Monday morning with perfect timing, and there was not a cloud in the sky when the race began. I tied my awesome new kerchief sweatband around my head.

There were lots of memorable things about that day. Joey McIntyre of New Kids on the Block was running, too.[63] People from every background and nationality were lined up together on either side of the course cheering, shouting, dancing,

---

[62] Kevin in a Land Rover? He was the guy who wore Converse Chuck Taylors throughout college; who owned, like, one pair of jeans that he wore every day until they fell apart; who listened to The Replacements and Guns N' Roses; who eschewed norms of etiquette and loathed small talk and bemoaned the ubiquity of Gucci loafers at his kids' soccer games and drank beer in lieu of fancy drinks; whose post-college Subaru was perpetually filled with beer cans and cassette tape cases with seats encrusted with vomit. We lived together in Boston in an apartment filled with dirt and barf. It was jarring to see him in a Land Rover.

[63] He's really fast.

74

handing out water, bananas, oranges, Gatorade, Advil, Twizzlers, towels, Vaseline, gummy bears, Sam Adams, and anything else that could conceivably provide any stranger or any someone else some comfort, some energy. Thousands of little kids held their hands out for high-fives and their faces lit up when they got one. The Wellesley girls' scream tunnel was like nothing I had ever experienced or will ever experience again.[64] There were people running with blind runners; Veterans marching in their boots in memory of fallen comrades; people pushing loved ones confined to wheelchairs; thousands of people running for charities. The signs along the course of the Boston Marathon were just a little bit cleverer than the signs you see at other marathons.

Geographically, the marathon route was the same for all thirty-thousand-something people running it. But inevitably, the scenery evokes different feelings and thoughts in each runner. My route was teeming with ghosts. I trotted past Green Line trains on which I had passed out, the school where I had gotten my Master's degree, the town where I met my wife, restaurants where we used to sit and talk and smoke and drink and discuss our hopes and make plans, friends' old apartments, apartments that had housed the girls—now they would be women approaching middle age—with whom I had one night stands. The people I had hurt, had tried to impress, of whom I had been envious—where were they now? The course took me through Brookline, my home for four years; where my wife and I had spent so many hours walking around; where we had made out for the first time; where I sat on the buffet table at our 1995 New Year's Eve party and it collapsed and salsa went all over me and my green velvet jacket; where I worried about being able

---

[64] Despite their collective intellect, or perhaps because of it, the Wellesley girls are very raunchy. At least on Marathon Monday. Though they still make great secretaries...of *state*. And one day, one will surely make a spectacular President of the United States.

to make rent. Anna's Taqueria, Vinny Testa's—favorite haunts.

At some point in the race I began to smell Grandma and Grandpa. It was disorienting at first, until I realized the smell was in my sweat, infused now with the smell of Grandpa's old kerchiefs and running over my face. The blend of mothballs and antiseptic and lavender powder and general dank mildewy basement; it smelled like drinks with fancy names like Diplomats and Stormy Weathers and Mamie Taylors; with perfumes whose names evoked purity, like Chantilly, Rose, White Shoulders, and Joy; with soaps named to evoke toughness, names like Borax and Lava and Lifebuoy. Their smell in the fabrics contained notes of grease and exhaust and dirt and lace and strawberries and Listerine and the damp shaken off wet plastic rain bonnets. It was one of the greatest things. Around mile twenty, in the Newton Hills, when I was beginning to feel exhausted, I stopped at the medical tents for Band-Aids for my blisters and began to be genuinely fearful that I might not finish. Grandpa's old smell pushed and prompted and inspired and cajoled and comforted. I began to pray to Grandpa, who had been dead for four years at that point. Long enough to remove the sting of the passing but not long enough so as to make him unreachable. The prayers went something like, "Grandpa I know you think I'm crazy for doing this but please help me keep running." "Grandpa I know you hate this city but it's important to me to finish this. Please understand, I know you get it." "Grandpa please help me."

They call it terror for a reason. Around mile twenty-three, I began to notice the crowds lining the marathon route were paying far less attention to the runners and far more attention to their phones. Then I passed the 40K marker—mile 24.8—and checked my own phone to gauge my time. There were dozens of voice messages from Kevin and Dave and everyone else who had been orchestrating my putative victory ride back to Kevin's house. That felt odd; they knew I was running a race. I listened to the messages and heard the words "bombs" and "body parts" and "stay where you are" and "stop running."

I called Kevin, and he told me to stop running. At that point, no one knew anything except that there were some explosions at the finish line. And body parts everywhere. I told him it seemed safe enough where I was and I would keep running. But then I began to notice the looks on the faces of the cops, and they looked scared; *everyone* was looking scared. I stopped running just before Kenmore Square, at about the 25.2-mile mark. From there I just started walking, stunned and stricken and suddenly alone. My phone no longer worked, as Boston police had shut down all cell towers in case the bombers were using them to set off explosions. I could not even cry. Yet. I just meandered about Kenmore Square, staring at my iPhone, waiting for a signal to return. I walked back up Beacon and past Fenway—where my wife and I had our first date. Then I cut over to Commonwealth Avenue and looked for the Nickelodeon Theater, where I had seen three movies—*Age of Innocence, The Piano,* and *Remains of the Day*—on the day after Thanksgiving 1993 when I couldn't go home because I had to work. The theater was no longer there. I walked up Commonwealth, past that kitchenette place I used to go to for pizza, past that parking lot at Boston University where I had tried out my new roller blades, past my old apartment on Pratt Street. Someone with a working cell phone let me borrow it to call Kevin. We planned to meet at the Trader Joe's on Beacon Street. I hitchhiked. A minivan stopped to pick me up. I apologized for being so gross and sweaty but the driver told me that she and her daughter—in a car seat in the middle row— were from Israel, and they understood the terror I was feeling. Her last name was Krueger. She drove me to the Trader Joe's parking lot and waited with me for Kevin to arrive. When he did, I said goodbye to her, and she said, "Give me a hug," and I said, "But I'm all sweaty," and she said, "I don't care," and so

I leaned over the cup holder and armrest thing and hugged her. I got in Kevin's Land Rover and then wept for twenty minutes. Out of anger, out of sadness, out of disappointment; out of gratitude; out of guilt that my disappointment in not finishing exceeded or was equal to my gratitude at being alive. Or at the very least was moderately disproportionate.

The next hours were filled with phone calls and disbelief and more terror and more gratitude. The kids back at Kevin's house had no idea what had happened. The group who had assembled to help me celebrate now stood around Kevin's kitchen island[65] and cried and hugged.

While it was nice to receive all the texts of people checking in on us, making sure we were okay, telling us they loved us, I could not stop crying. I took off the sweaty bandana headband. Long after he was gone, Grandpa had been squeezing and comforting me. Or my sweaty scalp, anyway. But me, too, in a celestial, spiritual way. On this day, this April 15, 2013, in this city he purported to hate, Grandpa's kerchiefs provided as much warmth and comfort and solace as the sun.

Striding through streets upon which I once only teetered and wobbled was both gratifying and disorienting. But mostly disorienting.

My son and I took a flight back to Baltimore the next day. I returned to work on Wednesday and spent the next three days refreshing CNN and the *Boston Globe* websites. That Friday when the city shut down to catch the Tsarnaev brothers, I got into a Twitter war with a state senator from Arkansas who tweeted, "I wonder how many stupid Boston liberals cowering in their basements right now wish they had guns!" In the days that followed, Boston showed me and the world what it meant to be resilient; what it meant to be strong; what it meant to be

---

[65] Kevin's kitchen island too was a wonder to behold, the Land Rover equivalent of kitchen islands. It was enormous, and the top was that thick marble. It had a sink in it and those drawers that you can't slam shut no matter how hard you try.

ferocious, proud, determined. What it meant to take care of the people and the things it valued. What it meant to give and not view the giving as a sacrifice. Rather, that giving is, most succinctly, what you do.

Like Grandpa.

Memory seems to me a transcendental function. Its objects are physical bodies, faces, the expressions on those faces, and tangible things, captured by our mind's camera and infused with an interior radiance. The bandana inhabits a complex space for me—an ordinary three-dimensional object that also serves as a portal to another world. I still have the Boston Marathon headband made from Grandpa's kerchiefs. I have also since used Grandpa's kerchiefs in other sartorial endeavors, including a bow tie. I wore the same headband for the 2014 Boston Marathon—though by then it had lost Grandpa's smell through the inevitable washings that followed the 2013 race. In 2014, it was a perfect day, with not even a cloud in the sky as runners wended their way from Hopkinton to the finish line. The security was actually inspiring, nothing like the pain in the ass that is airport security, as small-town sheriffs and Secret Service agents and state police and FBI all worked together to keep us safe. Again I prayed to Grandpa as the miles began to stretch my limits, but it was a far more joyous prayer than the fearful pleas of a year prior.

After Grandpa's house was sold and new people moved in, I wondered how long the old smell would linger. If only there was a way to bottle it. When asked, a realtor friend of mine typically tells her clients that how long a previous owner's smell lasts depends on the nature or source of the smell, the amount of carpeting and upholstery in the home, the previous owner's use of odor maskers and/or odor eliminators, and how much of the home is underground or situated vis-à-vis streams and trees. The couple who bought the house are now divorced. The farm and house on and in which we grew up is now inhabited by migrant workers.[66] The shutters are falling off. The barn doors through which the hay bales ascended on the elevator are falling off. I drove my kids there one day and drove into the driveway with the intention of telling them stories of where their daddy grew up. But they were terrified.

I don't make a habit of going over there anymore. The shimmery sparkly pool has caved in and been filled with years of muck and mud—the same sort of layers which archeologists use to distinguish the end of the Mesozoic era and the start of the Jurassic. If you look closely enough, you can still see some concrete underneath the mud, places where the bulldozer missed, but you have to be searching for them, cognizant of their existence. All signs of life have been sucked out of the windows of the house like an eternal tornado formed and sat still just outside of them.

In my mind is an indisputable fact: the soul of that home died when we left. It has never been the same since. It's hardly even a house today.

---

[66] Dad sold the house and farm to a neighboring family. That family's eldest son and his wife moved into the farmhouse, ostensibly to begin their lives together working the same farm we did. The eldest son's wife had an affair with our neighbor; eventually, the eldest son's wife moved in with the neighbor, and the eldest son moved back home with his parents. *See also FN8.* The family who bought our farm hired migrant workers to work on the land. Grandpa and Grandma had to witness their farm's slow demise. I never asked them what they thought about it.

Part II

Nobody

The Emperor of Ice-Cream

The title of this book comes from Wallace Stevens's poem, "The Emperor of Ice-Cream." I first read this in college, in a poetry anthology we read for a creative writing class. I was in college, so was likely hungover and ambivalent while reading it.

A couple decades later, a friend of mine posted a passage from Stevens's "Disillusionment at Ten O'Clock" in response to an essay I wrote called "The Man in the Green Puffy Coat." I liked the verse; liked its playfulness; liked being associated with it—and it prompted me to do some further investigation into Stevens's life and work. In my opinion, the most salient detail of his life was that he was an executive for the insurance company The Hartford in addition to being a poet. Furthermore, he declined a faculty position at Harvard after winning the Pulitzer Prize for Poetry to remain a Vice-President at The Hartford.

I reread "The Emperor of Ice-Cream," and it reminded me of Grandpa:

> Call the roller of big cigars,
> The muscular one, and bid him whip
> In kitchen cups concupiscent curds.
> Let the wenches dawdle in such dress
> As they are used to wear, and let the boys
> Bring flowers in last month's newspapers.
> Let be finale of seem.
> The only emperor is the emperor of ice-cream.
>
> Take from the dresser of deal,
> Lacking the three glass knobs, that sheet
> On which she embroidered fantails once
> And spread it so as to cover her face.

If her horny feet protrude, they come
To show how cold she is, and dumb.
Let the lamp affix its beam.
The only emperor is the emperor of ice-cream.

I was comforted to learn that many people find the poem puzzling; that there is no general consensus as to what the overarching point or theme of this poem is.

My synopsis goes as follows: a man—the neighbor of a poor dead woman—enters her house to find some carousing going on in the kitchen. He seems annoyed by this. Then he walks into the bedroom, finds the old woman on the bed, and covers her corpse with a too-small sheet. The poem, a narrative about preparations for the funeral of a poor woman, presents the reader with a question: choose death or choose life? Life is short, like ice cream, but can be really sweet and awesome. Not as simple as it might sound, though. Take, for example, the titular character in T.S. Eliot's "The Love Song of J. Alfred Prufrock," who asks himself, "Do I dare to eat a peach?" The suggestion is that it takes courage to treat oneself, or, if not courage, then certainly more self-determination than one would think necessary.

Part of the meaning of the poem comes from Stevens's zest for details, of which the most significant for me are the fantails embroidered on the sheet. Why notice the embroidery now? Are these details more or less important now that the woman is dead? She is dead, and the fact cannot be hidden by any sheet. The embroidery is superfluous. But it is also all that strikes the man. The woman was poor; why waste time and money on thread embroidering a sheet that is, at the outset, insufficient to even cover you?

When Grandpa died, my first concern was that I would forget what he looked like: the details that individuated him; all the physical attributes that had made Grandpa seem so peculiar to a five-year-old, like some sort of distant cousin to the animated Mister Geppetto. The red marks on his nose where his glasses rested; the impossibly intricate set of wrinkles in his big earlobes; the whisper of yellow in his shockingly full head of shockingly white hair; the precise angle at which he hunched when he walked; the way he sprinkled sugar on his tomatoes.

I feared too that I would forget what he sounded like; he sounded like the narrator of some stop-motion Christmas special—but more euphonious, with less of a crackle. And gentler.

Then my dad—Grandpa's son—and my aunts—his daughters—started giving my wife and me his stuff. The ring he wore; the watch he got from Grandma as a wedding gift with its impossibly tiny face with uncharacteristically ornate and sophisticated hands and numbers clouded by sixty plus years of wear. (Had he liked this gift? Did he think it unpractical? What had he gotten Grandma for a wedding gift?) These are what remained after death—the details, in the cold light of reality, of life.

Additionally, in the poem, the people mourning the dead woman have a thing for ice cream. Grandpa had a thing for ice cream. I realize that most everyone has a thing for ice cream. And I realize that in my emphasizing Grandpa's appreciation, I am only solidifying the conventionality of his appreciation. I like how the at first reticent man in the poem learns to have a thing for ice cream as well, accepting and appreciating both its sweetness and its luxury and the fact that its evanescent pleasures—like the evanescent pleasures of life—can be enjoyed but only for a short while. And certainly must be enjoyed in the face of anything else.

The narrative of Grandpa's life is filled with lots of scarcity, austerity, grief, worry, and even calamity. Of sheets too small to cover his feet. When I learned of that scarcity, austerity, grief, worry, and calamity, my reverence for Grandpa was diminished. I loathed scarcity.

Gary M. Almeter

Grandpa was rarely subversive (though the stories of when he was are good stories); he chose goodness over greatness and he chose kindness and simplicity over excess and frivolity. But in so doing, achieved greatness.

When you take your thumbnail and scratch beneath the surface just a little bit, you can find extravagance, joy, whimsy, and an overarching determination to bask in life's evanescence. Which might be true of anyone's story. They should all be simple; there's a beginning and a middle and an end. But stories tend to be made more complex by myth and fantasy.

The myth is that by any measure, Grandpa lived a life that was staid, conventional, and proper. Diligence incarnate. He worked hard. He was reverent.

To some degree, my grandpa was just like everyone else's grandpa. Maybe I was the anomaly to have a grandfather who was a fun-seeker and surrogate parent and reservoir of family wisdom and companion. How many people never even knew their grandfathers? Or lived away from them and saw them only at Christmas or for a week in the summer?

At the outset, when I was young, he was a mix of Santa Claus, Andy Griffith from *The Andy Griffith Show* era, Alan Funt of *Candid Camera,* the Monopoly Guy, the guy from *Bonanza,* Mr. Peanut, Ernest Borgnine, and the drawings of Norman Rockwell.[67]

Then he became a sad figure—like the grandparents in Tim Burton's *Charlie and the Chocolate Factory,* who lay head to toe, four in a bed with some sort of unidentified and hostile

---

[67] Later it occurs to me to ask, "Isn't that everyone's Grandpa?" The answer is: "Not necessarily." Who has lost a grandparent? Whose grandfather fought in World War II or Vietnam and never came back, or came back different, somehow diminished? Whose grandparents were always convalescing or contemplating death like Norman at the end of *On Golden Pond?* Whose grandpa beat them, or had to take on a parental role when their mom or dad died?

paralysis. Like Jimmy Stewart in *It's a Wonderful Life*, without the celestial intervention and the cinematic redemption at the end. He was a man who never got to reinvent himself. I realize that reinvention is not necessarily everyone's goal. Perhaps he neither wanted nor had to be anything but the man he was. But in light of the fact that I cherished those chances to be someone else, he struck me as a sad figure who lived in a literal valley his entire life. As I stood on the precipice of adulthood, eager to slip the surly bonds of my small town, I looked at him with pity. For despite the smile and the perpetual mirth, I assumed the immobility and lack of introspection must have made him a very sad man. But if it was there, it was a sadness I never saw. Until later.

Gary M. Almeter

The Last Largeness

"The Curtains in the House of the Metaphysician"

It comes about that the drifting of these curtains
Is full of long motions, as the ponderous
Deflations of distance; or as clouds
Inseparable from their afternoons;
Or the changing of light, the dropping
Of the silence, wide sleep and solitude
Of night, in which all motion
Is beyond us, as the firmament,
Up-rising and down-falling, bares
The last largeness, bold to see.

—Wallace Stevens

When I was still young enough to be appropriately and rightfully afraid of any and all things with which I was unfamiliar, I was afraid of all of Grandpa's stuff. The fear was multifaceted, from a vague fear that I had the wrong grandparents, to a real fear that I would sneeze the wrong way and break something. In their house, everything had a place; everything was organized and polished and categorized; everything stood at the ready, waiting for me to fuck it up. Everything was clean and shelved and organized and categorized and polished. Everything was daintier, lacier, fancier, more intricate, more fragrant, more pristine, more cherished than the things in my own home.

His garden looked different than ours, its rows straighter and completely clear of weeds, its plants more uniform and robust. His watering can, garden hose, garden tools, lawnmower, wrenches, hammer, pliers were all different than the ones we had. His garage smelled different than ours did. Their kitchen cabinets had white porcelain knobs on red cherry wood. Throughout their home, they had taupe level loop pile carpet with an amorphous infinite pattern. They had an organ; we had a piano. They had a blacktop driveway; ours was stone. They used an artificial Christmas tree with huge old-fashioned bulbs; we bought ours freshly cut every year and adorned it with modern mini-lights, placing a flashing star on top.

They chewed Chiclets and we chewed Trident.

Grandpa's lunchbox even had a different shape, and it was solid steel gray—nothing like our *Happy Days* and *The Dukes of Hazzard* and *The Osmonds'* lunchboxes. His thermos, too, looked more purposeful, seemingly made of some kind of supersonic titanium and, characteristically, lacking any adornment.

Their pans were different, and they stored them in odd places because their house was much smaller than the farmhouse. They never got a microwave. They popped corn in oil on the stove instead of with an air popper, and their salt-and-pepper shakers were crystal with sterling silver tops while ours were plastic and disposable, never intended to last a lifetime.

Their bathroom contained products of whose existence we had hitherto been unaware for ailments of whose existence Grandpa and Grandma would surely deny. They camouflaged sprays and lotions with crocheted covers. A big crocheted poodle covered Grandma's big can of Aqua-Net; and some sort of terrycloth-and-shag-carpet turtle covered the spare roll of toilet paper. They had soaps in the shapes of shells that they had never and would never use.

Their games were from another time and were housed in boxes displaying unfamiliar fonts, and the kids pictured on them looked like they belonged alongside Spanky and Alfalfa and Darla on *The Little Rascals*. There was a pinball machine

BAGATELLE[68] game with real glass and metal parts. Even their food tasted different: Grandma's spices had different and unfamiliar labels, and they bought different flavored ice cream than we did, and they mixed their TANG with more scoops of powder than we did, which made it syrupy and better. Their milk was just a little less cold. Their house was a modular home, so everything had compartments and sub-compartments; closet doors slid across tracks instead of opening on hinges like "normal" doors do. Their bedrooms contained knobby crocheted bedspreads. Every dresser and coffee table and end table had doilies on it. On all their windowsills, they had crystals and volcanic rocks and petrified wood from the many places they visited.

They watched their programs on a different TV, with different knobs and different numbers, and it sat on the floor as opposed to a stand like ours did. They had leather recliners—with which they seemed to have an obsession about how closely to the wall they could position them—while we had upholstered and reupholstered cloth chairs that neither reclined nor swiveled. They woke up early and read the paper. They cooked breakfast instead of eating cereal, and drank coffee in mugs with odd handles and circumferences that seemed disproportionate to their height.

My grandparents spoke a different language. Game shows like *The Price is Right* and *Sale of the Century* were called "quiz programs" and they watched them with vigor, expressing both disdain and disappointment when contestants did not do as well as Grandpa and Grandma thought they could have, or should have. They referred to garbage as rubbish and they referred to scissors as shears. They would unceasingly refer to

---

[68] The POOSH-M-UP Rodeo bagatelle game by Northwestern was manufactured in the 1930s. Inexplicably, it featured a rodeo theme but employed baseball scoring.

something called "the credenza" upon or in which everything resided, and I would have no fucking idea what they were talking about. I still don't. I think it's a piece of furniture of some kind.

How could they be so different from us? Geographically and genetically, we were as similar as two families could get. We shopped at the same stores, had the same hairline, went to the same church; we shared the same values, and yet bought completely different kinds of cereal. And yet the fear these differences could provoke and cultivate in me were substantial.

And then there was a day when all this stuff became familiar and comforting.

And then there was a day after that day when it was all so revolting: the artifice, the cheapness, the way everything was saved for and cared for. I am not certain when it happened. It is likely a symptom—a developmentally appropriate symptom—of adolescence that prompts and fosters independence. I likely asked the existential question "what's the point?" about fourteen bajillion times between fourteen and eighteen years old. I likely did so when I saw Grandpa coiling a garden hose perfectly, a hose that would inevitably be uncoiled the next day; when I saw him cleaning his garden tools; when I saw him organizing his garage; or when I saw Grandma's crocheted hairspray can cover. Everyone knows that it is a can of hairspray—why cover it up?

I am so proud of all the ways I am different from my forebears—this seems to me the natural order of things. And yet I get so hurt when my son exhibits traits different from mine—when he loves sports and demonstrates fearlessness and leadership qualities I do not fancy myself as having.

In August, 1991, on the night before I was to return to college for my senior year, I went to visit them. The night, windless and pale, moved only in their joyous voices as they exclaimed how happy they were to see me. We stood outside in front of the garage, the plastic doors illuminated from inside. I am wearing a green hooded sweatshirt from the Gap, and he is wearing green work clothes. Grandma is in a green pantsuit, one she made herself, and she remarks that everyone is wearing green. I just stopped by to hurriedly say goodbye, but they are so elated to see me that I capitulate a little bit and engage them in conversation. They say that they will miss me even though I didn't really see them that much that summer. I had a job and a girlfriend, and Dad had bought Sister Marie's car, which meant I basically had my own car all summer.

Something about this visit prompted me to think, "Wow. Grandpa is seventy-seven years old. Already past the average life expectancy." I think for the first time that this might be one of my last visits, and I ask Grandma to take our picture. I start to realize that every visit with Grandpa is in the nature of a farewell. There is a modicum of permanence to every goodbye; as though we are all practicing. Grandma takes a picture with her disc camera by Kodak of which she is so very proud. Grandpa and I stand side by side, and for a moment I think to put my arm around him as Grandma takes the picture. As soon as the thought arose, I decided against it. It felt—as I waited for Grandma to click the little button on her camera—as though I were imprisoned by that decision. In less than twenty-four hours, my friends and I would all be wasted and taking pictures of ourselves with arms wrapped tightly around each other. We will be playing Billy Joel's "Goodnight, Saigon" at an after-hours party, swearing our undying allegiance to one another. Why couldn't I do the same with Grandpa? Yet I was loathe to relinquish the standard protocols that had guided our relationship.

Despite the epiphany that this might very well be the last time I would ever see him, I am eager to go. Eager to meet the gang I worked with all summer later that evening at Erica's house for a party. Grandpa never went to college. He does not know what it is like—what it is like being freely independent and going to keg parties and cavorting with your friends and drinking beer and smoking cigarettes and skipping classes.

But they invite me into the kitchen for lemonade and cookies and I cannot say no and so I sit. And I wonder if this is the first time I had been in their kitchen all summer. It might be. As I looked around, I noticed again the color.

There is a color—it is the color of certain buildings, the kind that still have television antennae affixed to their roofs—that you see in vintage photographs of Castro's Cuba, and in some of the doorways in Morocco; it is the color of those pastel soft mints that restaurants used to keep in knobby glass bowls at their cash-register counters, before the days of hepatitis C and Ebola and all the other vicious ailments out there moved to the forefront of our minds, when restaurant patrons dug their grimy Ebola-ridden fingers into communal bowls without a second thought; it is the color (but not quite) of some 70s-era Jell-O mold concoctions—more specifically, that recipe that mixes green Jell-O and cottage cheese and/or whipped cream; it is the color of pistachio pudding and certain bridesmaids dresses from the 1970s, and also the oxidation that appears on certain metal fences. There is a mid-70s Volkswagen Vanagon in our neighborhood, and it is painted this color; its owners typically park it on the side of the road. The first time we saw it, my kids remarked at the color, and my wife said, "That was the color of your great-grandparents' kitchen."[69] There is no color in existence that so powerfully communicates the rural alienation of human beings inside the edifices they've created as this soothing-though-noxious green, which only came into being with the advent of the 1970s and is inextricably associated with the artifice of the period. I wish I had asked my grandparents how they went about selecting this

---

[69] For the deeply curious, the closest colors I have been able to identify are Pantone 3245U and Pantone 571U.

color. It was so unlike them, and almost garish in comparison to everything else in their home. But whenever I see that color, or anything close to it, I think of them.

Just before I left, Grandpa gave me a $2 bill. He told me that if you always keep one of these in your wallet, then you'll never be broke. Maybe that is what made this visit special? He had never done something like that before, despite the fact that I had been going to college for three years by then.[70] I still carry it with me. And I'm never broke.

I still recall them telling me to be careful as I backed out of their driveway.[71] And I still recall them waving to me as I drove away.

It wasn't the last time I saw them, as it turned out; not even close. But the notion that it *could* be fostered a whole new set of feelings.

There were great things about their house, too. The toys, once I got over the rusty springs and mildew and broken glass, were actually rather fun. My favorite thing was this clock they brought home from Las Vegas. It was approximately 12" x 12" in black lacquered tile and it had these super Art Deco hands and number markers in the middle and a super Art Deco script that said "Las Vegas, Nevada" just underneath the twelve. Clear red dice were glued to the perimeter of an imaginary circle to,

---

[70] Fourteen years later, I gave that same $2 bill to my friend J when he went to Iraq. J and I went to law school together. He was in the Army. On paper, we should not have been friends; he was, as I said, in the Army. And I am not. He was kindhearted and played football and probably never ever got drunk and puked. I did not play football and puked with some frequency. But we were friends. And still are. When he told me he was going to Iraq in late 2004, I literally could not believe it. The best thing that I could give him—the thing that ensured his return, because I was giving him something that I could not live without—was that $2 bill from Grandpa. I gave him the same admonition Grandpa gave me; and J brought back the same $2 bill.

[71] The fact that a person could go for days on that road and not run into another car never dispelled in them the belief that theirs was a treacherous thoroughfare.

in lieu of analog numbers to tell the time. It was shiny and decadent, and the gleam of the red and black stuck out in their home. I thought it was genius—that someone had thought to take a "six" die and a "five" die and glue them to a clock where the "11" should be. Grandma also took an hour or so to explain how dice are made so that the ink weighs the same as that which is removed from the dots so that the dice aren't weighted and are therefore truly and reliably random. It also struck me for the first time that they must have been to a city. And must have enjoyed it sufficiently to buy a clock.

Now that they are gone, their possessions adopt a new glittering evanescence. Even the most mildew-ridden Cootie box takes on a radiant sheen, albeit an imaginary one. What I wouldn't give to return them to their lackluster mustiness[72], if it meant I could return to that time and that house now.

---

[72] Grandma was a very proud woman but if you think that she'd be mad at me for telling the millions of people who will read this book that she had a musty basement you'd be wrong. She loved discussing, pondering, deliberating, dissertating, and explaining the hazards and hardships of domesticity and the methodologies she employed to conquer each. While her subterranean basement remained musty, it was significantly less musty than it would have been had she not employed various methodologies to make it less so.

Gary M. Almeter

The Sha-Na-Na Redemption

"The Good Man Has No Shape"

Through centuries he lived in poverty.
God only was his only elegance.

Then generation by generation he grew
Stronger and freer, a little better off.

He lived each life because, if it was bad,
He said a good life would be possible.

At last the good life came, good sleep, bright fruit,
And Lazarus betrayed him to the rest,

Who killed him, sticking feathers in his flesh
To mock him. They placed with him in his grave

Sour wine to warn him, an empty book to read;
And over it they set a jagged sign,

Epitaphium to his death, which read,
The Good Man Has No Shape, as if they knew.

—Wallace Stevens

Just over a decade ago, an alternative energy company identified my hometown in upstate New York as a viable site to construct its wind turbines.[73] The promise of such

---

[73] A wind turbine is a modern, more sophisticated windmill that converts wind into electrical power. The ones being considered for my hometown would have three large blades connected to a central rotor sitting atop an approximately 120-foot tall pole. To both simplify and echo a simpler time, I will call them windmills throughout this piece.

95

construction quickly metastasized into a threat. And the threat created some chaos. Throughout 2004 to 2006, town folks filled town hall meetings and voiced concerns that the windmills would, among other things: cause such a shortage of wind that there would be none left for drying laundry on the line; tarnish an otherwise flawless landscape; cause schools to close and hospitals to malfunction on non-windy days; and cause their children to "go" cross-eyed. The fight over the windmills pitted neighbor against neighbor in a town that, on the surface, had hitherto always been a serene and bucolic haven for all of God's creatures.

I asked my Grandpa, a resident of that small farming town for nine decades, what he thought of the whole hullabaloo. He laughed at the absurdity and hypocrisy of it all, acknowledging that the most vociferous opponents of the windmills were typically those with decades-old rusty trucks and tractors on their front lawns and dilapidated barns in their backyards. He recalled that there were similar—though less adversarial—concerns when electricity poles were first installed, and again when corn and grain silos reached such heights as to be considered a blot on the landscape. I asked him this in the midst of the controversy; we were sitting in Aunt Janet's living room. Grandpa opined that what differentiated the windmills from the landscape blots of yesteryear was that in the windmill scenario, certain people stood to make a great deal of money—money from doing positively nothing but providing a 400-square foot parcel of land upon which a company would erect a windmill. I was surprised to hear him say this. The town was as homogenous as a town could be, teeming with Roman Catholic farmers of German origin. It was rumored that such a lease along with the easement rights would garner about $25,000 per year. Some of these landowners—farmers, mostly—were poised to have as many as ten windmills installed on their properties. Such a windfall for their neighbors was, according to Grandpa, the real reason people were so upset. "People tend to get afraid when others get ahead," he said. "It makes them mad."[74]

Grandpa thought it silly, the whole windmill thing and the opposition thereto.[75] Particularly in light of the larger issues of the day: the war in Iraq, Hurricane Katrina, and the War on Terror.[76] Grandpa did not share the anger or feel such fear as that displayed by his neighbors; he felt no similar jealousy. Grandpa, unaccustomed to privilege, did not feel oppressed when he saw others advance. He was perpetually happy, a glass-half-full kind of guy. And if someone else's glass was maybe three quarters full, that was okay by him, because he still had his half glass. And that was plenty.

Like Grandpa, I've never "gotten" that general, overarching rage that seems to plague many others. I don't understand it. It is something to which I cannot relate. Perhaps because I have never really had anything about which I could be

---

[74] I think people learn this early. When you are a kid and your friend gets the video game you wanted. And then you might be secretly a little bit happy when the video game breaks. Perhaps this is character flaw unique to me but I do not think so. The sentiment is best expressed in Morrissey's "We Hate It When Our Friends Become Successful," a single from his 1992 album, *Your Arsenal.*

[75] The turbines were eventually constructed, about a hundred of them total. Each one soars, and each one can be seen for miles. They are majestic. They generate a great deal of clean energy as well, and they are no more a blemish on the landscape than the undergarments of those individuals who opposed them waving in the still-robust breezes on the still-functioning outdoor clotheslines. Their blades turn majestically, with the patience of a tree. They are simultaneously prehistoric and futuristic.

[76] Though he did say once, "If Osama bin Laden wanted to get attention, he probably wouldn't be much interested in Varysburg."

that angry. I know this is a luxury. As such, I have always witnessed rage from the periphery. I was born in 1970 and came of age well after the first wave of black rage had relevance as a political message and well before the Black Lives Matter movement of today. In the eighties and nineties, Public Enemy and NWA sold millions of records with their message of black power. This was almost instantaneously replaced by new hip-hop voices singing about wealth and sneakers and personal wish-fulfillment[77].

White rage is also surging. We saw it erupt at Trump campaign rallies when he talked about the wall and Muslims and making America white again. We see it in the surge and normalization of the "alt-right" movement. But you also see it on a less idealistic level in the suburbs in which I dwell outside of Baltimore. I see whites of all classes getting really, though subtly, upset when the right summer camp fills up too fast or when they are left on the pool waiting list for another summer or when their kids are assigned an unseasoned teacher. White people, as a whole, can get more—and less subtly—upset at things more nefarious, like poisoned Halloween candy, and anthrax powders, and storms, and black boys in pale hoodies walking home from a 7-11 where they have just purchased Skittles and a cold can of Arizona Fruit Juice, and Beyoncé's militant Super Bowl halftime show, and the suggestion that they relinquish their Confederate flags. All these things fill us with rage.

---

[77] In 2005, Kanye West infamously expressed some black frustration during a telethon for Hurricane Katrina, when he went off-script at a telethon and, after a long tirade, succinctly said, "George Bush doesn't care about black people" as Mike Myers stood impotently next to him. Such rage seemed to be assuaged by Obama's conciliatory race speech during the 2008 Presidential election and his subsequent message of hope. But such hope turned to despair, which eventually, following the arrest of Harvard professor Henry Louis Gates, Jr. when he tried to enter his own home, the killings of Trayvon Martin, Michael Brown, Freddie Gray, and nine people at a church in Charleston, South Carolina, turned to rage.

A majority of white people, I am learning, is afraid of everything; not just windmills. Things that we fear really and truly and thoroughly scare the hell out of us. And we use anger and defiance and our scant self-awareness to conceal our more vulnerable feelings.[78]

Our rage is camouflaged by alleged patriotism, and clothed in the niceties of law and order. When Donald Trump

---

[78] White rage will manifest itself following a "black" victory, like Obama's. Carol Anderson, an associate professor of African American studies at Emory University, posits that what we see today is not inexplicable black rage but white rage at the notion of black progress. She argues that such rage exploded after the Civil War, manifested itself to undermine the Supreme Court's *Brown v. Board of Education* decision, and recently took hold again following Obama's election in 2008. None of these victories brought much peace; rather, Emancipation brought white resentment that the good old days of slavery were over. As a result, legislatures throughout the South "scrambled to reinscribe and legitimize white supremacy via Black Codes." Nearly a century later, following *Brown v. Board of Education*'s ruling affirming that separate but equal schools for black and white children was unconstitutional, black children were met with mobs at schoolhouse doors and had bricks tossed at them. Governors of southern states launched massive resistance to the ruling, going so far as to withhold public funding from any school that complied with the *Brown* ruling. A little more than half a century later, the election of Barack Obama gave hope to the country and the world that a new racial climate had emerged in America, or that it inevitably would. A flurry of voter-suppression legislation, the Supreme Court's gutting of the Voting Rights Act with their decision in *Shelby County v. Holder*, the rise of "stand your ground" laws, and continuing police brutality make it clear that Obama's election unleashed a wave of fear. It is a subtler and less overtly racist form of fear. It's a remake of the Southern strategy, crafted in the wake of the civil rights movement to exploit white resentment against blacks, and deployed with precision by presidents Nixon and Reagan. As Reagan's key political strategist Lee Atwater explained in a 1981 interview, "You start out in 1954 by saying 'Nigger nigger nigger.' By 1968, you can't say 'nigger'—that hurts you. Backfires. So you say stuff like 'forced busing,' 'states' rights,' and all that stuff. You're getting so abstract now, you're talking about cutting taxes, and all these things you're talking about are totally economic things, and a product of them is blacks get hurt more than whites." *See* "Ferguson isn't about black rage against cops. It's white rage against progress." *Washington Post,* August 29, 2014.

wears a hat that says "Make America Great Again," we are inspired. When Colin Kaepernick suggests America isn't great by not standing for the National Anthem, he is vilified for somehow disrespecting our troops along with our flag. When Michelle Obama talked openly about how she feels waking up in a White House built by slaves, she was irreverently reminded those slaves were well fed.[79]

---

[79] I wrote this in August 2016 shortly after the Republican National Convention. I am writing this footnote in June 2018, shortly before the final manuscript of this book is due. I have thought about updating this section. But in the 22 months since, Donald J. Trump has said that professional athletes who do not stand for the anthem should not be in the country, called them sons of bitches, told Americans to do civic works on Martin Luther King, Jr. Day and then played golf at his private course, called white nationalists who killed a woman at a Nazi march in Charlottesville, VA "good people," lied more than 4000 times since taking office, kicked a journalist out of a press conference for asking a question he did not like, said that executive privilege affords him absolute power to pardon anyone, refused to answer questions and held meetings with Department of Justice officials encouraging them to halt a criminal investigation into his campaign, had his lawyer's office raided by the FBI, had a hush money payment to a porn star after having sex with her three months after his third wife gave birth acknowledged by his attorney, generally behaved like a tyrannical toddler on Twitter, blamed a high school massacre on the Department of Justice because they are spending too much time investigating him, attacked Amazon and other companies, acknowledged that he attacks the press to discredit them all, and lied, obstructed, pressured, humiliated, and fleeced countless people. So I would have difficulty even choosing which crime or *faux pas* is most analogous to the offensive way patriotism has been hijacked and warped in the face of Trump's treatment of Colin Kaepernick. And such analysis would be superfluous anyway since it is inevitable that by the time of this book's publication date, currently slated for March 2019, Trump will have orchestrated a whole new host of crimes and embarrassments. The one constant is the asterisk that follows all these things, "can you imagine of Obama had done this?" And no. I can't imagine if Obama had done this because had Obama had five children by three wives, had paid two porn stars $280,000 for two sexual interludes, acted like a buffoon on Twitter, wanted to build an Obama Tower in Moscow with the help of Putin, or sounded like a fucking moron every time he opened his mouth, he would never have been permitted to run for— much less elected as—president. Anyway, more succinctly, black men and white men are treated differently in this country. Anyone who cannot see it or refuses to

Protests and looting in New Orleans and Ferguson capture attention, but the real rage manifests itself in small towns where folks are considering whether or not to allow the construction of windmills on their beloved hills. They deify the past. People tell us to *be present*—but once we even become aware of the present, that present is gone. We are always dwelling, then, in the past. As recent a past as a nanosecond ago and as remote a past as a century ago.

Growing up, my family would typically watch *Sha-Na-Na* on Saturday nights. *Sha-Na-Na* was a syndicated variety series that ran from 1977 to 1981, hosted by the singing group of the same name. The group, whose name originates from the series of nonsense syllables in the doo-wop hit song "Get a Job," performed a song-and-dance repertoire of classic 50s rock and roll, simultaneously reviving and parodying that era's music and New York street culture.[80]

---

acknowledge it is either a weak person or an ignorant person or too chicken shit to come out and say what they really want to say. Anyone who says they only voted for Trump because he would appoint judges who would fight against abortion is also, similarly, too chicken shit to say what they really mean. I doubt many Trump voters are reading this awesome book. My book likely only appeals to educated, genuinely kind people. If you are a Trump voter and you are reading this book, stop what you are doing, close this book, roll it so that it is as close to cylindrical as you can metaphysically make it, and shove it up your ass.

[80] The group began singing as part of the long-standing Columbia University a cappella group The Kingsmen, but changed their name due to the Pacific Northwest group of the same name, famous for covering "Louie, Louie." Sha-Na-Na began performing in 1969 and achieved national fame after playing at the Woodstock Festival, where they preceded Jimi Hendrix. They had a syndicated variety series featured the group performing hits from the 1950s and 1960s, along with comedy skits. The show typically opened in a concert scene, and then moved through various street and ice cream parlor scenes where they and their guests performed several songs. The members of Sha Na Na during the TV series were Jon "Bowzer" Bauman, Lennie Baker, Johnny Contardo, Frederick "Dennis" Greene, "Dirty Dan" McBride,

The Emperor of Ice-Cream

One of the members of Sha-Na-Na was a man named Frederick "Dennis" Greene. Greene, known as simply "Denny" on the show, choreographed most of Sha-Na-Na's dance moves; he was typically one of the three band members who wore gold lamé suits and was generally portrayed in the series as the most intelligent member of Sha-Na-Na—the one who had the lowest amount of tolerance for the group's tomfoolery.

On those weekends when my siblings and I had some sort of Sunday morning commitment and could not attend Sunday morning church, we would have to go to church with Grandpa and Grandma on Saturday night, as they *religiously* attended Saturday service at eight p.m.[81] One night, in the summer of 1980, I went to church with Grandpa and Grandma.

That evening it was just going to be me accompanying them to church. I walked to their house, freely entered, and sat down in their living room. I sat down in Grandpa's chair and started watching TV. Grandpa and Grandma had just gotten a television with a remote control when remote controls were still excitingly new, and anomalous. I took the remote and started flipping among the four channels they got: 2, 4, 7, and 29. I stopped on 4 to watch *Sha-Na-Na*. By this time, Grandpa and Grandma had joined me in the living room. Grandpa, upon seeing Dennis Greene singing in his dazzling gold lamé jumpsuit, asked me, "Do you like to watch those black niggers, Gary?"

My nine-year-old self just sat there. My ears got hot and I said nothing. Whenever I close my eyes and think about that

---

Jocko Marcellino, Dave "Chico" Ryan, "Screamin'" Scott Simon, Scott "Santini" Powel, and Donald "Donny" York (vocals).

[81] We loved Grandpa and Grandma, but I use the term "have to" because going to church with them meant that we had to behave. Also, there were typically no children at church on Saturday nights, so there wasn't even anyone to see or at whom we might make funny faces.

evening—that evening when I heard my Grandpa, for the first and only time, say the word "nigger," my ears still get hot. I can still see the pattern in their rug as I stared down at the floor; still feel the vinyl upholstery of the chair I was sitting in crinkle as I shifted in it. I can feel my hands getting sweaty as I gripped the remote, and see my belly rising up and down through my red, white, and blue stars-and-stripes tank top[82] as I tried to formulate words in response to Grandpa asking me about the black man on his television set.

After what felt like several minutes, Grandpa said, "I asked you a question, Gary." I managed to meekly mutter, "It's just a TV show, Grandpa."

Hearing him say *that* word seemed to make the earth stop spinning on its axis.

We went to church as though nothing happened. We rode home from church in silence. Grandpa and Grandma dropped me off at home. I can still see the slight rumor of a hint of yellow in his otherwise white hair, illuminated by the dome light of their Pontiac Bonneville when I opened the car door as they pulled into my driveway. I can still see myself run up the stairs to our kitchen and feel the relief that swept over me at being home. More precisely, a mix of relief and shame. I was devastated. I did not sleep that night. But I told no one.

In the intervening decades, I have tried to reconcile the man—the kind, loving man—with the word. I have rationalized. I have told myself that Grandpa's use of the word was more the result of some sort of momentary lapse of reason and less the result of inherent racism; that he was just mad at me for sitting in his chair and taking his new remote and wanted to give me a verbal jolt. That he was merely the product of his

---

[82] My cousin Tim is four years older than I am. This hand-me-down stars-and-stripes red, white, and blue tank top was one of my favorite articles of clothing of all time. The fact that I was wearing it in 1980 suggests that he wore it in 1976, in the midst of our country's bicentennial celebration.

upbringing—born between the Emancipation Proclamation and *Brown v. Board of Education,* when it was not uncommon for ordinary people to speak that word—and it still emerged now and again (though that one evening in 1980 is the only time I ever heard him say that word) much the same way he would sometimes still call the refrigerator the "icebox." I've tried to tell myself that he was just in a rare bad mood; or that, to him, by virtue of some incident of which I am unaware, he perceived black men as dangerous, and to be presumed guilty.

I did sometimes wonder if he was racist—if he had the capacity to hate an entire group of people because of the color of their skin.

Hatred is a strong word. I'm certain he didn't hate an entire group of people. But what if he just thought them inferior? Thought them less intelligent? Years later, after Grandma died and Grandpa was living with Aunt Janet, I went to visit him for the weekend. Aunt Janet had just hosted a priest from Africa for a week and he and Grandpa had been roommates in her upstairs bedrooms. Grandpa sometimes referred to the priest as "the Darky Priest." He spoke with reverence and great affection and said that he and "the Darky Priest" had great talks and enjoyed sharing meals. We all sort of giggled about this. I giggled and wondered if I was giggling at Grandpa, at the word "darky"—which, phonetically speaking, is just an odd word—or if I was actually giggling at the black priest, at what I perceived as audacity.

"Darky" is a different word than the n-word, though Grandpa's use of the former helped inform his use of the latter two decades before. "Darky" connotes an Al Jolson sort of amusement, but it doesn't connote hate. And of course Grandpa didn't hate. But would it be any better if blacks simply amused him?[83] Are black priests somehow less black? Are black priests

---

[83] In his 1989 film, *Do The Right Thing,* Spike Lee explores the way whites perceive blacks, the way whites categorize blacks, the way whites use blacks for

exempted from racism? Or at least the sort of ugly racism prompted by something more nefarious than amusement?

As mentioned, Grandpa was a farmer. Is a farmer from Buffalo entitled to make assessments of others? They are not the most sophisticated bunch. I am aware of this. Farmers are likely the subject of scorn—or something less than scorn, something resembling ridicule—in more sophisticated circles. And then when we keep following the ripples, are people who went to the lesser-Ivies (sorry Brown and Cornell) subject to the scorn of those who went to Harvard and Yale (and maybe Princeton)? Where does it end?

Sometimes I wonder if I am racist. If the word Grandpa used somehow nuzzled its way into my cerebral cortex and set up camp there.

I was recently walking down the street in Towson, Maryland on a sunny afternoon, when I heard someone whistling Kate Bush's "Running Up That Hill." The whistler sounded like he or she was about fifteen to twenty feet behind me. I listened for a little bit. The whistler was flawless. And the

---

entertainment. In one particularly poignant scene, pizzeria employee and black man Mookie and his boss's white Italian son Pino have the following exchange:

Mookie: Who's your favorite basketball player?
Pino: Magic Johnson.
Mookie: And not Larry Bird? Who's your favorite movie star?
Pino: Eddie Murphy.
Mookie (smiling): Who's your favorite rock star?
Pino: (says nothing because he sees the trap Mookie has laid for him)
Mookie: Barry Manilow? (laughing) Pino, no joke. C'mon, answer.
Vito (Pino's brother): It's Prince. He's a Prince freak.
Pino: Shut up. The Boss! Bruce!
Mookie: Sounds funny to me. As much as you say nigger this and nigger that, all your favorite people are niggers.
Pino: It's different. Magic, Eddie, Prince are not niggers, I mean, are not black. I mean, they're black but not really black. They're more than black. It's different.

song is unmistakable. I turned around to see who it was and was surprised to see that it was a twenty-something black male whistling the 1980s alternative classic by the sprightly British chanteuse.

I immediately thought of Brent Staples's essay "Walk on By," wherein he writes about his efforts to assuage white people's fears of him when they meet him on the sidewalk by whistling Beethoven or Vivaldi. Then I wondered if maybe a modern rapper had sampled the salient melodies of "Running Up That Hill" in a contemporary rap song, and that explained how the black man walking behind me knew it. Then I thought that maybe the black man was doing some sort of meta-toying with me—that he was Brent Staplesing me and whistling Kate Bush because he knew that I knew that he could not possibly know who Kate Bush was. Then I said, "Fuck. I'm racist."

But I'm not. I find racism abhorrent. And the evidence thereto weighs heavily in my favor: I taught scores of urban youth in an inner-city high school and loved them all and hugged them and am still in touch with many of them today. I actually taught them "Walk On By." I encouraged them to not tolerate being treated with disdain when they walked into stores and tried to teach them that, though racism is real, rising above it was the best way to combat it.

I watched HBO's *The Loving Story* about Mildred and Richard Loving, who fought to eradicate Virginia's miscegenation statute, and I watched Spike Lee's *Four Little Girls*; I watch all those documentaries. I read *To Kill a Mockingbird* and *The Color of Water* and *Their Eyes Were Watching God* and *Invisible Man* and, more recently, Colson Whitehead's *The Underground Railroad.* I read Randall Kennedy and law review articles about racist sports teams' names, interracial adoption, Thomas Jefferson and Sally Hemmings,[84] and Strom Thurmond. I've advocated for

---

[84] Sally Hemmings, herself the daughter of a white plantation owner and one of his

reparations at family Thanksgiving dinners, and I voted for Obama twice. I would have voted for him a third time were I able! I have a black dentist and enthusiastically refer people to him. He is the best dentist I have ever had, and I want him to succeed.

I have read Peggy Macintosh's essay, "White Privilege: Unpacking the Invisible Knapsack," and it took me awhile, but I think I have a working knowledge of what it means to have white privilege. Just last week I bought four avocados from the grocery store and forgot to bring them home. I called the grocery store and spoke with a young woman named Courtney at customer service, who told me to come in and talk with her. When I got to the store there was a long line at customer service, so I just walked to the produce section, took four avocados, and walked out. I received nary a passing glance. Furthermore, on the eve of a snowstorm, when stores are packed with people preparing for Armageddon, I can pull into any Home Depot or Lowe's, load up my SUV with firewood, and drive away. Anyone who sees me, my sophisticated tortoiseshell glasses and white skin, just assumes that I am supposed to be taking the firewood. I have never tried it, but I suspect that I could walk into any convenience store and take a pack Skittles and a can of cold Arizona Fruit Juice and walk out with it without anyone saying anything to me. I know I could carry a pack of Skittles and a can of cold Arizona Fruit Juice to my house without being shot,[85] whether or not my sweatshirt was hooded and whether or not the hood was on my head.

Furthermore, I rejoice when my kids are oblivious to race. When she was in kindergarten, my daughter told me that she wanted to be a lunch lady. When I asked her why she said that

---

slaves, was one of Jefferson's slaves with whom he had six children.
[85] I am not advocating theft; or anarchy by avocado; or mutiny by Skittles. I am just letting you know that I understand white privilege.

she liked the clickety-clacking sound of the lunch lady's fingernails on the cash register. When I asked her to describe the lunch lady, the lunch lady's dark skin was the eighth characteristic she mentioned, only after her dangly earrings, long fingernails, curly hair, Ravens jerseys, purple glasses, necklace with her name on it, and jingly bracelets.

But then, on an ordinary humdrum afternoon, I instinctively think that a black man wouldn't—couldn't—whistle a Kate Bush tune. And then I wonder if my three years teaching at that urban public school was just a cliché, the Caucasian man eager to make a difference by saving the poor youth, but only for three years and also with a way to extricate himself from such. Think Sandra Bullock in *The Blind Side*. But me. And then I wonder if there were lots of things that rubbed off on me, like if one day I might say, "nigger."

On a continuum of attitudes toward race—one end composed of people completely oblivious to the concept and who see only human beings, and the other composed of Ku Klux Klan members—where do I fall? How do we quantify all these nuances? Who am I?

I think at the very least I have some implicit racial bias. And I am sorry for that. I don't know how that happened. I tried. At least I am thinking about my thoughts on race, which suggests that I maintain a modicum of self-awareness. Is this anomalous? Do most white men think about this?

A friend told me not to beat myself up—that it would actually be rather odd for a twenty-something of any race to whistle Kate Bush. While I realize that age might have something to do with this, age is not a factor when I hear someone my age (forty) whistling a Beatles song or a Rolling Stones song. Both of which, while not as obscure as Kate Bush, are as removed from a forty-something as Kate Bush is from a twenty-something. So that factor only serves to erode my racial bias just a little bit.

I will shamelessly employ the tired argument that I have black friends. With whom I hug and laugh and share dinner. But sometimes I playfully tease them about Chaka Kahn, or Stevie Wonder—just presuming that they like Chaka Kahn or Stevie Wonder. Once, a black friend and I were talking about how she was perceived in the neighborhood. I made a joke about how the other moms in the neighborhood think she is going to car jack them. She laughed. But I think that qualifies as a microaggression; harmless on its face but secretly more corrosive than I realize. I also work near the courthouse. Once, a pair of black men asked me where Washington Street was. I replied, "Are you looking for the public defender's office?" They weren't. They were looking for a building adjacent to mine. I directed them to that building's entrance. But I walked away feeling shitty.

Historian E. H. Carr, in his book *What is History?* writes:

Every human being at every stage of history is born into a society and from his earliest years is moulded by that society. Both language and environment help to determine the character of his thought; his earliest ideas come to him from others. The individual apart from society would be both speechless and mindless.

Everybody has a story. It is through this prism of vignettes that we frame our take on the world.

Curious thing, the blood we inherit. It sloshes around in our veins and makes us who we are, underneath our skin, along with the landscapes we inhabit and the people with whom we interact. It swishes and sloshes through our veins carrying with it our DNA, DNA susceptible to a panoply of flaws of kinds both character and physical. My DNA tells me if I will get cancer or diabetes, and it tells me if I will be easygoing and relaxed or prone to temper tantrums.

The Emperor of Ice-Cream

Similarly, we do not cut our politics from cloth but weave it from the material we have at hand. Everybody has their own tics, affiliations, idiosyncrasies, grudges, connections, and connotations, which, added together, comprise their identity. The tension between who we are and what we make of it and what we might do with it is rarely resolved.

So, I have room for improvement. There are more "unseen dimensions" to my gestalt than I realized. I think the thing that bothers me most is that for all my post-Kate Bush analysis, I never stopped and engaged the whistler. I never nodded and mouthed "cool song" or gave him a thumbs-up. There's a story there—the story of how this black man came to know Kate Bush. It probably took and takes courage for him to listen to Kate Bush. I didn't earn Kate Bush. She was just always there, at college keg parties, on the radio stations I listened to. She was a natural extension of what was expected of me. The whistler's story remains unknown, and that suggests how we might fix these things—by engaging with one another; by talking and telling each other's stories. I am just doing the best I can; I've been told this is all I could do.

A friend recently told me about the time he corrected his mother who, during a conversation about Indians asked, "Dots or feathers?" There was silence and then he said, "Mom, you just can't say that." The irony, he said, is that he recalls when he was 11 years old and, upon returning from the Washington Zoo with his mom, heard his grandfather ask, "Did you see any jigaboos?" He heard his mom scold his grandfather, a man, he said, that no one ever scolded. That is progress, I guess. For what will my kids correct me? Will we be vilified for wearing Washington Redskins sweatshirts? Referring to everyone in the Middle East as Middle Eastern? Will my kids find me revolting for having ever referred to anyone as "thin" or "fat"? Will science yield new astonishing information about the corrosive effects of terms like "chubby" and "skinny"? Will the term "obese" become verboten? So many things to think about when

110

considering how to treat a person.

In the Spring of 1995, I was working in Boston as a Sales Assistant in the Law School Books Department of Little, Brown and Company. This was my dream job, as I had wanted to work for a publisher ever since I could remember. Though I was selling books to law school professors and not green-lighting manuscripts of hot new fiction writers like I had envisioned, I was still working for a book publisher; in Boston; talking about books all day. Typically, law professors would call the 800 number, and I would answer it and talk to them about casebooks that we offered in the subjects that they would be teaching in forthcoming semesters. One evening, a man who identified himself as Professor Greene, from the University of Oregon's School of Law, called the 800 number. He asked about casebooks we had in Entertainment Law. Sadly, we had no such casebooks, but I liked the friendly sound of Prof. Greene's voice and so asked him what else he was teaching. He was teaching Torts in the fall, so I told him about all our Torts books, and arranged to have him receive complimentary copies of each. A few weeks later, Prof. Greene called back to say thanks. This—a call back to say thanks—was rare. He said that he had had no luck in finding an entertainment law casebook and had decided to assemble his own materials for the class by piecing together portions of other books. I located some practitioner's law books related to entertainment law, some contracts casebooks which included entertainment contracts, and threw in some race and American Law books since he mentioned that he would be integrating a racism component in the course. A few weeks later he called to say thanks again. I told him how rare this was. And he said he was new. We chatted. I told him that his students would surely be enraptured with a voice like his. And then he told me that he was Dennis Greene from Sha-Na-Na. I told him I remembered Sha-Na-Na. He made sure I knew that he was Denny—the guy who typically wore the gold lamé suit.

Turns out the black guy in the gold lamé from Sha-Na-Na received a BA degree from Columbia University in 1971, an Ed.M. from Harvard University in 1984, and a JD from Yale Law School in 1987. I was astounded, and did my best to convey my awe and incredulity and profoundest admiration.[86]

It was after hours. The office was empty. Perhaps a bit dumbfounded by the coincidence of the whole exchange, I took a deep breath and proceeded to tell him the story of how one day in the summer of 1980 I was going to church with my grandparents on a Saturday night, and I was watching TV while waiting for them to get ready, and then how my Grandpa asked me if I liked to watch those black niggers. And I told him that I was sorry. That I didn't know why I was telling him this; that I had thought about that night a lot since it happened; and that he had a right to know that for several weeks, he had been communicating with the grandson of a man who once said the n-word.

I think also that I believed in the world's ability to right itself, just like that, with a solitary kindness; a solitary admission.

If Emily Post had ever written a chapter on the proper etiquette in this situation, neither one of us had read it at the time. He was silent for what felt like minutes. In those moments, I thought, "Oh shit, I am about to get fired." And then I felt my ears get hot. He sort of laughed, thanked me, and said, "Don't sweat it, man. I think most people have had an experience like that. We are all just doing the best we can." That was it. I thanked him for his kindness and understanding. It was a turning point for me. We are all just people. And because he told me that he would be adopting Richard

---

[86] The job of selling law books to law school professors requires great obsequiousness. I can be very obsequious. But I was even more so—and perhaps a little authentically—upon hearing this.

Epstein's *Cases and Materials On Torts* casebook, I also thanked him for his business. We talked for a few minutes more about school-related minutia.

In addition to being astounded by the coincidence of the exchange, I am simultaneously proud of and embarrassed by it also. I think it took courage. I think it shows an earnest attempt to foster understanding. But I also realize how self-important it was to think Prof. Greene had time for me; to think that he wanted to engage a self-absorbed Gen X-er in his quest for forgiveness. It's embarrassing to think I could pepper business calls with personal reflections, and perhaps it was a little narcissistic of me to think that Prof. Greene would care. The self-absorption it took to think of my need for forgiveness over the potential hurt it would cause Prof. Greene is embarrassing. I see now that I was acting less from kindness and more from a need to expunge some of my own feelings of shame.

Greene later taught at law schools all over the country, at Ohio State University, Seton Hall, University of Connecticut, and the University of Dayton. Greene died in Dayton, Ohio, on September 5, 2015 from esophageal cancer just a few weeks after his diagnosis. He was sixty-six.

But I never spoke with him again after that evening in which I revealed myself to be the grandson of a man who once said the n-word. And I have come to know that the world doesn't necessarily right itself with a single admission.

Prof. Greene's assessment and forgiveness was sufficient for a time for me to leave the Sha-Na-Na incident alone. The news cycle is always peppering us with little reminders that no one is perfect, and that helped also. Helpful also is the rage we see at Trump rallies. Grandpa would never have succumbed to such hatred. He was incapable of such hatred. He would think it despicable. I am comforted by the fact that Grandpa never delighted in anyone else's misfortune. He never begrudged anyone their good fortune.

But isn't that everyone's Grandpa? Isn't everyone's Grandpa the perfect hybrid of Santa Claus, *Bonanza*'s Ben Cartwright, Mr. Peanut, and the host of CBS's *Password* Allen Ludden?

I still expected more from Grandpa than what I got in his living room that one evening in 1980. I expected him to be immune from such words, expected him to be more sophisticated, to be more loving. And there were also perpetual reminders that attitudes toward race are not as innocuous as we think, like the way I assume someone's race by what they whistle.

It's harder than we realize to shake off the dust of where we have been.

In families, facts often come to us belatedly. Rarely are we told the most crucial facts of our ancestors' lives when we are most intimate with them, usually as young children. Such knowledge comes, if it comes at all, when we are older. When we appreciate how it feels to worry about a mortgage, to fret about a child, to get aches and pains. And what exactly are facts? Do they have the power to explain the world to us? On the contrary, it is the facts that must be explained.[87]

E. H. Carr is right. We are the sum of all our vignettes. All our vignettes—assembled, played, and replayed in slow

---

[87] Regrettably, I never asked Grandpa how his concepts of race were formed. He spoke frequently about how members of FDR's Civilian Conservation Corps planted all the trees in the woods that peppered the farm and circumnavigated the fields. But talk then quickly turned to rationing sugar and tires during World War II. I never asked him if he talked to any of the CCC workers, or brought them lemonade, or played baseball with them, or what their racial make-up was; never asked him what they looked like. CCC camps in the north were integrated and of the 3 million men who participated, 200,000 of them were black. My maternal grandfather, a man who seemed to loathe just about everyone, told me with some frequency about how he played baseball with the coloreds and how they were some of the nicest people he had ever met. I never followed up with him on this point.

motion, fast-forwarded and paused—make us who we are. The narrative of my personal history is distinguished by lots of Grandpa vignettes, and lots of things of which I am proud; but also lots of things of which I am ashamed. Lots of things to which I owe Grandpa.

But in one of my most distinct memories of him, he is on his hands and knees on the floor of the very same living room in which he asked me about Dennis Green. We are playing "Blockhead," a popular game in the 70s made by Milton Bradley. The object is for players to stack multicolored and oddly shaped wooden pieces atop one another until they all fell. Even back then, when he was only in his sixties, Grandpa's Parkinson's caused his hands to shake with some vigor. So I always won. And Grandpa always acted surprised and disappointed when I did. I think the love it took for him to get down on the floor with his aching knees and play this stupid game with his trembling hands far outweighs whatever residual racism made him say that word. I also think of him making eggs for the priest with whom he bunked at Aunt Janet's house in 2006, and of Grandpa sharing a pint of Ben & Jerry's with him.

In September 2004, I was clerking for a judge in Baltimore City Circuit Court. I rode the same bus to and from work every day: the Maryland Transit Authority's Bus Number Eight. And every day the Express picked up the same people—mostly black ladies, nurses and state workers. After a few weeks, one of those ladies, Miss Lynn, asked me my name. I told her. The next day she called me "Greg," and I couldn't bring myself to correct her, as she had already looked away and we were brand new friends. Then she called me Greg again the next day, and I was unable to correct her because she was several seats away and the chatter between the two seats made a succinct correction implausible. She called me Greg again, and by that point, correcting her would have been just plain rude. So I was Greg. And then everyone started calling me Greg. We chatted every day for a couple years. They were elated when I told them my wife was pregnant. One evening, I got on the bus and they had organized a baby shower for me, replete with cupcakes for the whole bus and a big shopping bag full of onesies and washcloths and baby wipes. We spent the entire bus ride eating cupcakes, and I opened gifts, and those with kids told baby stories. This baby shower my fellow bus riders threw for me just before my son was born is among the things in my life for which I am most proud.

I also know now that it was the Grandpa in me who chatted with them every day. It was the Grandpa in me who decided not to make a big deal of the fact that they were calling me the wrong name. It was the Grandpa in me who shared and laughed and chatted with these ladies. It was the Grandpa in me who cried at the kindness and goodness and thoughtfulness of it all. For all the flaws in my DNA, there are, thanks to his bits of basic code sloshing around in my veins, some good things as well. I too have whatever genetic mutation he had which made him immune from the rage so many white men feel, prevented him from feeling put upon when others obtained more.

I came to see that in many respects there were two Grandpas; that there had always been two Grandpas; two distinct models of what it means to grow into and be a man. The first model demands one to grow up adhering to the mores of the world; to be as susceptible to momentum as anyone else; to be as erodible as that sedimentary rock which forms the Grand Canyon. When Grandpa was done with farming, he worked for our small town's Department of Public Works, paving roads and filling potholes. I would see him and a half dozen other men driving trucks around and shoveling asphalt, and, knowing what I know now about the way men speak with one another, I have little doubt that Grandpa heard, and perhaps even took part in, racist stuff. The second model encourages one to not really grow up at all—to pursue frivolity and bemusement; to show everyone such remarkable dedication and sacrifice that you never really show yourself to be human. Grandpa embodied both. The latter clarifies how Grandpa became a myth—a great narrative for a while, one you can laugh at as you recount the memories. A myth is so much better than a person, but as we repeat the myth over and over again, the legend begs to be more closely scrutinized, and the myth doesn't hold. It's too inhuman. Yet it is natural for children to mythologize their grandparents. They are giants on the landscapes into which we are born; we cast our eyes upon them as we lie in our cribs and totter at their feet. As mysterious as parents are, the greatest of infantile mysteries must be the sudden appearance of these older giants, our own parents' parents.

I have debated whether or not to tell the story I have just told you. I am sometimes bewildered by my compulsion to do so for a host of reasons. In a world where Syrian children wash up on the shores of the Mediterranean and parents are torn from families and sent back to countries of origin from which they never originated, how can such a story even be relevant? To dwell so preciously on a word used three decades ago by someone I love seems almost vulgar. Furthermore, as his grandson, I want to protect Grandpa. That is what families do, right? Protect one another? I think that's why I had to preface this essay with the windmill story, to let you know that Grandpa was neither bitter nor hateful. He did not get angry when others sought equality. He did not hate. But all heroes are flawed.

The tipping point for me was realizing that, when talking about race, it's usually not the stories we tell that get us into trouble—that foster shame and the threat of rebuke—it's the stories we *don't* tell. So I'm telling you about Grandpa. It's not completely benign, but the Sha-Na-Na incident pales in comparison to the treatment of slaves, the lynchings, the degradation of the black citizen in the United States. My silence would thusly pale in comparison to the scope of others' silences as they watched the unknown multitudes who swung silently from the trees to which they were hung.

In thinking about the Sha-Na-Na Incident—trying to digest it, identify why it has stuck with me, process it, inhale it, apologize for it, get angry about it, get sad about it, try to empathize with my grandpa, generally identify and develop an understanding of the truth—I think of other truths that our country desperately needs to explore. If everyone knew the truth about slavery, if we all actually stopped to ponder and digest and inhale the idea that families were split apart and sold, women were raped, whipped, killed; if we pondered the idea of Jesuit universities selling slaves to stay afloat;[88] if we really stop to think about what happened to the Central Park Five;[89] if we take our thumbnail and scratch beneath the surface of what we are saying when we talk about Thomas Jefferson fathering children with Sally Hemmings; if we explore the story of Emmett Till[90]—we would be different people. We would be ashamed, aghast, astounded. More understanding. More empathetic.

Some would surely call it looking backward. I call it an eagerness to move forward; hopefully as a more enlightened culture. And I am just trying to understand my Grandpa, the man, as well. A man, I know for certain, who was just doing the best he could.

---

[88] In 1838, the nation's premier Catholic educational institution, now known as Georgetown University, sold 272 men, women, and children to raise money to pay off the debts of the then-struggling college.

[89] In April 1989, Trisha Meili was raped and beaten while jogging in Central Park. Five juveniles, four black and one Latino, were tried and convicted for the highly publicized crime. They were later exonerated after DNA evidence cleared them.

[90] Emmett Till was a fourteen-year-old boy from Chicago who, in 1955, was kidnapped, beaten, shot, killed, and thrown into a river for speaking with a white woman while visiting relatives in Mississippi.

But this did all happen as I was learning that Grandpa was human; or merely human. And with that epiphany came the acknowledgment that human beings—even the ones you revere—are flawed. Furthermore, there are those flaws and those errors in judgment which can be forgiven and those that cannot. I think Grandpa's is the former. Being human, in fact, means being flawed. Additionally, it is becoming clear that while where you are never fully determines who you are, no one is completely and absolutely immune from the where of where they come from. In all its beauty, toxicity, joy, sorrow, and everything else.

This Is How the Wind Shifts

"The Glass of Water"

That the glass would melt in heat,
That the water would freeze in cold,
Shows that this object is merely a state,
One of many, between two poles. So,
In the metaphysical, there are these poles.

Here in the centre stands the glass. Light
Is the lion that comes down to drink. There
And in that state, the glass is a pool.
Ruddy are his eyes and ruddy are his claws
When light comes down to wet his frothy jaws

And in the water winding weeds move round.
And there and in another state—the refractions,
The *metaphysica*, the plastic parts of poems
Crash in the mind—But, fat Jocundus, worrying
About what stands here in the centre, not the glass,

But in the centre of our lives, this time, this day,
It is a state, this spring among the politicians
Playing cards. In a village of the indigenes,
One would have still to discover. Among the dogs and dung,
One would continue to contend with one's ideas.

—Wallace Stevens

I never saw Grandpa drunk. Never saw him even tipsy. Later, when the self-consciousness prompted by his Parkinson's-induced shaking hands made eating in public uncomfortable, he would drink some brandy prior to the meal

120

to relax.[91] I never saw him gamble. Though once a year he would play the games of chance at the Sheldon Volunteer Fireman's Picnic, and he would always buy a raffle ticket that whatever Catholic school we were in at the time forced us to sell for some piece of shit bullshit prize. I never saw him smoke. Anything. No pipe, no cigar, no cigarettes, no joints handcrafted with EZ Wider rolling papers. The only indulgence[92] he had of which I am aware was ice cream.[93] And I am starting to understand it.

---

[91] Additionally, when he was in his eighties, he had elective surgery to help correct this hand shaking from Parkinson's. I don't know what the surgery was called, but it involved going into the brain stem and making some adjustments in an effort to alleviate the pressure, or whatever it was that created the shaking. It almost sounded like a lobotomy, but in the back. Anyway, the surgery worked. A little bit. For a little while. The shaking came back gradually and within a couple years was just as severe as it had been before the surgery. But he did it. He said to himself, "I am important enough, and my feelings are important enough to have elective surgery on my fucking brain when I am an octogenarian." He didn't really say that. Or maybe he did, and I just don't know it. Anyway, it is unlikely he said that but that is what I heard when Mom told me that he was having the surgery. Your feelings are important.

[92] Every two or three years, Grandpa bought a new car. It was typically a Pontiac Bonneville or Oldsmobile Cutlass Supreme or something like that. Never a Cadillac or anything from the Ford Lincoln Mercury family. Some might consider this an indulgence, since each car seemed to be nicer than the one before it, marked by plush seats and a perpetual new car smell. A few of them even had a compass. But insofar as the car itself was necessary for them to get from point A to point B, I have determined this not to be an indulgence.

[93] Americans love ice cream. Every single idiot American loves ice cream. And every year the average American eats twenty-three quarts of it. Me telling you that my Grandpa loved it is like me telling you that Grandpa liked to breathe. Or that he drank water. But Grandpa's love for it took on a different hue. I understand that this is the very definition of fandom, that every fan thinks their devotion is the "most significant," the "most authentic," the "most severe," and/or the "most important." But Grandpa's love for ice cream seemed to be a fundamental part of who he was.

The Emperor of Ice-Cream

Grandpa ate ice cream no matter what the temperature was outside. Typically, an individual's love for ice cream waxes and wanes with the weather. A few cool weeks in the summer and ice cream sales plummet. Grandpa always ate Maple Walnut; if it were on sale, however, he would settle for Butter Pecan. I still consider these two flavors "old people's flavors."

And always the cheapest possible ice cream in the largest possible container. No Ben & Jerry's or Haagen-Dazs for him despite the fact that in the summer of 1981, *Time* magazine, in the opening paragraph of a cover story on ice cream, said, "What you must understand at the outset is that Ben & Jerry's in Burlington, Vt., makes the best ice cream in the world"; in fact, the lower the level of cachet, the better. And he gave not one hoot whether the egg whites used to prepare the ice cream came from locally-sourced grain-fed chickens or whether the walnuts used were organic or whether the corporation that manufactured the ice cream used slave labor to make it or how many chemicals were used to approximate the flavor. So long as whatever technician or flavorist that assembled the flavor respected and adhered to the deeply held conservatism to which Grandpa held when it came to putting food in his mouth, it was good enough for Grandpa.

It's hard to know exactly when alcohol begins to have an effect on you. When the evanescent feeling of indomitability begins to take hold. When the warmth replaces the shame. When the conviviality replaces the chronic isolation. But it does have its effect.

The first time I got drunk was Saturday, April 4, 1987. I was a junior in high school, and my friends and I all took the ACT at Genesee Community College that morning. Afterward, we went to the Taco Joint for lunch, and then I went home with Spud. That year it had been noted that I would be a "riot" when drunk. Neil Cummings's earth science class was the perfect confluence of people around whom I was not afraid to

122

be funny, and people had taken note. So, after months of efforts and orchestrations to rival the Manhattan Project, there was to be a party in the greenhouses across the street from Tuan and Phouc's house. I wore my new Adidas T-shirt and drank four cans of Coors Light before blacking out, and then I woke up at Spud's house. I could go on about the greenhouses—about how we listened to Pink Floyd and Steve Miller and the Scorpions, and how thrilling it was to be wasted and to walk around a town in which I was anonymously smoking cigarettes—and about high school in general. About the warmth I felt getting wasted with people who had up to that point felt like distant strangers.

I woke up on Sunday morning filled with dread and walked out into Spud's kitchen to find his father, working like a demon alchemist, cooking chicken cacciatore.[94] My first time drunk coincided with my first real glimpse into what we will call "culinary diversity." It was clear that Spud's father dredged each pinch of salt and each tomato and each piece of basil from the depths of his very soul. It was a celebration of heritage; of family; it was an all-day affair. It was also probably the first time I had ever seen a man cook, and it was definitely the first time I had ever seen a man cook with such authority and enthusiasm. It was also the first time I recall being acutely aware of how different my family was. I had always been aware of my family's overarching normalcy; seeing Spud's dad cook cacciatore prompted me to wonder if our normalcy actually

---

[94] This feeling would repeat itself over and over for the next several decades. The feeling of waking up and wondering what the hell I did, who the hell I would have to call to apologize, which co-workers I had offended, checking my wallet to see how much I had spent the night before and to make sure credit cards were still there, making sure I knew where my glasses were, whether the screen of my iPhone was smashed again, how I was going to function that day, how I was going to replenish the liquor cabinet with what I had drank the night before so my wife would not became suspicious.

made us not normal. There were times I would bemoan the fact that our family lacked proprietorship over anything.

Spud's dad greeted me cheerfully. I was relieved to know I would not be admonished for what I can only assume was inappropriate behavior the night before. My family, farmers eight or ten generations removed from our ancestors' arrival from Belgium or Germany or one of those places, did no such dredging of basil from the depths of our soul. For us, food was less of a celebration, less a form of reverence for the past than it was merely something to ingest in the most utilitarian way. That day cemented for me that our family did not have what Spud's family had.[95]

Nowhere it seems do we encounter the question of what we like so broadly, so forcefully, so instinctively, as when we sit down to eat a meal. The meal is not just a ritual of nourishment, but a kind of story. Venturing through the course of a meal, we encounter a narrative, with its prologues, climaxes, and slow resolutions. But a meal is also a concentrated exercise in choice and pleasure, longing and regret, the satisfaction of wants and the creation of desires.

A meal at Grandpa and Grandma's was both a narrative and the satisfaction of wants, but also an extended skirmish between Grandma and myself. Each mouthful was just a series of passive-aggressive skirmishes punctuated with hyper-compressed disappointment that I was failing to try new things, and backhanded boasts and compliments regarding how inexpensively each thing that we were eating was purchased. Failure to fully embrace Grandma's hard work or diligent gardening fostered profound feelings of inadequacy and shame. At least for me. And it was scary. For I knew that I would have to try some of Grandma's pickled cauliflower.[96] Typically, on

---

[95] Also cemented that day was the fact that I loved getting wasted.
[96] The word "try" suggests doing something for the first time. I tried pickled

those days I was sent to spend with Grandma and Grandpa, we would sit down at the kitchen table when Grandma would take a quart-sized mason jar out of the cupboard and set it down on the table with a sound that was no less devastating than what the *Enola Gay* must have created with its casual delivery over Nagasaki. The mason jar contained pickled cauliflower—its bulbs or florets or whatever the fuck they are called jammed into the mason jar and soaked in its urine-esque pickle juice and looking like brains—and this signaled to me that ingestion was both imminent and inevitable.

Grandpa would observe the ritual with what I interpreted to be a mix of sympathy and amusement. And perhaps a little bit of gratitude that he would be spared. Indeed, in the course of their sixty-two-year marriage, Grandpa refused to capitulate to Grandma on only one item of which I am aware. One. On everything else, he acquiesced. The one item on which they could not—and would never—agree was what a tomato was. They grew them by the bushel in their garden. They worked together flawlessly, watering, cultivating, planting and weeding and harvesting. They had bushels of enormous fire-engine red tomatoes that they would eat as is. Grandpa thought (correctly) that it was a fruit, while Grandma believed it to be a vegetable. I recall dinners at their house when Grandpa would go out to the garden and pick a big beefsteak tomato, so red it nearly glowed, and bring it into the house. Grandma would wash it and, with the knowledge that what she was washing was a vegetable, sliced the tomato and put half on a plate for her and half on a plate for Grandpa. She would salt her half, cut it, and eat it. Grandpa, knowing that tomatoes were a fruit, put sugar

---

cauliflower no fewer than 88 bazillion times. Each with the same results. If insanity is doing the same thing over and over again and expecting a different result, Grandma was positively insane. Perhaps criminally so. Once I tried to explain this to her. It didn't go well.

on his.[97] Mountains of sugar from the Tupperware sugar dispenser.[98] Then they each ate their tomato halves.[99]

We are born knowing two things: sweet is good and bitter is bad. We also arrive into the world with a curious blend of full-spectrum liking and disliking. We are on the one hand omnivores, and yet on the other we are also neophobic when it comes to foods. A few days out of the womb, and we are already expressing preferences.

In my hometown, there were no Chinese restaurants; not even those storefronts that merely deliver food and purport to be Chinese. There were no pizzerias. I didn't like pizza for the majority of my childhood, so we never ate it, ordered it, took it out or took it home, anyway. Our diet had no diversity. There was no ethnicity or exotic spices or African peanut butter, Greek moussaka, Reuben, B.L.T., asparagus and caviar,

---

[97] Botanically, the tomato is a fruit, as it is the ovary and the seeds of a flowering plant. However, the tomato has a much lower sugar content than other edible fruits and is therefore not as sweet. Since it is typically served as part of a salad or main course of a meal, rather than as a dessert, it is generally considered a culinary vegetable. Further complicating matters, however, is that tomatoes are as acidic as fruits. Lots of foods share this sort of ambiguity: bell peppers, cucumbers, green beans, eggplants, avocados, zucchini, and pumpkins are all botanically fruits yet treated as vegetables. I think, technically, then, Grandpa was right.

[98] The Tupperware sugar dispenser to which I refer are now considered vintage. Grandpa and Grandma had the double-ended sugar dispenser, about four inches high and five inches wide. One end had an airtight opening for a spoon; the other end had an airtight opening for pouring. Theirs was turquoise; like their kitchen. They had a ton of Tupperware stuff.

[99] Perhaps you are wondering where my half was. I did not like tomatoes back then. And apparently, tomatoes were valuable enough to not waste on making me try them.

Japanese shrimp miso, chicken chili, Irish corned beef and cabbage, Polish pierogis, Swiss chocolate, French frog legs, Korean beef ball, Italian shrimp and eggplant Parmesan, ham and egg, short rib, Russian beef Stroganoff, turkey cacciatore, or Indian mulligatawny.

It was not just us; there was a lack of diversity wherever I went. There were two black kids in my high school class. Mark was adopted by the Caucasian owners of the Colonel West Motel; Madelyn—we called her "Mad Dog"—was the daughter of a custodian and a cafeteria worker. There were no Latinos or Muslims or Asians. TV was not helpful in expanding our horizons. I recall one episode of *Happy Days* when Marion Cunningham tries to spice up her relationship with Howard by making couscous. Lavern DiFazio's father owned a pizza joint. But otherwise, TV families seemed as entrenched in pot roast as we were. Though the *Brady Bunch* did have that episode where they put beans and hot dogs in a flashlight and brought it to a Native American boy.

My wife is the daughter of Polish immigrants.[100] Meals for them are an event. They make pierogis and *flakki* and *gwumpke* and a host of traditional Polish dishes. This is who they are. Food is the epicenter of their world. My mother-in-law orders kielbasa from Chicago and goes to the market for the right kind of cheese with which to make her pierogi.[101] She

---

[100] Stefan "Steve" Wichlinski came to the United States via boat in 1947 at the age of eleven. This is the age of my son as I sit here and write this. His family settled in Patterson, NJ. Amelia Stankiewic arrived in New York in 1968 following the death of her mother. She was twenty-six and worked at the Avon in Rockland County, just north of New York City. She and Steve got married in 1972 and settled in Hawthorne, NJ, twenty-one miles from the George Washington Bridge. He worked at the Ford plant in Mahwah, NJ, and she raised my wife and cooked.

[101] Additionally, my in-laws lived in close proximity to the Nabisco factory in Fairlawn, NJ. This factory produced what she calls "the smell." "The smell" was the scent of cookies that drifted through and around Fairlawn, Hawthorne and Paramus,

savors her pursuit of the best mushrooms and then savors the mushrooms themselves and then savors the things she makes with them—things as close to identical as possible to what her mother made. Again, after being immersed in this world, the absence of our family's food narrative began to gnaw at me.

If one were to place meals on a continuum, with one end being "festive" and the other end being "obligatory," meals for Grandpa and Grandpa would have been about halfway between the midway point and the obligatory endpoint. There was never too much spice or an exorbitant amount of cheese or dizzying displays of seafood. While there was never excess, things were never Spartan either. There was always *plenty;* there were always fruits and vegetables in bowls; they always had Chiclets in the drawer and in the car. And they always, *always* had ice cream.

It is challenging, then, to identify a food narrative for my family. To say my family lacks a food narrative seems at odds with my memories because it seems like all we did was talk about food. We talked about what was for dinner and supper. We cut coupons and leafed through circulars chronicling weekly sales at Super Duper and Tops, this before Wegman's began their advance toward world domination beginning in the Buffalo–Rochester area of New York. But this seemed so utilitarian to me. Purely the manifestation of a basic human need—the first level of Maslow's hierarchy having nothing to do with identity and heritage and history and everything to do with nourishment and subsistence. But I am realizing now that we were not normal. At least not normal by twentieth-century standards. This brings me comfort.[102]

NJ. Several of my wife's aunts and cousins worked at the Nabisco factory too.

[102] Though I'm wondering if, like a white guy at Dartmouth or Duke claiming to add diversity because he's wearing green seersucker instead of blue, we really have something to add to the diversity conversation.

Gary M. Almeter

We had a large chest freezer in our basement that we filled with meat. We grew up on a dairy farm, and every time Dad butchered a cow, a man would come and drag the cow away to his lair and presumably cut it up. It came back to our house as chunks of putative pot roast wrapped in white paper. It was always Mom who would venture down into the cellar and come back upstairs with several pounds of meat.

Geographically, we lived about forty miles east of Buffalo, which gave us claim to the Buffalo wing and beef-on-weck and the hot dogs and soft pretzels and whatever else they serve at bowling alleys and Buffalo Bills football games.

In 1978, my aunt and uncle gave me a subscription to *National Geographic World* for Christmas.[103] I was bored once in the summer of 1979 and identified a recipe for fortune cookies in an old issue of *World*. Somehow, my siblings and I convinced my mother that we needed to make these fortune cookies. The recipe said it made four dozen. While my older brother and my mother set about making the dough, my sister and I set about cutting slips of paper and composing fortunes. Having never eaten a fortune cookie, we could not have mimicked one of the Chinese fortunes—its cadence, its certainty, its insufficient conjunctions—and instead wrote innocuous things like, "You are nice," and "You are kind," and "We like you." Every now and again we deviated and wrote things like "Swimming is fun" and "The sun is bright."

On one such fortune slip, I covertly wrote, "You're gonna

---

[103] *World,* published by National Geographic Partners, features stories for kids about animals, science, technology, archaeology, geography, and pop culture. There were jokes, games, and activities in every issue. I loathed all those things as a kid—still do—but I loved getting a magazine in the mail once a month. And so I have maintained a certain enthusiasm for the physical magazine.

die on the 4th of July."

We made the fortune cookies and invited Grandpa to come down for a swim and to eat them with us. He picked one and it was the one that said "You're gonna die on the Fourth of July." We were terrified. But he laughed. Like a belly-rolling, jolly laugh. It surprised me that he laughed. But then it also didn't surprise me either. For the rest of the afternoon we sang the words "You're gonna to die on the Fourth of July" with a breezy melody reminiscent of "Afternoon Delight" or "Horse with No Name" or some other ubiquitous soft rock hit from the 70s. And we went swimming for hours. When Grandpa left, he said, "I hope the Fourth of July never comes!" and drove away.

Grandpa and Grandma took us blackberry picking at least once per summer. Grandma's dad planted a number of blackberry bushes between a couple fields about a half-mile walk away from our house. Grandpa and Grandma also took us strawberry picking at any one of the pick-your-own farms which dotted the ten-mile radius around our house. Grandma bent at the waist to pick strawberries because her knees were bad. She picked the most, and she scolded us if we picked strawberries that were not yet ripe. As a result, I was too scared to pick any strawberries. This is another reason why in the first chapter of this book I wrote that Grandpa probably didn't like me that much; I was a shitty strawberry picker. Additionally, Grandpa and Grandma had raspberry bushes behind the Blessed Mother statue adjacent to their porch. Whenever we were there in the summer, we could and would pick raspberries. Sometimes we brought them to Grandpa and Grandma and sometimes we just ate them all ourselves.

During the 1970s, a sage innkeeper named Sarah Tucker shilled Cool Whip non-dairy whipped topping.[104] Thirty-

---

[104] Tucker was played by Marge Redmond, best known for playing Sister Jacqueline in *The Flying Nun,* which aired on ABC from 1967 to 1970. She was nominated for an

second commercials depicted her running an inn somewhere in the Northeast. Guests came, and she would serve them strawberry shortcake. The guests were always surprised when Sarah Tucker topped the shortcake not with authentic whipped cream, but with Cool Whip non-dairy whipped topping that she effortlessly and flawlessly lobbed onto the cake with a perfectly peaked dollop. For decades, every time Grandma put cool whip on something, she would attempt to replicate Sarah Tucker's perfect dollop. And she never once succeeded.

At family parties, aunts would inevitably bring Jell-O molds. There was typically a green one with cottage cheese. Always an orange or red one filled with strawberries and marshmallows. This was not unique to our family, but it is part of the narrative. Deviled eggs were ubiquitous, as were baked beans with bacon on top and peanut butter cookies with a Hershey's Kiss at the center. Also famous were Grandma's extremely sweet pickles. And her ginger molasses cookies, which, when baked, maintained an indelible series of circles from the sugar-coated Tupperware glass with which they were stamped before baking.

We ate a ton of corn on the cob. We had holders shaped like corn on the cobs that would pierce the ends of the corn on the cob, so you could hold it. We had special butter reserved so that we could roll the corn on the cob in the butter, and we salted the fuck out of it. One day a year, we would husk about 5000[105] ears of corn on the cob, and Mom would boil them and cut the corn off and freeze it. One summer, my brother had braces and he couldn't eat corn on the cob, and it was agony

---

Emmy for Outstanding Supporting Actress in a Comedy Series for the Sister Jacqueline role during the 1967–68 season but lost to Marion Lorne, who won posthumously for her role as "Aunt Clara" on *Bewitched.*

[105] I am completely manufacturing, and likely exaggerating, this number. It could have been 5000 or it could have been 100. It was likely somewhere between the two.

for him.

In his short story, "Barn Burning," Faulkner reflects on behalf of a character about Abner Snopes's use of fire to burn down neighbors' barns, writing, "the element of fire spoke to some deep mainspring of his father's being, as the element of steel or of powder spoke to other men, as the one weapon for the preservation of integrity, else breath were not worth the breathing, and hence to be regarded with respect and used with discretion."

Basil spoke to Spud's father in this way. Mushrooms speak to my mother-in-law. Ice cream spoke to Grandpa.[106]

But everyone likes ice cream. So what, if anything, makes Grandpa's devotion to it so special? Makes it something worth exploring?

Grandpa spent his whole life watching people leave. At every single stage of his life, at every opportunity, friends and family and neighbors and mere people he saw once a week at church departed. For some elsewhere. I think of him waving at me when I was a young boy as I crossed the creek in the back of our farm; I think about him waving goodbye to me on the eve of when I was to move to Boston. And while this is a common characteristic of a certain generation of post-industrial farmers who stayed in their hometowns, it seems even more profound when I think of it being so with Grandpa. I understand that he is my Grandpa. Perhaps it is symptomatic of something resembling narcissism that I think that my

---

[106] My mom's dad, Grandpa L., made maple syrup in his sugar shanty for as many years as he was alive. This is a book about Grandpa A. But should you be interested, I would love to tell you about Grandpa L. and the way he made maple syrup—and, more generally, his devotion to the maple tree—sometime. He made maple syrup for decades. It was both something he loved and something he was compelled, as though required, to do.

ancestor doing something makes it somehow and generally
more so. Perhaps it is just human nature. Grandpa lived in only
three houses his whole life—each no more than a mile from the
other. A farmhouse as a boy; a farmhouse he bought from his
new in-laws; a ranch house that arrived prefabricated and that
he set up about fifty yards from this second farmhouse.

To complain about not having enough or not liking what
you had was considered disrespectful. So we grew up having to
eat *everything* on our plate.[107] And I counterbalanced that by

---

[107] Many of us were raised by parents who experienced the Great Depression and,
therefore, became members of the "clean plate club." The notion of "waste not, want
not" was instilled during mealtime at a very early age. Also, there was an ever-
popular motivational tool used to remind youngsters how fortunate they were to
have food to eat while other children were starving around the world. With obesity
on the rise in America, a new philosophy has replaced the old standard, and parents
no longer force children to clean their plates. Dieters are encouraged to eat until
they are satisfied but not stuffed. Still, there are many who believe overeating for
politeness's sake is wrong. Considering today's restaurant portions, it's easy to
understand why food is often left behind.

In some European cultures, a clean plate indicates that you're still hungry and are
ready for a second serving. Leaving food behind can mean several things, depending
on local tradition: you didn't care for the food, you are completely satisfied with your
portion, or you're acting in a gracious manner to show that you haven't "pigged out."
In China, clearing a plate is considered rude, yet in America, it can send a non-verbal
message that your food was delicious and much appreciated. There is no hard-and-
fast rule as to whether one should finish food or leave a little behind. When Emily
Post undertook the enormous task of establishing behavioral guidelines all but
ninety years ago, two things she believed to be most important were: etiquette
should always be practical and considerate of others. Her code has not changed and
is still relevant to our modern lives. When it comes to the clean plate debate, I would
suggest you use your common sense. To purposely leave food on a plate would be
considered wasteful. However, it seems perfectly acceptable and practical to leave
food if, for some reason, you were unable to eat everything.

drinking as much as I could, whenever I could, for twenty-three years.

I am now the grandson looking to make sense of a life fading from memory. Nine years' worth of fading.

Ice cream provided contentment and consolation. An escape from the loss of parents; the rigors of farm life; the necessary sacrifices of parenthood; the little humiliations people suffer. The right bowl of ice cream at the right moment in one's life can have a profound impact, and when paired with difficult circumstances, ice cream can be a refuge.

Despite its evanescence, the ice cream has stayed with me.[108]

I know that there can be something unsettling, perhaps even grotesque, about a writer extolling the effects of ice cream without reservation. So much ice cream in so many of its forms is so silly and so flippant and so needlessly decadent, and so little ice cream is really *about* anything beyond the standard summertime tropes and clichés. And in many respects, ice cream can be dangerous: too much cholesterol and too much sugar, too fattening. Like drugs and alcohol, it can create a debilitating dependency.

I recall the evening of May 2, 2011. It was a Sunday, and my wife had been gone for the weekend for the First Communion of our goddaughter and then would be gone for the rest of the week for a series of high school visits. I was so proud of myself that I hadn't gotten drunk in her absence. We spoke on the phone Sunday night and said goodnight. Then Brian Williams's authoritative yet friendly visage pops onto the television screen and says that breaking news just happened, and a report is imminent. I went to the kitchen and got a pint of Ben & Jerry's "What a Cluster" to eat while I waited for the

---

[108] And I don't mean that it has stayed with me in an extra-pounds-on-my-frame sort of way. I mean that it has stayed with me in a memory kind of way.

imminent report. I finished the pint, and still no report, so I absentmindedly got another pint—this one, "Chubby Hubby"—and ate it while waiting for the promised report. I finished that pint, too. Still no report from Brian Williams. So I got another pint— "Cinnamon Buns"—and began to eat it. Obama came on the television and told us that he had killed Osama bin Laden. What great news. As Facebook and Twitter erupted I solemnly reflected on the fact that I had just eaten three pints of Ben & Jerry's in one evening. I was no different than a junkie.

It's a challenge to write about ice cream, the same way it's a challenge to write about anything as evanescent as the mood of a Grateful Dead concert or the thrill that Civil War re-enactors might get in the midst of recreating the Battle of Gettysburg. You can't put it in a museum or bottle it or recapture it any way but by trying it.

It's a challenge to write about alcohol, too. It all seems so silly, the *need* to take a drink. The need to hide beers in the back of the fridge at a party so in case they run out of beer, you are sure to still have some. The destroyed relationships, the risk, the money, the shame, the guilt.

Still, ice cream lingers. And the things we remember matter. Still, the thing about things you love and try to recapture is the nagging questions of whether they are they really that great, or are they great because of the life you were living when you first heard them or tasted them?

Once when he was living with Aunt Janet, I sent Grandpa a half dozen pints of Ben & Jerry's from their factory in Burlington, VT. I was delighted to learn that when they arrived—via overnight shipping packed in a big Styrofoam cooler of dry ice—they were hard as rock, and even more delighted to learn that this mystified and enchanted and perplexed Grandpa. I sent him five flavors that I thought he would like, but also sent him "Boston Cream Pie" just to be a pain in the ass. When I visited, half of that pint was still left

135

The Emperor of Ice-Cream
over, so we ate it together in Aunt Janet's kitchen.

Gary M. Almeter

The Loneliness of the Dodgeball Player

"Of the Surface of Things"

I

In my room, the world is beyond my understanding,
But when I walk, I see that it consists of three or four hills and
    a cloud.

II

From my balcony, I survey the yellow air,
Reading where I have written,
'The spring is like a belle undressing.'

III

The gold tree is blue.
The singer has pulled his cloak over his head.
The moon is in the folds of the cloak.

—Wallace Stevens

When I was in its sixth grade, St. Vincent's Catholic
School hired Coach Wendy[109] to teach gym class. The students

---

[109] Coach Wendy, thusly named because she was the girls' softball coach at Attica
High School, was lauded for her tenacity and her arsenal of Nikes. Coach Wendy
was the perfect hybrid of Mike Rice, the disgraced Rutgers University women's
basketball coach who was fired for berating and abusing his players, and Ursula the
Sea Witch from Disney's *The Little Mermaid*—but in grey sweats and myriad Nikes in
lieu of an iridescent aquatic bustier. To obtain the most thorough description, you'd
be best served by watching the *Saturday Night Live* clip of Melissa McCarthy as
coach Sheila Kelly at Middle Delaware State University. You can watch the clip here:
http://www.nbc.com/saturday-night-live/video/outside-the-lines/n35031

thusly got a new taste of just how barbaric gym could be. Theretofore, gym class had been coeducational and fun. Coach Wendy's pedagogy included grouping sixth, seventh, and eighth grade boys together to generally engage in forty-five minutes of misandry.

But mostly all the bitch did was make us play dodgeball.

The Coach Wendy dodgeball era began the fall of 1981. I was ten years old and would turn eleven at the end of October. The cutoff birth date for our school district was November 1, which meant that I was always the youngest in my class. I was also the shortest. And I was generally small to begin with. Recall that I spent days reading books instead of tossing hay bales and lifting pigs to increase muscle mass. There was an eighth-grader named Chuck Merkel who had been held back two years. He was sixteen years old in September 1981 when Coach Wendy began her new, torturous physical education regime—I mean *regimen*. Chuck was a farm boy and really strong. He was more like a sixteen-year-old man than a sixteen-year-old boy; like a post-adolescent Dennis the Menace, but even more nefarious— like Heath Ledger as the Joker kind of nefarious. And like the Joker, Chuck still had traits of boyhood: really bad acne and chronically tousled dirty blond hair. He also had a faint moustache and every sort of sociopathy ever contemplated by the then-newly published third edition of the Diagnostic and Statistical Manual of Mental Disorders.[110] Chuck, as bullies are wont to do, targeted the smallest kid for the two classes per week we played dodgeball. The smallest kid was me.

I had an enormous head and a teeny weeny little body. Like a Pete Rose bobblehead on a Celine Dion body. Coach

---

[110] Later, while in high school, Chuck was sent to a juvenile facility for dropping cats from the top of silos. I couldn't make that up.

Wendy had an infinite supply of those red rubber playground balls in varying sizes; the ones with the basket-weave design on the surface, which served to inflict the maximum amount of pain when it struck your bare skin. The big ones were easy to dodge; Chuck could throw the tiny ones so fast and so hard that they would almost knock me out when they hit me in the head. Coach Wendy loved every minute of the ninety minutes of dodgeball to which I was subjected per week: forty-five minutes on Tuesday and forty-five minutes on Thursday. What a great time to be a gym teacher—Coach Wendy was clearly emboldened by new President Ronald Reagan's perpetual references to Knute Rockne's famed Gipper. And while at this point, Gen X-ers lamenting their old dodgeball experiences is cliché, with respect to early 1980s gym teachers (as supposed to today's teachers of physical education), these clichés exist for a reason—like those of real estate agents and wedding planners.

Outsmarting Chuck was not difficult. I had a friend named Michael Kaizer, also tiny, and also adept and more at ease doing things outside the norm—he was into drawing, and therefore appreciated the fact that I was more into reading and writing. When we were on separate teams, he would throw a ball at me gently, and I would get out. I have never forgotten this kindness.[111] But an early exit from the dodgeball mirth only antagonized Chuck. He would call me names like *sissy* and *faggot* and now and again throw balls at me even though I was safely out. As you might suspect, the names stung more than the balls did. Michael and I weren't successful in getting on the same team all the time. Coach Wendy vigorously exercised her progressive pedagogy and frequently varied the dodgeball team-selection process. Sometimes she would pit all sixth graders against all seventh and eighth graders; sometimes she would

---

[111] Michael and his family moved to Buffalo the next year. I have no doubt that had he stayed, we would have been good friends through high school.

have team captains;[112] sometimes we would count off by twos;[113] sometimes she would do something pedagogically unexpected like, "Everyone born between January and June on this side, everyone between July and December on that side," and teams would form their lineups as instructed.

Fundamentalist army officers assassinated Egyptian President Anwar Sadat six weeks into Coach Wendy's dodgeball regime. All news on Wednesday, October 7, 1981, was devoted to the Egyptian president's death the day before. This was the time when there were only three channels to choose from, and at six p.m. the only thing to watch was news, and the news that day was filled with video of soldiers firing guns into a crowd watching a parade in Cairo. Those images— along with the shame of being targeted by Chuck the previous day, the shame of being laughed at by Coach Wendy, and the dread of what the next day would bring—brought me to tears: I started crying. I remember my mom asking me what was wrong, and all I could do was sob: lip-quivering, snot-flying, red-splotchy-necked bawling. She held me and asked me what was wrong. I recall trying to explain about Anwar Sadat and Chuck Merkel and Wendy Miller and how the whole world was just an awful unjust unsafe horrible place.

I realize now that I was probably depressed. And ashamed that, contrary to the oft-recited aphorism of my youth that I tried desperately to take to heart, names—just like sticks and stones—actually did hurt me. Not only did they hurt, they *stung*, and burrowed below my epidermis to sting and strike my bone marrow. Names *did* hurt, and in the same way it would

---

[112] Chuck was always first one picked. He would histrionically tell his captain not to pick me, so he could "whale on me."

[113] It took Chuck a few classes, but eventually he would line up in such a way so as to guarantee that he was not on my team, so he could "whale on me".

hurt if someone sawed off the top of my head and poured hot tar into my cerebral cortex. That's how much the names fucking hurt. What was wrong with me?

The following Saturday, Grandpa rode his three-wheeler the few hundred feet from his house to the farm to help us rake leaves. He asked me how I was, and I lied, told him I felt good. Then I felt more shame: shame for not being able to tell Grandpa the truth, and shame that I was such a dodgeball wimp. See, Grandpa was revered in our town. He was strong. He would never have tolerated a Chuck Merkel throwing dodgeballs at his fucking head. He never would have been afraid of the men in Egypt who killed Anwar Sadat. He might've initially been afraid of Coach Wendy, but eventually and inevitably, he would've vanquished her, too. I recall setting the rake against the giant maple tree around which we were raking, telling Grandpa I had to go to the bathroom, then going to the bathroom and weeping. I remember thinking: What is wrong with me? Pursuant to the aphorism, sticks and stones will break bones, yet names aren't supposed to hurt, so why do the names Chuck calls me hurt so much?

I wonder now what would have happened if I had just started crying in front of Grandpa, told him that there was a mean boy who made dodgeball a death match and a gym teacher who derived pleasure from it, that there were evil soldiers killing world leaders for trying to improve lives, and that I just had no idea what the fuck what was going on. I wish I would have. I wish I had told him that nowhere really felt safe anymore. If the goal in life is to be authentic—and I think it is—I wish I would have been more authentic with Grandpa from the outset. I still wonder if Grandpa had ever been bullied. As I got older, he became more human—more flawed—and this only made me like him the more.

Later that year, I would become the bully. There was a kid named Tim who could barely read. I called him *stupid* about

400 times a day, and encouraged others to do so. I realize now that it was because I was bullied; that I was merely rolling the pain downhill, as it were. A big part of the bullying was about being smart—a trait generally associated with physical weakness. But "bullying," especially as we understand it now, wasn't part of the conversation in 1981. I had no idea what was happening. But I knew Grandpa would have been really ashamed of me. I also know now that this need to bully was the result of keeping all that shame and indignity inside.

About a year after the day I broke down weeping from Anwar Sadat's assassination I saw Grandpa cry for the first time. It was during the mass my mom and dad and his sisters had for Grandpa and Grandma for their fortieth wedding anniversary. During the communion meditation, Mom played "Bring Me a Rose" by Carey Landry.[114] Grandpa didn't weep so much as sort of lost his composure for a few minutes. But he definitely cried.

I don't think I can overstate how important this moment

---

[114] Mr. Landry is a composer of Catholic liturgical music. Among his better-known compositions are "Abba, Father," "Hail Mary, Gentle Woman," and "Peace Is Flowing Like a River." He is ubiquitous in liturgical music circles. The lyrics to "Bring me a Rose" are as follows:

Bring me a rose in the wintertime, When they're hard to find. Bring me a rose in the wintertime, I've got roses on my mind / For a rose is sweet, Most anytime and yet. Bring me a rose in the wintertime, How easily we forget. / Bring me a friend when I'm all alone, When they're hard to find. Bring me a friend when I'm all alone, I've got friendship on my mind. / For a friend is sweet, Most anytime and yet. Bring me a friend when I'm all alone, How easily we forget. / Bring me a smile when I'm far from home, When they're hard to find. Bring me a smile when I'm far from home, I've got smilin' on my mind. / For a smile is sweet, Most anytime and yet. Bring me a smile when I'm far from home, How easily we forget. / Bring me peace when there's talk of war, When it's hard to find. Bring me peace when there's talk of war, I've got peace on my mind. / For peace is sweet, Most anytime and yet. Bring me peace when there's talk of war, How easily we forget.

was for me. It was the first time I saw Grandpa cry. It was the first time I had seen any grandpa cry.[115] It might have been the first time I had seen any man cry in person. I can still see his shoulders quake as I sit here today.

He couldn't know about Chuck throwing dodgeballs at my head or me crying about Anwar Sadat. He would've been ashamed of me. I couldn't be vulnerable around Grandpa. But then he made himself vulnerable. What a gift to see that. What a gift he gave us.

At the end of his life, when he was in the nursing home and we weren't sure what he could understand and what he was thinking, he cried like he did at his fortieth anniversary—but even more so. He engaged in uncontrollable sobbing. We had some hypotheses about why; the one to which I subscribed was that he was letting out all the sadness that had been festering in his subconscious for decades, sadness that he had held in for so many decades because "big boys don't cry" and/or because he had to be strong for other people. Other theories were that the elderly are "emotionally incontinent"; that he was a crier his whole life and that this was just the natural and logical extension of that.

A few theorized that he was depressed.

People always said how brave and happy Grandpa was. Everyone agreed. Like the more Grandpa could dodge or bury or suppress the pain, the more heroic he was.

This seemed to be a formula for living a life full of secrets among many men from that town from that era. I know this now: people constantly hid. And still do. It was a sickness no less worse and no less corrosive than his Parkinson's. Grandpa had so many things he never told anyone. The look on his face and the look on the faces of so many people seemed to be the

---

[115] My mom said that my maternal grandfather cried at the funerals of his parents.

same: the resolve gets almost etched into the contours of your face.

Same with Nicholas Perry, whose son fell into a silo filled with corn silage and died from the toxic gases. And Ernie Glaus, whose one son went swimming in the pond adjacent to their house after school one day and drowned, and whose other son's leg was caught in a corn chopper assemblage unit and had to be amputated. Or PJ Almeter, whose two sons both killed themselves with a shotgun in the cornfield, a decade apart. And Bernard Perl, whose son was killed in a car accident a mile or so up the road.

None of them said anything about their losses again. And I wonder how they feel—how that resolve works on a person from the inside over all the years. I wonder if they will die the same way Grandpa did—after exhaling a flurry of raw emotion.

There is a hint of disgrace associated with crying, especially among older men. The stigma is not surprising, since most associate crying with depression and depression with weakness. What emerges is that we know very little about crying. Not only is there no clear-cut association between crying and depression, there are also very few studies reporting the opposite assertions that one commonly hears about it—that crying has healing benefits when it is not a response to pain or anger.

There was lots of pain and anger and humiliation in that town. I could see it then even as a child but didn't know what it was. There was a woman named Judy who always seemed sad to me. She had two kids and no husband, or a husband that we never ever saw, which was unimaginable at the time since everyone went to church. One of her kids was my age and named Randolph. Randolph could have been an extra from the 1950s portions of *Back to the Future,* so perfect was his perfectly parted and pomaded hair and flannel shirts and penny loafers. But so misplaced too; and so smiley and effervescent as to let even a seven- or eight-year-old kid know that something was amiss. And Judy was always sad. Once she was the waitress serving us at this diner in East Aurora that we would sometimes go to after my biweekly allergy shots. It startled me to see a woman from church in a waitress uniform. And it was even more startling to see how she moved—so timidly, so slowly, so frightened. They moved shortly after Randolph and I made our First Communion in 1978.

There was a woman named Rosie who was married to a guy whose family ran a lawnmower service shop. Rosie was always sad, too. At least she always looked sad. Exhibited the same sort of timidity and perpetual fear that Judy always did. Her daughter went to my high school and told me once that her father beat her mother. After her two daughters graduated high school, she left her husband and died shortly thereafter from breast cancer. This exists everywhere; there is literally some manifestation of sadness and sadness in varying degrees in every single town and village and city and megalopolis in the world. But there was something extra sad about it being in a place where it was ostensibly *wrong* to be sad.

I grew a beard my senior year in college. It was something to do; some new way to exhibit independence, some new way to rationalize, perhaps even celebrate my sparse ambition. A new way to give voice to the absolute lack of direction I was feeling. I now see this as fear. This was 1991 before beards were *de rigueur* amongst the millennial hipster set. This beard was also the only one of its kind amongst my preppy J. Crew. It was a departure for all of us.[116]

When I went home for Thanksgiving, I visited Grandpa and Grandma that first night, Wednesday evening. They were delighted to see the beard, said I looked handsome, said I always reminded them of Abraham Lincoln—you know, things

---

[116] I really can't emphasize enough how earth-shattering my beard was, what a seismic impact it had on the student body of Le Moyne College.

grandparents say to their grandchildren. Then Grandpa said something that really floored me. He said, "I expected you to have a beard this week." Astonished and disbelieving, I said, "No way, Grandpa. You expected me to have a beard?" He said, "Yeah—I know you, Gary."

For a while I chalked this up to the sort of broad and innocuous claim that fortunetellers typically make when any new potential clients walk in; their strategy to imply they know more about the person than they actually do. They look for clues about a person's identity via body language, clothing, age, hairstyle, race, and ethnicity, and then identify one of the standard introductory statements in their oeuvre to startle the potential client into submission. Something as broad and innocuous as "You've had a bad experience with water," or "There's a friend in your life who has caused you great pain," which could generally apply to anyone. So was Grandpa using some sort of fortune-telling cold-read on me? Just saying, "I knew you'd [do something]" as some way to cultivate closeness? Because at the time, I thought, "Grandpa doesn't know me at all."

For most of my life I wanted very much not to be where I was. Most of the time I felt in danger of vanishing altogether. If I could have put what I was feeling onto words, the words would have been an infant's wail: *I don't want to be alone; I want someone to want me; I'm lonely; I'm scared.*

Or did he? Know me, I mean. There is no way Grandpa knew me well enough to predict I'd have a beard. There were so many things he did not know about me. Things I thought he couldn't know. I was always so ashamed to tell him anything. I frequently told him nothing of some of the most pertinent things about my life. There were also some things that he couldn't know; for example, there is no way that Grandpa knew what it was like to be targeted in dodgeball, because he didn't play dodgeball, because their one-room schoolhouse didn't have a gym. And even if he *had* played dodgeball, it is unlikely

146

Grandpa would have let himself be targeted like I was by Chuck. But then again, maybe every generation has its dodgeball. Maybe he felt something like it every time he helped a neighbor fell a tree. Or shoot a cow. Maybe a neighbor saw him flinch once before putting a bullet in a cow's head.

But after engaging in this analysis and finding the whole thing so unsatisfactory, I thought, "Of course Grandpa knows me." Maybe all those things that I thought he could not know were actually things that people instinctively know. Maybe all the traits we exhibit as toddlers when under the impression no one is watching are really who we are. To the extent that a man—any man—can understand what another man goes through just by virtue of the fact that the older man once went through it himself, then I guess yeah, Grandpa knew me.

I get so much from him. I loathe people who began ahead of me. I really have a problem with people who were born wealthy. So did he.[117] The one time he lost his temper was because a man of greater means, the owner of the golf course down the road, stole hay from him. He never lost his temper otherwise, not even when my brother and I painted his Arctic

---

[117] My siblings and I used to make fun of Grandma and Grandpa for the way they cut out obituaries and wedding announcements of prominent people and put them in scrapbooks. Today, 2016, when the Sunday *New York Times* arrives, the first sections I look at and the only sections I read every week from beginning to end are the Obituaries and Vows sections. I hate that I do this. It makes me loathe the people in each for the opportunities they have been given. The newly married people are all the sons and daughters of neurosurgeons and executives. They are all on the cusp of greatness. The dead people were all founders of something; they all had multiple homes and all their children and grandchildren are "devoted" to them. Why do I do this? I both blame and thank Grandma and Grandpa for this. I suspect their obituary and wedding-announcement books were like some homemade embryonic versions of Facebook. Identifying who they knew and the best faces those people could put forward. I wonder now if Grandpa and Grandma did that for their own validation, the same way we (or I) often use Facebook. "These are the people I know"; the functional equivalent of Facebook.

Cat snowmobile with motor oil. I also don't know for certain that he wasn't the target of playground taunts. I don't think he had gym class at his school. But I know that if he did, he would not have been okay with it. And I wasn't okay with it either. I didn't have the strength to really do anything about it, but I knew that it was not okay to be treated this way. And I've worked through the feelings, schadenfreude included, that come from knowing that Chuck was in juvie while I was working my way toward college, grad school, law school—a life of which I can be proud. I have tried to locate Chuck but have been unable to. And I did start with New York State prison rosters.

And maybe Grandpa knew what it was like to be depressed. Maybe even surely he did. Maybe he recognized it in me. Maybe when we were raking leaves and he asked me how I was, he could hear it in my voice; that even though I said, "Good," I wasn't really that good. Maybe without me even knowing it, he raked all the leaves that day. Technically, I saw him cry thrice. Once at his fortieth-anniversary mass and twice at the senior care center. I have cried hundreds of times. I wept for three weeks when I was depressed in May—June 2010. Four partners at my former big law firm saw me cry.[118] I cried when I saw Phillip Seymour Hoffman in Arthur Miller's *Death*

---

[118] These include the time I returned from a deposition positive that I had really fucked up by inculpating a client in a lung cancer asbestos exposure case. My boss was furious. And when I started to cry, he said, "Would you please stop fucking crying and help me fix this fuckery?" It was funny. Another partner saw me and my son at Petco the day before we were giving our cat away. We were there buying our cat his favorite treats. The partner asked my son how he was, and he said that we were there buying our cat his favorite treats before we gave him away, and I started to cry. The biggest cry happened when I left the firm and realized my new job was awful, so I called a partner at the old firm and told him I had made a big mistake and started to cry. The fourth cry was when a partner and I were at a deposition on the twenty-something floor at Cleary Gottlieb Steen and Hamilton in lower Manhattan in 2006, and I was looking at the massive holes that were once the World Trade Center.

of a Salesman, both at the end of it and when I first walked into the theater, just knowing I was about to see Phillip Seymour Hoffman. I cried when my three children were born. I cried when I saw Alan Kurdi's body on the shore of the Mediterranean Sea and anonymously made a $100 donation to Save the Children. I cry every time I see *It's A Wonderful Life.* I've become quite a crier. I don't think it's such a big deal anymore, to see men cry. We watched September 11 happen. And everyone cried. Former Speaker of the House John Boehner cried on national television with some frequency. David Letterman cried when he was thanking the doctors who performed his open-heart surgery. And how could you not? How can you not let yourself be vulnerable every now and again?

My son is at an age where his friends' birthday parties are often held at bouncy trampoline places. He loves going to these because he loves dodgeball. I asked him why, and he went on and on about how fun it was to whip the balls and yada yada yada. I told him I hated dodgeball, and he asked why, and I was almost going to tell him about Wendy Miller and Chuck and having a giant Pete Rose bobblehead head on a teeny Celine Dion body, but I decided to wait on that.

The Emperor of Ice-Cream

Gary M. Almeter

Part III

Conundrum

Wallace Stevens was both an insurance executive and a poet, and the way he occupied these two worlds intrigues me. I generally like people who possess two seemingly incompatible characteristics. I think everyone has the capacity to inhabit seemingly inapposite worlds. Or maybe I just think that people should. While I am uncertain as to precisely why, I can theorize that people like this are just inherently more interesting. Examples: my law school classmate—who graduated at the top of the class—with the giant scorpion tattoo covering three-quarters of his leg; the client who donates to both Planned Parenthood and the National Rifle Association; my friend with a PhD in history who also plays in a thrash metal band. Stevens's poetry celebrates creativity and whimsy; the life of an insurance company executive would seemingly not.

The myth of Grandpa's willingness to sacrifice—of his adhering strictly to a regimen of austerity and scarcity—is still there, but I'm learning of random acts of extravagance. Grandpa, sometimes as an act of whimsy and sometimes as an act of subtle defiance, could succumb to indulgence now and again. As I tend to. With great frequency. In many ways, trying to find out who Grandpa was is an exploration of how indulgence in its many forms is positive and positively necessary; and how what typically feels like escapism is more often really an effort to live more deeply in the life you have. That where you are does not necessarily determine who you are.

Grandpa became a triumphant figure. Like Andy Griffith in *Matlock*. Like Alan Arkin as Edwin Hoover, the potty-mouthed heroin addict in *Little Miss Sunshine* who teaches his granddaughter to dance unabashedly to Rick James's "Superfreak." Or Henry Fonda's Norman Thayer of *On Golden Pond*, who, as it turns out, was quietly defiant and authoritative the whole time the viewer believed he had been weak and reticent. When you take your thumbnail and scratch a little bit beneath the surface of Grandpa's life, you see a man who found ways to infuse his life with that thing between defiance and whimsy; a refined anti-authoritarianism; and something resembling self-indulgence.

Put A Little Something In Our Lemonade and Take It With Us[119]

"A Quiet Normal Life"

His place, as he sat and as he thought, was not
In anything that he constructed, so frail,
So barely lit, so shadowed over and naught,

As, for example, a world in which, like snow,
He became an inhabitant, obedient
To gallant notions on the part of cold.

It was here. This was the setting and the time
Of year. Here in his house and in his room,
In his chair, the most tranquil thought grew peaked

And the oldest and the warmest heart was cut
By gallant notions on the part of night—
Both late and alone, above the crickets' chords,

---

[119] The more obvious title for this piece would be "Roller Skating With Jesus." But who wants to read about a man who merely roller-skates *in close proximity* to Jesus and not even actually *with* Jesus? Such a title would be wholly accurate, for indeed, Jesus is with us always. However, the problem with that title is that it connotes the idea that the reader is about to read a story of a small child who was roller skating down the street, was hit by a potato chip truck, and is now—literally—roller skating with Jesus in heaven. Dwelling with him and among the saints in all of their glory. Listening to Rupert Holmes's "Escape (the Piña Colada Song)" and Kim Carnes's "Bette Davis Eyes" during the heavenly All-Skates and listening to Journey's "Open Arms" during the Couple-Skates and not even worrying about her hands sweating during the Couple-Skates because it's heaven and palms don't sweat in heaven. The best song to skate to was Quiet Riot's "Cum on Feel the Noize," but there is likely no Quiet Riot in heaven. Anyway, no one died in this story. Presumably, Grandpa could now be roller-skating with Jesus if he so chose. I suspect he is square dancing with Jesus. Which is probably pretty annoying since Jesus has surely mastered *all the square dancing calls* and does them all flawlessly.

Babbling, each one, the uniqueness of its sound.
There was no fury in transcendent forms.
But his actual candle blazed with artifice.

—Wallace Stevens

I.   Finger

Kevin B. fingered Carla F. on Saturday, April 7, 1984. I know this to be so because (a) Kevin told us all and (b) Kevin told us on the Monday of the last week of school before the two-week Easter break that he fingered Carla the Saturday before. Easter Sunday fell on April 22 that year. It's a matter of simple arithmetic and the complex system of synapses that make us have memories. We were in eighth grade, and it was Kevin's inaugural fingering, done whilst he and Carla were out riding dirt bikes through the muddy and as-yet-unplanted spring fields of our hometown. I do not know if it was also Carla's inaugural fingering. Kevin told all of us, the four other boys with whom he went to St. Vincent's School, that he fingered Carla while we ate lunch that Monday. I had no idea what he was talking about. But then Craig asked to smell Kevin's fingers—a request to which Kevin readily assented—and I began to understand what had transpired.[120] Craig

---

[120] For the record, Kevin also asked me if I wanted to sniff his fingers; I had to make a split-second decision—risk being mocked for *not* wanting to smell his fingers, or actually smell his fingers and risk getting some sort of digitally transmitted STD from the likes of someone who let boys penetrate her whilst dirt-biking. I politely declined. The first of many such declarations of independence. My laser-like analysis went something like this: first, I had no interest in learning what Carla's hoo-hoo smelled like. Additionally, I was really confused about what I would actually smell. Had Kevin not washed his hands in the intervening forty-eight hours between his inaugural fingering and school on Monday? If not, then gross. And also if not, wouldn't

vigorously sniffed Kevin's fingers with the same enthusiasm an oenophile might sniff a 1787 Chateau Lafite Bordeaux once owned by Thomas Jefferson[121]; Craig also pretended that the scent of Kevin's fingers, replete with the residual scent of Carla's hoo-hoo, rendered him intoxicated, as though he had actually consumed the 1787 Chateau Lafite Bordeaux once owned by Thomas Jefferson. At least I think he was pretending. Perhaps Carla's hoo-hoo really was an intoxicant.

We, the five young men who comprised St. Vincent's eighth grade, spent the rest of the lunch period ascertaining the details of and reliving the fingering: Kevin went riding dirt bikes with his friends, they saw Carla walking somewhere, Carla got on Kevin's dirt bike, Kevin and Carla rode on Kevin's dirt bike together, they let the other boys with whom they were dirt-biking go ahead of them so that they could stop and make out (though Kevin obviously would have been in the lead had he been trying to be in the lead); Kevin and Carla stopped near a patch of trees, ostensibly to pee but with the tacit understanding that he and Carla would be making out; Kevin and Carla made out on the ground; Kevin fingered Carla. Kevin was surprised that Carla let him finger her, but Carla was wearing sweatpants and so what was he supposed to do? Why, Carla had essentially encouraged the fingering.

For the remainder of that week, the last week of school before school ended so we could prepare to celebrate the risen savior, Craig asked Kevin if he could smell his fingers and Kevin always said yes and Craig sniffed the fingers for the next four

---

I also be smelling forty-eight additional hours of grime and grunge and who knows what else? If so, wouldn't the smell of Carla's hoo-hoo be diminished by whatever soap Kevin used to wash his hands and its residual lavender or jasmine or peach blossom essence?

[121] Thomas Jefferson was the nation's third president, our first ambassador to France, an inventor and master gardener. He was likely also America's first wine connoisseur.

days with the same enthusiasm with which an oenophile might sniff a 1787 Chateau Lafite Bordeaux once owned by Thomas Jefferson, and every day Craig pretended to be intoxicated by the scent of Carla's hoo-hoo.

School ended for a fortnight and there was no more sniffing and no more talk of fingering.

I watched *America's Top 10* with Casey Kasem religiously in those days. I loved seeing the songs move up and down the charts. We didn't have MTV yet, so the snippets of video on Casey's syndicated show were all I got to see. I watched *America's Top 10* on the Saturday before Easter; the second day that Christ was in his post-crucifixion tomb. "Against All Odds" was the number one song in the land that week[122], and in the video snippet of the song that Casey played, Jeff Bridges and Rachel Ward made out on the sand and in the waterfall and in a bedroom with flowing curtains. I wondered if Jeff fingered Rachel and assumed, in light of the fact that even a novice like Kevin fingered, that he did. Then I felt ashamed for thinking about fingering instead of spiritually preparing for the resurrection of the risen Savior.

---

[122] A mere five albums reached the number one spot in 1984: Michael Jackson's *Thriller*, the *Footloose Soundtrack*; *Sports* by Huey Lewis and the News; Bruce Springsteen's *Born in the U.S.A.*; and Prince's *Purple Rain Soundtrack*. Interestingly, Michael and Jackson and Prince both died from drug related causes.

II.   Overdose

On Thursday, April 26, 1984, a few days after Easter, I went roller-skating with Grandpa. It was unusually warm for April in Buffalo, so I walked to Grandpa and Grandma's house, the roller skates I bought for two dollars at a garage sale slung over my shoulder. It took just a few minutes to walk there, and when I arrived I found them sitting on the davenport,[123] drinking lemonade and reading the *Buffalo Evening News.* Grandma was still not emotionally over the fact that Buffalo had devolved into a city with but one newspaper. Their preferred paper, the *Courier Express* had ceased publication just a few years prior. I always got the sense that she read the *Buffalo Evening News* reluctantly and with suspicion. In that substandard paper that day was the story that alerted the world that police had found David Kennedy, son of Robert and Ethel, on the floor of his Palm Beach hotel room. He had died, presumably from a drug overdose. I knew who David Kennedy was because the twentieth anniversary of JFK's assassination was a few months prior, and I watched the twentieth-anniversary memorials and became fascinated.

---

[123] I now know that Davenport was the name of a series of sofas made by the Massachusetts furniture manufacturer A. H. Davenport and Company, now defunct. Due to the popularity of the furniture during the late nineteenth century and early twentieth century, especially in upstate New York, the name "davenport" became a genericized trademark. Grandpa and Grandma always said they were going to sit on the davenport. What they probably meant was the generic gliding sofa nestled in the little porch area adjacent to their unattached garage. What I thought "davenport" meant was the porch itself. In my defense, sometimes they would say "Let's go sit on the davenport" and then sit on chairs which were clearly not davenports. Either way, this porch they sat on was shielded from the road by the building in which it was encased, and served as the hub of summer activities. It was near the raspberry bushes and flowers.

The only other person I knew of who had overdosed was John Belushi. *Overdosing* as a concept was difficult to understand. Trying to reconcile Belushi's characteristic boorishness and untidiness with Kennedy's sophistication and refinement was impossible. Later I would learn that addiction does not discriminate; that it is wholly possible to consume too much of something; that if life was really fair, I would likely be dead, too; and that there are many who yearn not to feel the pain they feel and do not know what to do with it. Grandma seemed disgusted with the news. I recall her saying David's death was "such a shame." They had a picture of JFK in their dining room; the first Roman Catholic president.

I was thirteen at the time. The revelation that my friend Kevin—a friend with whom I had always had much in common—had done fingering was still with me. Frankly, I thought it sounded gross—that it didn't sound fun for anyone, neither the fingerer nor the fingeree. And for this I felt shame. That I did not yearn to finger. I also had no understanding of what drugs were. Nancy Reagan launched her "Just Say No" campaign in 1982, and we learned about the perils of drugs in school. We learned to identify and categorize drugs, e.g., morphine is an opiate, caffeine is a stimulant, LSD is a hallucinogen, etc. But we never learned what addiction was.

For the first time, I was acutely aware that in other parts of my small town, thirteen-year-olds were fingering. And enjoying the fingering. They were probably smoking and doing drugs, too. By extension, this meant that in other parts of the world, thirteen-year-olds were expected to be war-fighting, bread-winning, and baby-making. Maybe even stealing bags of morphine from their mom's purse. I thought of what life would be like if I lived somewhere else and was tasked with fingering and making babies with my teen wife. It didn't sound that fun. Especially when you factored in the necessary ancillary responsibilities to such an existence, like coal mining and possum hunting. There was a similarly seismic disruption when

I learned that a man to whom so much had been given could be lonely, could die alone in a hotel room in Palm Beach.

The world seemed like a horrible place that year. Political discourse was teeming with acrimony. Around dawn on October 23, 1983, a suicide bomber drove a truck laden with the equivalent of twenty-one thousand pounds of dynamite into the heart of a U.S. Marine compound in Beirut, Lebanon, killing two hundred and forty-one servicemen. And on November 23, 1983, ABC aired *The Day After*, a movie that postulates what the town of Lawrence, KS, would do during and after a full-scale nuclear exchange between the United States and Russia.

Roller-skating with Grandpa was fine with me in lieu of fingering and smoking drugs, but such contentment was tethered by the knowledge that these days of whimsy and frivolity were numbered. I would have to grow up and finger people and say no to drugs and face the problems of the world.[124] Roller-skating with Grandpa seemed like just the perfect antidote—or at least a minor respite—from the doom and gloom.

Grandpa was seventy in April 1984; in fact, he had just turned seventy that March. We had a party for him at our house—the farmhouse where Grandpa and Grandma once lived—and the grown-ups were joking about all the people who were running for president.[125] We were in the midst of the

---

[124] David Kennedy died of an overdose of cocaine and Demerol at the Brazilian Court Hotel in Palm Beach. Recently, a friend of mine flew to Palm Beach to orchestrate an intervention for an alcoholic friend of his. The alcoholic friend's wife paid for everyone to stay at the Breakers Hotel in Palm Beach, about 1.2 miles from the Brazilian Court. My friend asked me if I had ever been to Palm Beach. I haven't. He told me that it's both utopia and the saddest place on earth.

[125] It was a far cry from the seventeen Republicans who vied for the Republican Presidential nomination in 2016, but in March 1984, the eight men in the midst of the Democratic primaries vying to be the Democratic nominee for President of the

Democratic primaries; it was a funny time. I had cousins in high school. I wondered if they smoked drugs. And with the money he received, Grandpa did something unexpected and bought a pair of roller skates as a birthday present for himself.[126] I know they were expensive because I wanted a pair, too. I used to look at the roller skates in the Brand Names catalog.[127] The pair that I bought at a garage sale for two bucks weren't really that cool. They were brown and had wooden wheels. Grandpa bought a black pair with red wheels.

Roller-skating was big in 1984, at least in upstate New York—as big as something can metaphysically become in upstate New York, at least. I recall my siblings and I sort of looking at each other when Grandpa announced that he bought roller skates with his birthday money. It was a look that was the amalgamation of amusement and reverence and disbelief and embarrassment. It was similar to the look we all gave each other when my brother told us that Grandpa called one of Grandpa's own friends—a smaller man—a "little runt" at the

---

United States seemed like a multitude. Those men seeking to go up against Republican incumbent Ronald Reagan were Senator Ernest Hollings of South Carolina, Senator Alan Cranston of California, Governor Reubin Askew of Florida, Senator George McGovern of South Dakota, Senator John Glenn of Ohio, the Reverend Jesse Jackson of Illinois, Senator Gary Hart of Colorado, and former Vice President Walter Mondale of Minnesota, who ultimately won the Democratic nomination and lost to Reagan in an historic landslide.

[126] The fact that Grandpa used his birthday money to buy roller skates makes me really, really happy. It is hard for men to treat themselves. And Grandpa was astonishingly frugal.

[127] Brand Names was a regional catalog retailer with fourteen convenient locations in and around Buffalo. They had an enormous annual catalog filled with appliances, home furnishings, jewelry, and, in the very last pages, electronics, sports equipment, and toys. All stores closed in 2001. I can still recall its commercial jingle, "Bring Brand Names home for the holidays. . ."

Canandaigua Farm Show in 1982.

III.   Decay

The four corners formed by the intersection of Centerline and North Sheldon Roads, one of the busiest in my hometown, have each experienced some variety of decay, some variety of gone, each variety unique to it. At one time, these four corners were the epicenter of something more significant, something more bustling.

At one time the Sheldon Hotel stood at the northwest corner. It was not and had never been the Ritz, but it was a functioning hotel with a bar frequented by locals who had their own numbered mugs suspended from the ceiling. I recall the neon Budweiser signs that made my baseball uniform glow when I went there after little league games to play Space Invaders. The hotel burned to the ground in 1982. In the southwest corner of the intersection, there used to be a farm until its cows were sold, and eventually the barn collapsed. The house remains, and the people who live there now are not farmers—they work in Buffalo. They adopted three kids once they learned they were unable to have kids of their own. Mary Jane's old store sits on the southeast corner.[128] At one time, this was a fully functioning general store; the sales floor had several large display cases and shelves which contained, and presumably

---

[128] Interesting side note: Mary Jane and her fiancée Richard were engaged for forty-plus years and never married. They are both deceased now. I always used to wonder if they "did it." Interesting side note number two: my dad bought Mary Jane's old car, a 1979 two-door brown Chevrolet Monte Carlo, in 1991. I drove it to college in the winter of 1992 and used it until I moved to Boston in October 1993. Dad bought it for $750, and it had less than twenty thousand miles on it. Richard must have driven her everywhere. Or maybe she rolled the odometer back. If Mary Jane and Richard ever did "do it," I bet they did it in the back of my old Monte Carlo.

sold, motor oil, wires and twines of all sorts, coffee, fabric, egg beaters, and spoons and dishes of every kind. It had glass-front windows and a door with a bell attached to the top of it that rang. When the store was fully functioning, the bell would presumably rouse Mary Jane to emerge from her attached apartment and onto the sales floor. In my lifetime, Mary Jane only sold candy after church on Sundays. And she seemed to do so begrudgingly, flicking coins across the glass counter with her craggy knuckles as parishioners bought Three Musketeers bars. The store still stands but is empty of all provisions. A man named Norman now lives in Mary Jane's apartment. He was married to Gloria, who left him for Chet. One of Norman and Gloria's four children died in childbirth just a few years ago. The baby died, too.

St. Cecilia's Roman Catholic Church sits on the northeast corner. Standing on Mary Jane's storefront steps and looking across Centerline Road, from left to right the site contained a massive stone church built in the late 1800s, an open area with a statue of St. John Neumann[129] surrounded by flowers and benches upon which people could reflect, a two-story rectory, and a three-story school. The church is majestic. It stands seventy feet high and recently had a newly refurbished pipe organ installed in its choir loft. However, as the result of a generally declining and aging local population, declining rates of men entering the priesthood, declining global esteem for the

---

[129] The money for this statue was donated anonymously. Though I know who donated it. St. John Neumann was the Bishop of Philadelphia from 1852 until his death, at age forty-nine, in 1860. Prior to that, he was a priest in Elkridge, MD, Huron County, OH, and Buffalo, NY. While in Buffalo, he traveled the countryside to spread the Word to German dairy farmers and founded St. Cecilia's in 1842. Also, following my grandparents' sixtieth-anniversary mass, we had photos taken in front of the St. John Neumann statue. When my dipshit ex-sister-in-law asked me who the "man in the statue" was, I told her it was Johnny Appleseed and that Grandpa really liked him because they had the same initials, J.A. She said, "That's really neat."

church in general, the church community has dwindled. The parish has merged with the parish of an adjacent town; no one lives in the six-bedroom rectory; the school is rarely if ever used.

At one time, the school was fully functioning, and fielded a sufficient number of students for first through eighth grades. My dad and my aunts spent their first eight years of school there. It closed soon after my youngest aunt, Aunt Karen, graduated, and was just used for Sunday school and for meetings of church-related groups—ladies' sodality meetings, fundraising groups, Catholic Youth Organization meetings, and so forth. In the early 1980s, the two old sheds, once used as stables for parking your horse and buggy during mass, were converted to functional space. Wedding receptions, funeral dinners, and chicken BBQ fundraisers were held there in lieu of the school.

But even before the decay began in earnest it seemed like the corner was weathered. Weathered by the weather, weathered by falling milk prices, weathered by the decline of Buffalo which had recently become a one-newspaper city; barely a city at all.

Decay was a thing that shifted as you looked at it, the way a forest is dense with trees up close, but from outside, from the empty meadow, you see its true limits. Decay had little to do with the appearance of a thing—more to do with where the thing was relative to time and place. The town, once flourishing, now seems populated by weathered people; weathered Caucasians. Its homogeneousness and its industriousness, once the source of its pride, is now something sad and outdated.

IV.   Skate

On Thursday, April 26, 1984, Grandpa drove the two of us and our roller skates to the old St. Cecilia's school in his truck. We climbed the three stories to the top floor, which was at one time used as an auditorium. The first thing I noticed was not the vastness of the place, nor the twenty-foot ceilings and huge floor to ceiling windows, nor the craftsmanship of the old wooden stage and beautifully embroidered stage curtain with gold tassels; the first thing I noticed was the roughly fourteen trillion dead houseflies on the floor. Clearly the auditorium had not been used in years. We spent about an hour sweeping up the trillions of dead flies. We did not sweep them up and discard them, but rather we swept them into a giant heap in the middle of the floor.

Secretly, I also checked for the feral raccoons and feral cats and feral children that surely had taken residence in the school. Finding none, we put on our roller skates.

I was nervous when Grandpa stood up on his skates. What if he fell, and I had to carry him downstairs? What if I couldn't lift him, and a feral bear or the ghost of a murdered altar boy came and ate us? But Grandpa roller-skated well. He had a little bit of a hunched back, which made him always look like he was leaning forward a little too far when he skated. I was just as apprehensive about the fly carcasses on the floor. As we skated around them, the fly carcasses, weightless in their varying stages of decomposition, became airborne in our wake. As we skated, I could see bits and pieces of fly-carcass float through the air, the carcass wings sparkling in the sunshine beams that shined through the majestic school windows. I wondered if I was breathing in decomposed fly guts[130]. Mostly, though, I was nervous because I wanted to impress Grandpa so. That skating was something I could do. And that he wanted to do.

I am really lucky for a host of reasons; one of them is that I have a good imagination. While we skated I could let the shadows we created when passing the giant windows of the school be our high-tech light show. I could let the transistor

---

[130] Point of fact, I was definitely breathing in the newly airborne fly carcasses.

radio we brought be our AV system. I could let the old auditorium above the old church school be the hottest skating rink in all of the land. I could expect throngs of people to arrive any minute.

But the rudimentary and weathered wooden floor was not the super-waxed, super-smooth floor of a traditional skating rink. The sound of our wheels on the floor rendered the transistor radio inaudible; it only picked up AM radio anyway. There was no snack bar selling slushies and soft pretzels. We stopped for lemonade, and the song on the radio while we drank was Irene Cara's "Flashdance. . . What a Feeling." The incongruity of the whole scene made me laugh. Irene Cara, Grandpa, roller-skating in the sacred halls of Jesus. Grandma had supplied us with cups, but we didn't use them—electing instead to drink right from the Tupperware pitcher. Like the hardworking men in Steinbeck's *Of Mice and Men*. I suspect Grandma—ever the sleuth—admonished Grandpa for this breach when he got home.

We skated for about an hour total and then went home.

Grandpa never lived more than a mile from the small farm on which he was born. As such, Grandpa was part of the fabric of this decaying town. I think city folks (a group of which I proudly consider myself a member), for all their wisdom and sophistication, do not understand the pressure of what it's like to be known; to be relied upon; to be watched and considered and, in most instances, inevitably judged. In this decaying town, whimsy and folly were judged harshly.[131] Perfectly parallel rows

---

[131] I recall an event celebrating an anniversary of the priest of St. Cecilia's. Mike Almeter (no relation, or if there *is* relation, it is so remote as to be unidentifiable), a farmer and auctioneer and then-president of the parish council, recited a poem for the priest, Father Weber, an avid golfer. "And while we are out working and plowing the ground, you're out there swinging your golf clubs around." It was made in jest, but as Sigmund Freud suggested—and as the saying goes— "a joke is a truth wrapped in a smile." These people compared and judged and knew they were being judged.

of corn and healthy, milk-producing Holsteins were lauded. Cornfields were their own sort of battlefields. Young stalks, newly planted in April, that would appear in May (assuming Kevin and Carla's dirt-biking didn't kill the corn.) One's planting adeptness was readily determined by the straightness of the rows, how the planter navigated hills and curves and recesses that would inevitably get flooded. If the corn was not knee-high by the Fourth of July, then—in relation to the other farmers and considering any ancillary weather-related phenomena to account for the substandard corn—you were judged. Later, in November post-harvest, the depleted stalks appeared blanched and bonelike, cornstalks like femurs left on the battlefield awaiting the inevitable decay, the inevitable onslaught of worms.

It took courage, then, for Grandpa to go roller-skating in the school. Not the sort of courage necessary to raise the flag at Iwo Jima, or fly a plane over hostile territory, but courage nonetheless. People inevitably drove by and saw his truck in the school parking lot. They inevitably wondered what he was doing there; people in small towns just intrinsically and inevitably wonder that sort of shit.

What was he doing there? What was I doing there? We were just roller-skating. But I also think he was there because he knew that my growing up was nigh, and that I was uneasy and afraid and needed to know a grown-up could still have fun. That being grown up wasn't all fingering and overdosing and decaying.

This roller-skating day cemented for me—though I am uncertain if it was actually cemented that day or whether it merely congealed that day and solidified later, or whether it was merely the germination of an idea that day which later got cemented, but at some point in the intervening decades between April 26, 1984, and the present day, it was definitely cemented—the idea that a person can do whatever the fuck he or she wants to do. In fact, authenticity is necessary. You can skate when you're seventy if that's what you want to do. You can skate in the old parochial school. You can turn it into something extraordinary. The Successories®[132] poster says something like: "If you can dream it, you can do it." That is true. If you would rather roller-skate than work or finger Carla, then do so.

If you feel pain, find a way to deal with it. If you feel shame, then get the fuck rid of it.

It also made me think of Grandpa differently. He had always been a fixer; an analyst; a worker; a provider. His name, John, was similarly sturdy and indefatigable and monosyllabic. But it turned out he was also a poet in many respects. A man who valued imagination. As I've mentioned, Grandpa was seventy years old. And he was roller-skating on the top floor of the old schoolhouse. He bought roller skates, identified a flat open indoor area where he could roller-skate, and he fucking did it. He brought a battery-powered transistor radio in an effort to replicate the experience of a roller rink. He was a man who defied convention.

Grandpa seemed to occupy two worlds: in one he was the quintessential farmer, diligent father, and able-bodied worker; in the other he was the whimsical dreamer, prone to flights of fancy and an eagerness to explore. He was a rebel, too, in many ways. Grandpa also found and bought old cars—not necessarily classics, but teetering on the precipice of being such—and fixed them up. He called them "jibby cars," the act of naming them itself an act of creative rebellion. And pride. History was often in open rebellion on his front lawn—a car with fins for sale. Which had earlier been discarded.

Some more "truths" about Grandpa take on a new hue

---

[132] Successories is a company that makes motivational posters in an effort to inject personality and motivation into an office. My favorite is that poster depicting the photo of a bridge and a quote that says, "Be the Bridge: Problems become opportunities when the right people join together."

when I give them some additional consideration. For example, we have long held the near-mythical idea that he loved living in a small town, loved country life, loved country chicken barbecues and homemade pie. And to a large degree, I'm sure he did. But the origins of that are that he hated cities. When I went to visit him after Grandma died, he had just discovered all these old photo albums, and he was very eager to show them to me. One was devoted to his father's family. His father had a sister—Margaret—who married "an Italian from White Plains, New York," and left the farm to go live with "his people." She visited every few years; always in a fancy new car. Grandpa talked about "Aunt Margaret" with a wistfulness (not quite envy, but sort of approaching something resembling envy) and admiration that I didn't expect. Maybe it was just the fancy new cars. But maybe it was the fact she moved to an elsewhere. And maybe especially to a city.

I am of course looking at this day in April with some degree of euphoric recall. The truth is that the wood boards made the skating bumpy and made my feet vibrate; that when we were done, there were fly carcasses metabolically fused to our wheels that we had to scrape off; that while we were oblivious to them, we were almost certainly being stalked by the feral cats and feral raccoons and feral bats and anything feral which were all waiting to eat us should we fall down; that the school had asbestos and lead paint and probably rusty nails and all sorts of carcinogens too. The school was also adjacent to the cemetery. Which, at night, is surely the scene of all sorts of Michael Jackson *Thriller*-esque evil.

But even accounting for the euphoric recall, I loved being there. There is no greater use of a transistor radio to be had than carrying it to the top of an old school, pulling out the antenna, and finding a station that will play Irene Cara as I roller-skated with Grandpa; and seeing a new part of this person; indeed, a whole new way to be a person. There, amid the decay of the rotting housefly carcasses in the decaying schoolhouse belonging to a decaying institution on a decaying corner in a decaying town near a decaying city with but one newspaper, I learned one of the most valuable lessons I have ever learned: *Be authentic.*

In 1984, I wondered if Grandpa ever fingered Grandma. Or if his friends ever invited him to sniff their fingers. I wondered if he ever got so sad or filled with shame that he felt like smoking drugs. Or injecting drugs. Or snorting drugs. Later, when his Parkinson's made his hands shake to the point of not being able to hold silverware and he drank whiskey whenever he ate out to calm his nerves and ease the shaking, I would wonder if that was alcoholism. If he ever, had he lived in a different setting, could have overdosed.

Grandpa died in 2009. To be grandfather-less in this terrifying world still sometimes makes me shiver. When I think of him no longer near us, no longer among us, I still sometimes find it hard to breathe. I got lost once when I was six or seven. It was at the Niagara Falls Aquarium, and I got distracted by the promise of the electric eel, which was supposed to illuminate the numbers above its tank with its eel electricity. I wandered and couldn't see my mom or her college friend Peggy with whom we were visiting the aquarium. It was scary. That's sort of how being grandfather-less feels.

Gary M. Almeter

The Woman in Sunshine

"The Woman in Sunshine"[133]

It is only that this warmth and movement are like
The warmth and movement of a woman.

It is not that there is any image in the air
Nor the beginning nor end of a form:

It is empty. But a woman in threadless gold
Burns us with brushings of her dress

And a dissociated abundance of being,
More definite for what she is—

Because she is disembodied,
Bearing the odors of the summer fields,

Confessing the taciturn and yet indifferent,
Invisibly clear, the only love.

—Wallace Stevens

Grandma liked ice cream almost as much as Grandpa.

Before Grandma even got her ice cream scoop, they were doing a lot of planning about it. Typically, Grandpa would ask, "Do we have any ice cream, Ma?" and then look at me and

---

[133] My reading of this poem makes this perfect for a chapter on my Grandma. Different cultures attach different characteristics to different celestial bodies. Most ancient cultures considered the sun to be masculine, See, e.g., the Egyptian god Ra. In this poem, Stevens describes the "warmth and movement" of the sun as a woman who creates abundance.

wink. Grandma would typically answer, "Well, golly, I don't know, I will have to check, Pa." Both "Ma" and "Pa" knew there were gallons of maple walnut ice cream stashed in one of their two freezers.

Grandpa married Gladys Rose Glaser (hereafter "Grandma") on September 23, 1942.[134] They stayed married until Gladys died on October 9, 2004. Gladys, an only child, and her future husband John grew up about half a mile away from each other, in a small town whose only industry was dairy farming, situated about twenty-five miles east of Buffalo. I never asked if they knew each other as kids. Or maybe I did and have just forgotten the answer. I do recall Grandpa telling me how he went to visit Grandma when Grandma was a "domestic helper" to a wealthy family in Buffalo[135]. The wealthy family came home unexpectedly, and Grandpa had to hide in the kitchen. I like this story. I like to think that they were fun and flirty and mischievous as they courted.

She delighted in saying that she and Grandpa never fought. And I really think they never fought. I think most of the time Grandpa acquiesced. Famously, the one thing they disagreed over was whether a tomato was a fruit or a vegetable. But this was a fun and flirty sort of pseudo-skirmish.

In an infamous 1942 radio broadcast, a Professor Kunz, rector of Berlin University, explained, "Loss of limbs must be of no importance to German soldiers. For everyday life, a man

---

[134] "Gladys" was the twenty-third most popular name given to girls born in the United States in 1917. Gladys was not in the top 1,000 names for any year of birth beginning with the year 2000. Gladys is my daughter's middle name.

[135] Grandma also had a job on the Fisher-Price assembly line making wooden little people. She also made dresses that she would then sell to department stores for resale.

does not need two hands or two legs. Soldiers who lose both legs, for example, continue to ride horses." The Professor suggested that all that mutilated soldiers needed to return to their former lives was "an iron will. If their will is strong enough, they will be able to accomplish all sorts of manual work. One hand, in any case, is enough for every job, and with a strong will, the loss of two forearms will be no obstacle either."

Professor Kunz and Grandma had a great deal in common. Had she no forearms, she would have still discovered a way to pick quarts and quarts of strawberries in mere minutes. But that is an unsophisticated appreciation of her. And, like Grandpa, the story of her is quite necessarily the story of the evolution of my understanding of her.

She began in my consciousness as the perfect amalgamation of Tanta Kringle from the 1970 stop motion—"Animagic"—Christmas special *Santa Claus is Comin' To Town*; Sarah Tucker from the Cool Whip commercials; Betty White from the game show *Password*; and a lady Keebler elf. She could bake cookies and knit mittens and throw hay bales with equal parts ferocity and grace. As a child, she struck me as the perfect blend of femininity—everything smelled of vanilla and mouthwash and mothballs, and her vanity (such a paradoxical household item for a woman so prone to humility) table was topped with hundreds (that's hyperbole; it was probably more like three or four) of glass bottles and vials and spritzers and atomizers filled with perfumes and lotions and serums designed to keep her looking youthful – and indomitability. She gave us a dollar for each A on our report cards and could turn rubbish (cylindrical Quaker Oats canisters, tin foil, Mason Jar lids, bottle caps) into Christmas ornaments and birthday gifts for our parents. She once killed a woodchuck that had been harassing her by hitting it over the head with the stock of a rifle.[136] She loved things that were dainty—thimbles and pansies and little cactuses in little ceramic vases with a *burro* and ALBUQUERQUE, NEW MEXICO painted on the side, and little spoons and brooches and cloth-covered buttons.

Later, as I entered adolescence, Grandma's persona took on a more nefarious hue. I began to see how her "suggestions" were really criticisms. Minor corrections to speech and thoughts and ideas and minor admonitions about how one must comport oneself could, in the aggregate, have a debilitating effect. People's feelings weren't important. She was still wonderful, but fostering individuation was not her forte. I think she fostered a fear of failure. I remember her telling me that I was very insensitive for standing in her light. I remember the look on my brother's face when, after he criticized the way the Johnson & Johnson Company handled the press during the Tylenol capsule cyanide scare of the early 1980s, she corrected him and told him that Johnson & Johnson had done a great job. The memories I have of Grandpa and Grandma taking my sister and I to get our new dog are sullied by the fact that as I petted the dog for the first time, scratching her belly, back and forth, Grandma told me that I was doing it too rough since we didn't know the dog yet. Presumably, she didn't want the strange new dog to get mad and eat me—but that's not what an eleven-year-old boy hears.

---

[136] It should be noted that Grandma and Grandpa kept a couple of rifles in their home (I don't know what kinds they were—something like twelve-gauge or .22-caliber models—but one had a scope, and they shot real bullets). They were secured and secreted behind a curtain at the top of the stairs that led from the basement to the kitchen. When I say, "secured and secreted," I mean that you could see the guns easily, and if you had an inclination to do so, you could grab one any time you wanted. I am about as big a fan of the "well-regulated" phrase of the Second Amendment as they come, but the way they stored their guns is perfectly though inexplicably okay with me.

Older, and knowing a little more about what makes people behave the way they do, I began to view Grandma in a more sympathetic light. It must have been really hard growing up an only child on a farm, in what was clearly an unhappy home.[137]

The story of Grandma is also the story of the woods behind the farmhouse where she and I both grew up. When I was a kid, Grandma proudly told the story of how Franklin Delano Roosevelt's Civilian Conservation Corps planted each and every tree in that woods in the 1930s; spoke wistfully of how the CCC members would come and camp out and plant trees for weeks at a time. Later (perhaps she thought those listening were sufficiently mature to hear this, or maybe she was old enough to no longer care about artifice and image), she described how she would run to the woods as a little girl whenever her parents were fighting and how she would just stay there for hours, preferring the loneliness among the still trees to the fear that came from fighting at home.

---

[137] Grandma's paternal grandma committed suicide by jumping into the Niagara River and going over the falls. They never found her body. And Grandma never knew her. I don't even know her name—though I rely on that story with some frequency whenever called on to play "Two Truths and a Lie." That is when you name two truths and a lie, and people try to guess which one the lie is. I typically say: "One summer, I met and talked to Harrison Ford at Brooks Brothers; I proposed to my wife on top of the Empire State building; and my great-great-Grandma committed suicide by jumping into Niagara Falls." People always guess that I am lying about the great-great-Grandma—because there's no way that could happen, right? But that is true. It must have taken a great deal of effort for a poor country woman to orchestrate and execute her own demise; she must have been profoundly depressed. And that must have affected Grandma's dad. I suspect that people didn't reveal their emotions as readily back then as they seem to now. It's odd to me that something like this—something so potentially clinically relevant—warrants a mere footnote in this book. But there you have it. Maybe it is more relevant that I realize. Especially in a book about who I am in relation to grandparents. If I am ¼ Grandpa, then am I 1/16 this woman who threw herself into the Niagara River? Is there 1/16 of me that is capable of that?

175

The Emperor of Ice-Cream

When I was a kid, I thought of the woods as a dangerous place, filled with bears and hunters and steel-jawed traps that would snap off a boy's leg if he made one wrong step. While I now I appreciate the history and beauty of the woods, at the time it just seemed ominous and its allure distant and unknowable; as unknowable as how it might feel to be a domestic helper for a wealthy family in Buffalo.

One of my favorite things about Grandma was her friendship with a lady named Viola. They went to grade school together—they both boarded at the school—and then worked together at Fisher-Price making wooden toy people. It was a different kind of friendship. Even as a kid, I got the sense that each fulfilled a need in the other. Viola never married, and Grandma was an only child. They clung to each other. Grandma made herself vulnerable to Viola in a way that I had never seen before. It was a different kind of friendship than the ones I saw among adults—sitting around a card table playing cards and drinking whiskey sours and talking about electricity bills. There was a simplicity and an authenticity to the things Grandma and Viola shared. Viola was the only person I ever heard disagree with Grandma. Surely it was about something innocuous, like at what soil depth to plant tulips, but it was startling nonetheless. In spite of – or perhaps because of - Viola's defiance, she was treated as a member of the family. She was my aunt Karen's godmother. And was frequently invited to and attended family events. Knowing Grandma was capable of authenticity was confusing when the bulk of her interactions seemed so teeming with resolve. It made me wonder which one of her – the playful friend or the stern townsperson – was real. And if she had a choice in determining which persona to employ more often.

The myth is that Grandma—an only child, and valedictorian of her class—yearned to go to college, but when it came time to apply, her father said that they didn't have enough money to send her. And that the attraction between Grandma and Grandpa was this cognizance they shared of what it was like to be deprived, to have dreams deferred, to work every single day ungrudgingly because that is just what you did.

Grandma was very frugal. There is this one fabric—a brown-and-white plaid cotton—that she bought yards of to use in making a tablecloth for my mom, a set of pajamas for my younger brother, a nightgown for my sister, and button-down shirts for my brother and me. Even if she were to lose her limbs, she would have surely found a way to turn that brown and white fabric into clothing.

No loving relationship—unless two people die simultaneously in a plane crash while in their sleep—ends happily. That's just the way it is. Every friendship, marriage, romantic entanglement, employment situation, subcontractor, contractor, brotherhood, and sisterhood ends. Somehow. Every marriage ends.

Grandpa and Grandma's ended on their davenport on October 8, 2004. It was sunny and warm. They were discussing what to do next to winterize the garden. Grandpa went to the garden, and when he came back to the davenport, Grandma was slumped over on the glider. Grandpa drove his three-wheeler to Wayne's to ask him for help. He must have been terrified.

My aunt Janet told me once that she always thought that one of the things that attracted them to one another was the idea that they were both capable of so much more, but sacrificed for their families: he because his father died when he was sixteen, and she because her father promised—and then reneged on that promise—to send her to college. Later, after I was married, I saw how mutual rescue could be a necessary and galvanizing component in a marriage.

I agree with Aunt Janet, that recognizing this characteristic

177

of unrealized potential in the other brought a comfort that evolved into attraction. I think that when Grandma saw Grandpa, she saw a man who liked to be happy and was determined to be so. And this is what attracted her to him. I don't think she saw that in her own father.

At one point, she saw him, and he saw her. She saw his tall and angular frame—like the man in Edward Hopper's *Nighthawks* painting—and he saw her rounded features—round face, round nose, round eyes. They must have noticed this about each other when they met.[138] I bet she noticed his laughter and this drew her to him as well—a man who liked to be happy. I suspect she had never really been happy.

Their courtship must have been like something from Edith Wharton and Laura Ingalls Wilder —quiet dinners with her parents, working on the farm, chewing and making small talk with people she likely did not hold in the highest esteem. There is only one story I know of Grandpa interacting with his father-in-law. *See* page *214, infra.* I never asked Grandpa if he asked Grandma's dad for her hand. Or if he ever smoked a cigar with him, or had a glass of whiskey or brandy or hard apple cider out back of the barn. I never asked him if there were other girlfriends; I'm not sure he would have answered that one. It doesn't seem like people from their generation shared that stuff; they certainly didn't Instagram one-night stands. Like the kids do now.

There is this photo in one of Grandpa and Grandma's photo albums. Grandpa and Grandma are seated next to each other on the couch in the living room of the farmhouse. It is 1982, and the couch looks uncomfortable. There are no looks of displeasure on Grandpa and Grandma's faces to indicate the

---

[138] Where did they meet? The answer to this question is surely some sort of church mixer or mutual cousins or neighboring farmers, but when and how specifically? And why did I never ask them?

couch is uncomfortable, but I know that they are uncomfortable because the couch actually *is* highly uncomfortable, since my siblings and I spent a decade beating the shit out of it—making forts out of its cushions and jumping on it to turn on Side B of the Carpenters's LP *Now and Then*, the side that featured the oldies medley which was so very rock and roll—and just generally bouncing on it and fucking up all the couch springs.

The shag carpet[139] of the living room is prominent in the foreground of this photo—a shag carpet composed of billions of shags of shades of mustard, colors that, if they were paints or J. Crew blouses, would be called Tuscan sun, goldenrod, Black Eyed Susan, butterscotch, marigold. It is the sort of shag carpet that, if I hadn't been there to see it in real life, I wouldn't or couldn't believe that it ever really existed—like segregated water fountains or those big car phones that Wall Street men had in the 1980s or televisions without remote controls. From the time I first heard it, I think of this carpet every time I hear the part of "America the Beautiful" where they sing about amber waves of grain. This is the carpet that my brother and I pretended was a wheat field with the toy die-cast metal tractors we would get for Christmas. We would pretend to harvest the shag carpet; that each shag polyester tendril was a corn stalk of some kind. The tractors left marks in the shag—as though the polyester piles were really being harvested. I wonder now if by giving us these tractors Grandpa and Grandma were encouraging me to be a farmer when I grew up, or if these were simply the gifts people gave, out of habit or out of momentum or because it was just what they knew.

I think now of all the horrible things that Grandpa said about lawyers over the years. And how no one ever gave me a

---

[139] The name shag derives from the Old English *sceacga*, which means "beard." My sister in law Gretchen is a realtor and she tells me that shag carpeting is seeing a resurgence in popularity. As is wallpaper.

Fisher-Price toy that evoked or encouraged a career in the legal field. And I realize of course that no such toy even exists. They have fire trucks and rocket ships and even toy stethoscopes and microscopes. But no toy Westlaw subscriptions or toy legal briefs. No Lego courtrooms.

Anyway, I know this photo was taken at the party Mom and Dad had for Grandpa and Grandma's fortieth anniversary in 1982. The party where I first saw Grandpa cry when they played Carey Landry's "Bring me a Rose." Grandpa and Grandma are seated next to Harold and Marcella. Later, I will come to understand that Harold is Grandpa's brother. It takes a while—a couple decades, really—to learn that your Grandpa is a *person*. And it takes a while longer to think of him as someone's brother—as a brother's brother. It is hard to see Grandpa as some brother's brother because he is my Grandpa. Brothers have flaws and have fights and are generally a pain in the ass. Was Grandpa ever a pain in the ass? Did they fight? Were they jealous of each other? Did they compete?

In the photo, Grandpa is opening a picture I drew of him driving a tractor and Grandma baking cookies. I know that it is September. I know that my aunts bought them two Happy 40th Anniversary plates as a gift. One was painted by a friend of Aunt Karen's and was deemed unacceptable; I recall my aunt saying, "I wouldn't let my dog eat off this plate," and it was funny and made me think about how important it was for the adults to still get their parents' approval. How seeking such approval never ever stopped. Aunt Joan had to stop at Como Mall in Cheektowaga to get a professionally-made plate. Father Weber came to say mass in our dining room.

I remember a full bar in our dining room. It was odd to see bottles of whiskey and vodka since family parties usually consisted solely of wine and beer. And maybe whiskey sours, but Mom made those in the blender. I recall my aunt complaining that vodka tasted terrible; that it was made from fermented potatoes. Later, as people's problems with alcohol began to manifest themselves, Grandma would make alcohol verboten at family parties.

After cutting the cake, people hushed as she recalled her wedding day. It was sunny, and she wore a light blue velvet dress. I wish I would have asked her if that was an act of defiance or an act of frugality (was blue velvet fabric on sale? was she so eager to move out of her parents' house that she said, "Fuck this, I ain't wearing white"?). She loved her bouquet. I recall her looking down at the kitchen floor—our kitchen floor, which had once been her kitchen floor—and pointing at the yellow stripe which ran along the perimeter[140] and recalling to the guests how much she wanted that yellow stripe and how hard it was to configure as they were tiling the floor with the asphalt and asbestos floor tiles. It would have been much easier to make the entire floor the gray-and-burgundy linoleum tile, but she really wanted the yellow stripe.

Grandpa and Grandma's wedding photo stands next to the cake. In the photo, Grandpa is wearing a morning suit, and Grandma is wearing the blue velvet wedding dress of which she just spoke. The dress is splayed out before her in regal fashion. The photo is black-and-white, but now we all know that the dress is a light blue velvet. I knew this before because Grandma used the fabric from her wedding dress to make things for her grandchildren: plush Christmas ornaments, stuffed animals and throw pillows, and even a shirt. A light blue velvet shirt that, when I wore it, must've made me the perfect hybrid of Prince Valiant and Little Lord Fauntleroy.

They were married on the morning of September 22, 1942.

In the photo, they are happy; but not overly so. But neither do they appear nervous or sad, like the bride and groom

---

[140] I wonder now if the tile floor with the yellow stripe had asbestos in it; I'm rather certain that it did and that one of us will contract mesothelioma form the kitchen floor, but I can't worry about that now.

in so many wedding photos of that era appear to be. There is no trepidation at the imminent and instant integration of lives, laundry, DNA, baggage, fears, hopes.

Grandma said they had a wedding reception at the farmhouse, and it lasted all afternoon and all evening. I wonder what wedding receptions were like back then—before the days of the Electric Slide and the Hokey Pokey and the Macarena, before compulsory Save the Date cards and destination bachelorette parties with penis straws and penis squirt guns and online registries where you can buy the couple a meal on their honeymoon. I wonder if someone played the piano in the front room. I wonder if there was a piano. Or even a front room. I wonder what they would even play at a wedding reception before the American songbook was written, and all I can even think of is the Boogie Woogie Boy from Company C. But no reception would have lasted all afternoon and all evening if the only song they would have played was "Boogie Woogie Bugle Boy (From Company C)." What other types of music did they even have back then? If not "Boogie Woogie Bugle Boy (From Company C)," then what? One of Chopin's easier pieces? Or Beethoven?

In the photo, Grandpa has the earnestness of a boarding school boy, as though he grew up in a world of knickers, coal furnaces fed by servants, trolley cars, neckties worn on golf courses, and croquet matches in Newport. There is a slight hardness to his stare—the sort of look that military officers cultivate. He seems proud of his station, and I wonder what he wanted for his progeny. Grandma appears truly happy. I never thought of her as the sort of woman who would look forward to her wedding day her whole life—such a woman seems so contrary to everything else that she espoused. But on the other side of that coin, it also was a perfect opportunity for her to revel in the things she loved, like flowers and lace and little bite-sized radishes.

I wonder if they were virgins when they got married, and then I wonder if I am weird for wondering that, or if I am some kind of deviant. But then I think that probably everyone wonders that, because how could you not? I wonder if they were in love, and suspect that they were. They were young by today's standards; Grandpa was twenty-seven, Grandma twenty-four. I wonder if their courtship was like mine. What they talked about. If they shared embarrassing moments or if they remained stoic. If they shared stories about how they learned to ride bicycles; thoughts on FDR; thoughts on Charlie Chaplin; thoughts on parenthood; if they gossiped about the members of their wedding party. As I've mentioned, Grandma was an only child. I wonder if she was nervous about being someone's sister-in-law; about sharing space; about compromising over China patterns.[141]

There's a photo of Grandpa and Grandma in the receiving line outside of St. Anthony's parish in Hawthorne, New Jersey. They are standing in front of my new wife's grandma and are waiting to say congratulations to her and me on our wedding. He is smiling. He looks proud and happy.

I notice his posture. It is not good posture. I realize that this posture is a perfect metaphor for him—how he is tall and strong, but lurking beneath a few vertebrae is the notion that he could have been just a little taller and stronger and more perfect had he the tools and confidence to do so. I sometimes wonder if the not-good-posture happened in the way that trees bend over time or as rocks erode after decades of being hit with waves, or if it happened one day as a result of a particular loss he endured. Or a couple losses. I wonder if he had friends with whom to share those losses. I wonder if the not-good-

[141] Grandpa would never have been adamant about a china pattern. The idea that they compromised on china patterns is mere speculation and likely a complete fiction.

183

posture—*slouch* would not be too strong of a word—would be as pronounced if he had spent his youth in a different locale, on different lists, on the right lists, lists for coming-out parties at the Ritz-Carlton or parties at the Plaza.

I hope he is proud of me. I forget what he said to me as he walked through the line. I remember we hugged in a way we had not ever hugged before.

In the years following the wedding, when remembering my own wedding, Grandpa and Grandma talked repeatedly about how the bus we had chartered to take people from the Pearl River Hilton to St. Anthony's got lost and that a busload of people was late. I recall being little and them telling me about weddings and the band was too loud or the buffet line was too long or all the food tasted like sterno or the food was not good and the portions were too small.

Grandma made everything. She made draperies and blouses and First Communion dresses to sell at the fancy department stores in Batavia, and she made shirts for my brothers and I, and knitted sweater vests—a red one of which I wore in my school photos in first, second, and third grades. She made nightgowns and she reupholstered chairs and sofas, and whenever I needed a gift for my mother or father, she would help me make an ornament out of a Mason jar cap, or a pencil holder out of a Quaker Oats box. She made relish and soup and pickled the fuck out of everything that metaphysically might or could be pickled; she made cookies and cakes and punch, and everything she made had some sort of secret ingredient or substitution or secret process or special nuance. She made hers and Grandpa's square-dancing outfits, and she made all of her own clothes, and she made signs for her own garage sales, and she crocheted afghans with both ferocity and nonchalance.[142]

---

[142] My family and I regularly use two such afghans—those classic zigzag, chevron-patterned afghans. We have one with zigzags with shades of green and brown, and

She made my parents a quilt for their fifteenth anniversary.

She was astonishingly creative, great at math, and determined to use every last scrap of fabric and yarn and thread. She made dresses from old feedbags—part of this was creativity, part of this was because she seemed certain that financial ruin was imminent if she didn't.

She was fond of aphorisms. Whenever we made anything, she would say, "Measure twice, cut once." She was right, but damn, that got so annoying. As a result, I never measure anything. And I fuck up everything I try to make. Luckily, Microsoft Word permits me to highlight and delete large swaths of garbage. It's almost encouraged.

We visited Grandpa in 2005, the first summer without Grandma. I recall sitting with my son and Grandpa on the davenport. I recall trying to be extra silly so as not to have to think about the fact that we are all sitting on the davenport— the same davenport on the same porch on the same back lawn on which for decades I sat with Grandma and the same davenport on which she died—without her. It's almost like no one even knows *how* to sit on this or any other davenport without Grandma; there is no script for what to say, and who is supposed to ask about replenishing the lemonade and getting cookies, or comment on the horseflies or the houseflies or any sort of fly? Are there even any cookies in the house?

But then Grandpa sort of springs to life, in a way I had never seen before. And since I am a husband and am beginning to understand the gravitational pull of a spouse, how what they say and how they say it in one minute can change an entire day and how those days can become months and the months become years and the years become decades and the decades

---

another with zigzags with shades of gray and red.

become a marriage; a spouse can change a lifetime relatively easily. With mere words that function as innocuous comments but quickly become corrosive. Anyway, in the absence of Grandma's criticism, there is a new buoyancy to Grandpa. A new confidence that is both startling and sad. While Grandma could get under my skin now and again, the fact that she got under Grandpa's skin in a way that I had until then only viewed as flirtatious was jarring.

The gardens look the same and the lawn looks the same and the garage to which the davenport is adjacent looks and smells the same—same blend of weed killer and motor oil and fertilizers and insecticides and garage accoutrements. Grandpa smiles. He is really, really good at teasing and holding our son. He knows what to do.

Gary M. Almeter

Goodbye Grandpa

"An Old Man Asleep"

The two worlds are asleep, are sleeping, now.
A dumb sense possesses them in a kind of solemnity.

The self and the earth—your thoughts, your feelings,
Your beliefs and disbeliefs, your whole peculiar plot;

The redness of your reddish chestnut trees,
The river motion, the drowsy motion of the river R.

—Wallace Stevens

When he died, I was most afraid of forgetting what he looked and sounded like. Or maybe not afraid so much of forgetting outright, but afraid of the memories I had of him diminishing or fading like some oft-trampled garden. So I prepared a mental rolodex of attributes of which I would think: the rumor of yellow in his hair, the red marks on the bridge of his nose where his glasses sat, the wrinkles in his ear lobes, the way hayseeds got stuck in his arm hair when we unloaded hay, his posture, his silver fillings. I also wrote a quick list of things and stories to be sure I wouldn't forget:[143]

Roller-skating
Bandanas
Sha-Na-Na
Little Runt

---

[143] It is noted that everything on this list might also be found in Britney Spears's weekend day planner for any given weekend.

The Emperor of Ice-Cream

Jibby cars

Three-wheeler

$2 Bill

Swimming pool

Plain hamburgers

Pizza[144]

My voice mailbox is always ninety-two percent full, as I have voicemails saved from people I love just in case they die. I guess I am fortunate to have so many saved voicemails. I have voicemails from my wife reminding me to pick up milk and telling me that I got another speeding ticket in the regular mail. As I anticipatorily navigate the anticipated grief of when she goes, I know that I will miss the most mundane things the most. Grandpa never left me a voicemail. But I do recall his voice. And we have home movies with him, both 35mm ones and the ones that recorded directly to VHS, the latter replete with the sound of him speaking. Voices provide authenticity. My mom gave us CDs of her 1967 senior thesis; she was a music major at Nazareth College. Even though I have heard her sing and play music gajillions of times, hearing her do it as a 21-year-old somehow magically provided new insight.

Grandpa fell and bumped his head while shoveling snow in December 2007. He had an operation to relieve some swelling and was never the same. He entered a nursing home in Rochester, New York, in January 2008. I flew there to say goodbye in February and saw him receive his last rites, the Catholic way of saying goodbye in which the priest blesses someone on the cusp of their demise and relinquishes their soul to heaven. But for the next year, Grandpa lived on—none of us truly *knowing* how much he was understanding and observing.

---

[144] The pizza isn't really a story. I just wanted to remember that, for a time, he and I both disliked pizza.

Gary M. Almeter

As I said earlier, he cried for much of the year.

He died on January 26, 2009. It was a Monday. I recall being ready to go to work and the phone ringing and mom and dad said hello and then were just sort of silent and sniffling. And then through tears, they told me that Grandpa died. There is no blueprint for what to do with news like this. And even if there was, it would be superfluous since whatever reaction you have just sort of happens. I recall weeping a heaving, red splotchy faced, weeping. Even though cognitively I knew that the day was imminent – it's impossible to anticipate or plan for such news. I was working in the Towson office of a large law firm and could not be late. A partner had just retired on January 1, and we were moving offices in June, so for a time I got to enjoy his big corner office with big mahogany bookcases and oriental rugs. Since I was in the corner, I was in clear view of everyone. Six days prior to Grandpa's death, I had watched the inauguration of Barack Obama and cried, and there I was crying again all day that Monday. My boss came in my office and saw me crying and said, "Are you going to do anything besides sit here and fucking cry?" I told him my grandpa died, and he said he was sorry.

I flew home for the wake and funeral. After the wake, my brother-in-law and I asked Dad to stop at the liquor store and get a bottle of Grey Goose[145]. I still had to write a eulogy and wasn't going to be able to do so without some assistance. He triumphantly returned from the liquor store with some sort of generic vodka. I said, "Did they not have Grey Goose?" and he said, "They did, but this was a lot cheaper." It was hard to be mad at him since he had just lost his dad, but I *was* sort of mad at him. Which only added to the confusion of the day. I made some mint and lime martinis and sat down to write the eulogy. The thing is, when I woke up the next morning, I had that

---

[145] Grey Goose fancies itself the best tasting vodka in the world. It was an extravagance but felt necessary.

189

moment of panic that happened whenever I blacked out the night before. What did I do? Did I do anything for which I need to apologize? How the fuck did I get here? In the case of the day of Grandpa's funeral, for a few seconds I thought I hadn't written the eulogy at all—I had to check my briefcase to be reassured that I had. I had written my grandpa's eulogy in a blackout. Here it is:

He was our Grandpa. In the last week we have seen just how much people were drawn to Grandpa; and how much people loved and respected him. Not just because of his good looks and great hair, but because he was a good person. We thank you for that. And we thank you for acknowledging his spirit and for the many ways you have each shown that you care.

It is very comforting to see your faces here this morning. Presumably and hopefully you all knew Grandpa in some capacity. Maybe you met him at senior citizens or worked with him when he worked for the town or maybe when asked, you might say, "I don't even know how I know John. He's just always been there!" Because I think the fact that you are sitting here means you recognize, at least to some degree, the impossibility of capturing such a bountiful and wonderful life in a few minutes. And that to summarize exactly what Grandpa means to us, when the "us" by virtue of God's good grace has expanded to include people across multiple generations of family and friends across the continent, would be impossible.

So hopefully you'll forgive me when I inevitably fail at doing so. A neighbor and friend of Grandpa's said it best last night when he said, "You know, when you're ninety years old and you're riding your three-wheeler up and down the road, you know you've lived a great life." And I agree. And could not say anything more apt than that. So I could stop there. But I am an Almeter, so I am going to keep talking.

One of the great ironies about Grandpa is that he learned at such an early age, and learned rather abruptly, that life was not always going to be fair and that life was certainly not going to be care-free. And that in fact, life can really be painful. Most of us inevitably learn these lessons, but have the luxury of learning them gradually. Most of us can only imagine how Grandpa must have felt when he was a teenager and his dad died.

There are those, who, when confronted with such a tragedy and the subsequent epiphany that life wouldn't always be merry, would wither at its sheer force, would succumb to it, would give in, give up, or just become bitter. But in the face of whatever force would make a lesser person give up, Grandpa summoned a greater strength of character; he picked himself up, dusted himself off, and set about the business of keeping his family together. Grandpa, quite simply, chose to be happy. And while it was a defining moment, Grandpa chose to not let it define him.

Grandpa, on the other hand, left school, set about providing for his mother and siblings during what we now call the Great Depression, and somehow—though it must have been exhausting—never tired. In the wake of this great tragedy, Grandpa worked tirelessly to make the lives of those he loved as carefree as possible. And he did so for decades to come. Grandpa became determined to make sure that the lives of the people he loved would be filled with as much merriment and laughter, sunshine and lemonade, whimsy and hope as was humanly possible.

191

And, Grandpa, we are all here to say that that is exactly what you did.

As a result, and more generally speaking, we loved Grandpa. He gave us candy. He was an easy man to love. But there came a day when, just as importantly and significantly, we learned that we liked Grandpa too. We liked him because he was nice and sweet and he let us win at games, he gave us things, and still he let us eat candy. And there was this time when Grandpa evolved from being "Grandpa" to being a man who was more complex, someone really and genuinely interesting. In addition to what he gave us, we started to like him for what he taught us. Much of what we learned from him, and much of what we liked about him, had to do with many additional ironies that surrounded him.

Grandpa was both profoundly humble and extremely proud. Humble enough to let Grandma make his clothes and put patches on his jeans; proud enough to buy, one day in 1941, an overcoat for $100. Humble enough to buy an old jalopy and spend months polishing it to a jibby car sheen, but proud enough to demand the largest, gas guzzlingest car on the lot.

He could simultaneously be both pious and irreverent. Grandpa had a strong and unwavering faith. I think his family can all recall a time when they knew Grandpa was saying a rosary just for them. And it helped. I think we can also recall when Grandpa wore a shirt to a family picnic with rows of bulls across it and the word *bullshirt* written underneath them. Just to wear his bullshirt.

He worked hard, but he liked to play as well. How many summer afternoons would Grandpa drive tractor all day, help us unload the last load of hay, which, as Kris said, was always the best because, well, it was the last; but also because Grandpa was there cracking jokes and telling us to slow down. And we knew when that last load was done, Grandpa would go swimming with us and let us drink beer underneath the big maple tree.

Grandpa adhered to rules, but he recognized when they could be broken; he encouraged us to break a few now and again. Particularly rules about swimming in the deep end. And staying up past our bedtime too. And riding the three-wheeler without a helmet. And not saying anything when he heard the candy drawer squeak. And Grandpa let us drive the cool stuff way before Mom and Dad said that we were ready.

He could be both dignified and silly. He was always there to send us off on our next adventure, whether that adventure was across the creek or across the country, and he was always there to welcome us home.

He was both devoted to Grandma but also alarmingly adept at flirting with the ladies at the picnics and the ham dinners. He knew when to tease Grandma and he knew when to acquiesce.

He was frugal, but always recognized the importance of occasional frivolity.

He couldn't see too well, but inexplicably had a knack for finding four-leaf clovers.

He would frequently pretend that he didn't know anything; but he was a spectacular teacher.

And he continued teaching everyone around him, valuable and profound lessons until he drew his very last breath.

He had no tolerance for stupidity, but he was also very forgiving when one of us did something stupid. Like when Jeff painted the Arctic Cat snowmobile with motor oil.

He could be invincible, like when he was stood at the corner of Utah, Colorado, New Mexico, and Arizona. And he could be vulnerable, like during those times when he would cry. And Grandpa knew that it was okay to cry.

Like Grandma, he loved his home, loved the scenery, loved the farm—but also somehow loved to travel. And as much as he loved looking at the stars on a clear country evening, I suspect every once in a while he wondered what it would have been like to live in the big cities I sometimes suspect he only pretended to loathe, to appease Grandma.

Later, his hands would shake; but he was always sturdy and somehow never frail. And certainly not frail when he decided to take up roller-skating at the age of seventy. And we will never forget the way he laughed when he got up after the three-wheeler tipped over with him and Andy riding on it.

Grandpa liked everything with wheels on it.

Which is poignant; because whenever you saw Grandpa, it was always very apparent that he was the happiest guy in the room—just being exactly where he was.

Generally speaking, Grandpa had a way of making us feel like we were the most important people in the world.

More specifically, whenever he would see us, he would give us a look of such astonishment and such happiness that it was like he was seeing us for the first time. Every day as we waited for the bus, Grandpa would drive down the driveway on his three-wheeler and talk to us like the minutiae of our elementary school lives was truly earth-shattering news.

As has been happening for generations in every American family, there came a time when Grandpa evolved further from being "Grandpa" to a man who we admired and wanted to be more like. And we try.

But as it turns out, it is very tough to be like Grandpa. Every once in a while, I try to be nice, I try not to fight with my spouse, I try to save for my kids' college educations, and try to say "By golly that little whippersnapper" when someone pulls out in front of me in traffic, and not curse and give them a lewd gesture. It is not easy. And as hard as it is to be nice, Grandpa made it look that much easier. Those attributes—indeed the most laudable attributes— just came naturally for Grandpa. And on those days when I try to be nice and inevitably fail, I'm left with the same feeling I had when I was a kid and it became apparent that every dog, every cat, indeed, every animal we would ever own, just liked Grandpa more than it liked us. And we would just scratch our little kid chins and say, "What does that guy got that I haven't got?"

But maybe replicating Grandpa should not be the goal. Maybe it is enough that Grandpa at least makes us want to try to be better. And he does.

Maybe it was just his character. I suspect it grew from that determination to make sure the lives of those around him were as carefree as possible and filled with laughter and sunshine and lemonade and whimsy. And I bet Grandpa never knew that what he was doing was that difficult for others. It was just who he was.

The good thing is, that even though replicating Grandpa is impossible, remembering him will be easy. Because he is impossible to forget. Passing on the words he used and the things he did, and sharing memories of the many things that made him special—things unique to everyone here—is and will be an honor; and he will continue to spread merriment even when he is not here.

To his friends, we hope you miss him—but not in a melancholy way. Please think of him now and again. At chicken BBQ's or senior citizens meetings, or a lazy afternoon when you wish John was around. Or if you see a woodchuck trotting across the road, maybe swerve just a little to try and hit it.

We already have and will continue to see him in his great-grandchildren; their fierce determination, their sweet tooths, their sense of wonderment at bugs and flowers and machines—all comes from somewhere.

His grandchildren all carry loads of their own memories, ranging from the grand to the ordinary. From hugs at graduations to the way he let us eat raspberries right off the bush to the way he would find worms for Krissy to put on the hook whenever she had a hankering to go fishing. We'll think of him when we see something as marvelous as the Grand Canyon or as plain as one of those red handkerchiefs he used. And we will think of him when our own children develop a seemingly inexplicable taste for tomatoes with sugar on them or a penchant for keeping a sprig of grass between their teeth.

And for his children, who, in the past year, taught us all a thing or two about devotion and what it means to be someone's child, your memories will inevitably and rightly be more special than anything we could either invoke or understand. And while the general consensus among the five of you is that he was a great dad, you should also understand that you are great kids too. So tomorrow afternoon when you get together to celebrate Aunt Linda's fortieth birthday, in addition to the birthday cake, splurge and enjoy a little bit of the whimsy Grandpa always endorsed, and enjoy an extra helping of ice cream for dessert. Nothing says carefree and merry like ice cream in February.

In short, we loved every minute we spent with Grandpa. And there will be a day when we think about Grandpa in heaven, with steady hands, square dancing with Grandma and, during square dancing breaks, listening to his dad tell him how proud he is of him—or maybe not saying anything at all—and those thoughts will make us smile. And he will be there to welcome us home again.

God Bless you, Grandpa. We love you and we always will.

It's a perfectly good eulogy, even if written by a sober person. But I wrote that wasted. Don't even recall writing it. For the entire year following, this fact shamed me; I couldn't believe that I had done something so disrespectful. So in addition to grief, there is lots of shame associated with the day. Getting mad at dad for not buying Grey Goose and then writing a eulogy while wasted created a tsunami of shame.

The Emperor of Ice-Cream

Sometimes death extinguishes questions that lingered over the decedent in life; other times, death raises new questions about the decedent. Grandpa's death made the questions people didn't ask themselves in 1942— *What do I want to be when I grow up? What would make me happy? What is standing in the way between me and complete happiness?* —altogether superfluous. Would he have been a better mechanic? Baker? Carpenter? Priest? Travelling salesman for some long-forgotten relic of the days when there were travelling salesmen? It was of no consequence. Rather than continue to ask these questions about Grandpa's happiness, I realized how his job—being a farmer—must have fashioned his temperament. Or maybe he was born with the temperament, and being a farmer fit him perfectly. Though that is unlikely, in light of his asthma. Anyway, Grandpa was perfectly content not being in control. He let Grandma lead conversations. He let the rain fall and the sun shine with nary a concern. He let his kids be the center of attention. He let the bugs and diseases and boll weevils and parasites attack his crops and animals and did not get angry. The withering sun, the petulant child, the damaging rain, the domineering spouse—you can't control any of it. Might as well just enjoy it.

His death was the perfect punctuation mark to his life; his very, very good life. His death was the startling realization of every truth, every natural law, every Biblical pronunciation, every long-held conventional thought about death. Every aphorism about reaping what you sow, about the life in your years, about dancing like no one was watching—all were true. He knew there was nothing that he had that he could or would keep forever. He knew there is nothing you keep when you go.

During that life he lived, he made things and he helped people and he loved and he was good and he casted his reflection. And as a result, people, as they are wont to do, came to honor him.

After mass, there was a dinner in the church shed. For all

of my histrionic disdain for the town and the townspeople and their backward ways and their love-hate relationship with literacy and their horrific clothing and their lack of personal hygiene, they really know how to put on a wonderful funeral dinner. Everyone brought a dish to pass—tons of casseroles with bubbling cheeses and creams and sauces in nine-by-thirteen Pyrex casserole dishes; macaroni salads and ham salads and potato salads of every kind—each with its own nuance though each, evincing an excess of something—its maker clearly exhibiting an eagerness to please; three-bean salads and five-bean salads and seven-bean salads but no nine-bean salads, for that would be sinful; and cheesy scalloped potatoes and cheesy spinach bacon dips and cheesy onion dips with ingredients containing everything extra fat; and cookies of every shape and size. Along with the casseroles, the people brought genuine sorrow and genuine concern and genuine love.

The casserole dishes and the Tupperware containers were all marked with the names of their owners in Scotch tape on the bottom—hard-working German folks with names like Becker and Kibler and Glaus and Kraus and Schiltz and Muller and Meyer—with whom Grandpa had worked and worshipped and eaten and played and guffawed and worried and prayed and helped.

There were a few hours between the end of the funeral dinner and my flight back to Baltimore. What does one do between a funeral dinner and a flight back to Baltimore? I had a few beers at my maternal grandparents' house as I waited for my flight home, and then had some more beers at the airport. There are things humans do instinctively to make themselves feel better. My daughter rubs a special extra-fuzzy part of her home-made blanket. Adults aren't all that different.

And then I drank the rest of that year. His death was harder than I thought it would be.

His death created a world of grief so oppressive, so perplexing, so incendiary that I found it difficult to breathe much of the next year. All the years I had spent trying to evade the life he had crafted for himself, all the years I spent validating the choices I had made, all the years I spent escaping and reinventing and yearning for some sort of transmogrification were suddenly and clearly for naught. It just ends in death. The fact that I was filled with such grief despite the fact that he died at ninety-four after a life spent riding his three-wheeler and playing with dogs and eating ice cream made me feel guilty and ashamed for having such feelings.

All this culminated in a depression that hit me in May 2010. I had always thought that depression was for weak people who couldn't handle their own lives. I was wrong. After a rough day on May 19, 2010, one where I had fought with a contractor who was doing work on our driveway; fought with a visiting attorney who stopped into my office, saw the signed picture of Ted Kennedy on my wall, and called him a murderer; and then in the evening fought with the woman selling Girl Scout cookies with her daughter, who accosted me twice—first as I made ingress and second on my egress from the grocery store—it was clear that all civility I'd once possessed had dissipated. I didn't sleep at all that night. At some point I started weeping while lying awake and then I wept for three straight weeks.

How fleeting life is. How impermanent.

I stopped drinking on May 23—not because I ever thought I had a problem, but because we went to a neighbor's for dinner and were eating outside. As was my custom when eating outside, I waited until everyone was seated and then excused myself to go inside to guzzle whatever intoxicating beverage I could find. I found a pitcher of mojitos in the fridge and guzzled directly from it until a giant mint branch came out of the pitcher and impaled me in the eyeball. Then I said, "Why am I doing this?"

After some self-assessment, a new job, a selective serotonin reuptake inhibitor, among other things, I got better. It's astonishing, really, the variety and amounts of shit I (and people in general) could carry around with me without even realizing that I was carrying it around, and how heavy and omnipresent and corrosive it all was, and what would happen when I endeavored to get rid of it.

A new life started.

Oddly, and simultaneously surprisingly and not surprisingly at all, Grandpa, the man I had always believed to be inert and compliant, turned out to be directly responsible for a transfiguration of sorts. It was certainly a period of the most fruitful and most substantive reinvention I've ever experienced. And the most unexpected. I had chided him for the way he seemed to live his life, saving and working as though imminent ruin waited just around the corner; acquiescing and capitulating; stagnating. Until I experienced depressions and began to appreciate the precariousness of things, the comfort of that which is familiar, and to understand that while not imminent, ruin of every sort might very well be waiting. Just around some corner or other. While the ruin that threatened me was far less Biblical than the drought and locusts and famine which had threatened Grandpa's livelihood, the omnipresence of the threat felt astonishingly similar. As would have been the result.

I knew that I could never ever feel that way again—could never allow myself to.

I decided to stop drinking wine or beer or martinis made with Grey Goose and cucumbers and sprigs of rosemary or gin and tonics out of mason jars or any of the other palliative cocktails that people use to reward themselves for whatever it is they feel they did that warrants a reward. This prompted a renewed enthusiasm for ice cream. I understood the need to comfort and reward myself somehow; I understood the need to pay five dollars for a pint of Ben & Jerry's merely because I *could.* I began to view Grandpa's affinity for ice cream—and Grandpa—in a new way.

The Emperor of Ice-Cream

It was comfort. It was defiance. It was indulgence. It was escape. It was something separate and apart from meat. It was something separate and apart from potatoes. It was something that he did not have to harvest, water, plant, cultivate, or expend efforts on in any way whatsoever. It was rebellion and insubordination and sass. It was lavishness and extravagance. It was contentment. It was abatement.

Gary M. Almeter

Catching Tigers in Red Weather

"Disillusionment of Ten O'Clock"

The houses are haunted
By white night-gowns.
None are green,
Or purple with green rings,
Or green with yellow rings,
Or yellow with blue rings.
None of them are strange,
With socks of lace
And beaded ceintures.
People are not going
To dream of baboons and periwinkles.
Only, here and there, an old sailor,
Drunk and asleep in his boots,
Catches tigers
In red weather.

—Wallace Stevens

To the best of my knowledge, Grandpa did not wear a "night-gown" to bed. If he did, it likely would have been white. Or light blue. It would definitely not have been purple with green rings or green with yellow rings.

Behind poems like Stevens's "Disillusionment of Ten O'Clock" lies an imagination tearing at its reins, just waiting to work its wonderful wizardry on the world. Stevens thought that people didn't understand how they saw the world. For Stevens, the average Joe saw the world in black and white, because the man on the street didn't realize that a beguiling maze called the brain filtered everything he saw or felt or heard or touched or tasted. The mind, for Stevens, is a world of infinite possibilities, one that is limited only by a person's weak imagination.

Typically, disillusionment is a bad thing. It suggests that we've become disenfranchised from the wonder that makes life, well, wonderful. We've become unable to think outside the box, believe in something more, and free up our imaginations. There's just the boring old nightgown and the boring old bed.

There are those, however, who dream of catching tigers in red weather.

Grandpa and Grandma were always preparing for things: during the summer, they would be pickling and canning and redoing the blacktop driveway so as to prevent water from seeping into the cracks and making even bigger cracks; during the winter, they would be ordering seeds for spring planting and preparing pillows and seat cushions for the outdoor patio. A nuclear holocaust was perpetually on the horizon, and a debilitating injury was surely always nigh. They were always budgeting, saving, searching for bargains. Driving twenty-six miles to Batavia to get yarn on sale. Buying cheap fabric no one liked and then making curtains, blazers, shirts, skirts, and tablecloths out of it. They were always checking their insurance premiums. Getting *more* insurance. They hated pogo sticks because once Grandma heard of someone who lost her front teeth after falling from one. Once, I went with them to a store called Gold Circle[146] because Campbell's soup was on sale and there was a limit of ten cans per customer; Grandpa, Grandma, and I each waited in a separate line, so we could carry away thirty cans of soup.

It was a yearly tradition for Grandpa to strip the paint from the iron railings of his back steps. He would then replace it with any color that my grandma wanted. Usually, she settled

---

[146] Gold Circle was a discount department store chain based in Ohio. It covered mostly New York, Ohio, Kentucky and Western Pennsylvania, It was founded in 1967. When it was sold and dismantled in 1988, it was a division of Federated Department Stores and had 76 stores.

on brown, but it was every shade of that color imaginable. Some years, the difference was so subtle that I couldn't be convinced it was any different at all. Every now and again he would then paint the awning and trim of the house to match the stairs It was a long process that he started over again after the final frost of the year. I still remember watching him out there, steam rising from his back as he labored over the staircase with great affection. A man of few words, he showed his love for my grandmother by *doing* things for her. Things that he just didn't have to do.

I loathe all such preparations. When asked if I wanted disability insurance at my job, I saw that it was about the cost of six lattes per month and said, "Fuck no." I loathe austerity. I hate saving. I hate preparing. I hate weatherproofing. And I sure as fuck am not going to walk an extra ten feet down Aisle 12—much less an extra twenty-six miles—to save a dime on a jar of fucking peanut butter. Does this make me a shitty person? Probably.

I wonder if Grandpa was happy. He was always smiling, but a lot of who he was suggested that he was the type to just keep soldiering on.

But through this myth of austerity, I find elements of Grandpa's defiance—of his commitment to whimsy, and to satisfying a guilty pleasure now and again. Of being entitled to happiness. Of saying, "I deserve this."

I say that all the time.

It is difficult for men to be vulnerable; to say, "I want to treat myself." For men, it feels like cheating somehow to say, "I deserve this just because."

In wondering what kind of life Grandpa had, and whether it was the kind of life he wanted, we look to the evidence. And the overwhelming evidence is that his life was filled with scarcity and self-deprivation, which makes it appear that our case is doomed and that the jury will rule against us. And if you have never been to Buffalo during the months of November, December, January, February, March, or April, then you know that it can be really fucking cold; and windy; and when it is windy and cold, it is even fucking colder. Adding to the assault is that, before Lake Erie freezes, the cold wind sweeps the water off the lake and dumps snow on the city and outlying areas that the people measure in feet.

Even when it doesn't snow, the psychological effect of knowing that it *can*, and likely will, has a very debilitating effect on one's mental state.[147] It is impossible to plan anything—any holiday or cocktail or dinner or birthday or anniversary party or bar mitzvah—in light of the fact that it can be cancelled at a moment's notice. And, of course, the people are prepared for it. Everyone has chains on their tires and big four-by-four trucks and plows attached to the grills of those trucks, and they have wool sweaters and puffy down coats and hats and mittens and scarves and shovels with ergonomic handles so your back doesn't hurt so much and snow-blowers and bins of rock salt outside their doors.

But it can still be hard.

So when it's time to put on our case—defending Grandpa and telling ourselves he is a man to be emulated and that he did have a good life, we look for and find more evidence.

The Pool

There's a photo of Grandpa where he is treading water in the pool. His glasses are off, and he is squinting. A person

---

[147] To be sure, every area of the country endures some sort of perpetual threat. Earthquakes and the unending shifts in tectonic plates on the west coast; forest fires in the west; tornados in the midwest; hurricanes in the southwest and Gulf Coast regions; flooding along the Mississippi and Atlantic coast; New England has its own relationship with snow and cold.

looking at the photo can't see them, but I know there are the red marks that the silicone nose pads of his glasses always left on the bridge of his nose. The sun is setting in the background. Me and my brother and sister are splashing about. I know Grandpa is treading water because of his proximity to the diving board, which I know to be the deep end. I recall how labored Grandpa's breath was when he treaded water and how that—in addition to the red marks left by the nose pads on his glasses—was the first indication I had that he was not immortal.

He is swimming in the pool he built in 1959. When I was a kid, the pool now belonged to my parents but since Grandpa lived a few hundred feet away he was there, too. A pool seems like such a luxury for a farmer to have in the 1950s—like something only Frank Sinatra and Dean Martin and Peter Lawford and Ava Gardner should have had. When Grandpa swam, I could go in the deep end without one of the Styrofoam bubbles strapped to my back. Grandpa declined to jump off the diving board, and I always wondered why.

The pool was ovular: twenty feet by forty feet. It went from two-and-a-half to eight feet deep. Lancaster Silo Company once came on the farm to build a new silo. At some point, Grandpa asked them if they could also build a pool.

In 1960, the U.S. population was 179,325,657. Of those, 13,474,771 lived on a rural farm. In 2013, of the 75,650,000 homes and farms in which their owners lived, only 12,104,000, or sixteen percent, of them had swimming pools, tennis courts, and/or other recreational structures. Sixteen percent of those had pools.

I was unable to locate any statistics on how many homes had swimming pools in 1959. No one knows how much it cost. When asked if Grandpa or Grandma were equal advocates for the pool, or if one advocated more ardently, or if one was even against the swimming pool, my dad and his sisters seem to agree that they both were equal advocates.

The Emperor of Ice-Cream

What prompted such a luxury? Such an *indulgence*. And so unnecessary when there was (and continues to be) a perfectly good and refreshing creek behind the barn[148].

I think some of it was pride. Mixed with a need for approval. And a certain kind of competitiveness. I have it as well. I love being the first person on my block to get something. And I am more competitive than I realize. Growing up on a farm fostered a real need to make sure I was not perceived as a farmer in college. I wore tons of J. Crew.[149]

That comes from somewhere.

And do you know how many fucking hours we spent in that pool? Thousands and thousands. He used it with some frequency and played with us (it would be impossible for me to overstate how fun swimming with Grandpa following the last load of hay truly was).

The pool was next to the cow pasture, which meant that sometimes the air around the pool smelled like feces. But not often.[150] And there were thorn bushes of some kind growing in

---

[148] Refreshing despite the fact that it is polluted with cow urine and fecal matter.

[149] A colleague has a single friend in her forties. The colleague always tells her that when deciding who to date, she should look at the men's watches. The men with the nicest watches are the ones who feel they have something to prove and are likely either broke or super-leveraged or worse, merely nouveau riche. The ones with watches that might have been nice at one time but are shitty and all scratched up now are the ones to date, for they are wealthy enough to not care what people think of their watches. This sort of analysis pervades lots of areas.

[150] Besides, of all the feces, bovine feces is the least offensive. Bovine feces was just a little less pungent and a little less nasty than all the other feces. Even canine and feline feces are worse. We also had porcine feces and equine feces in the village, and they were far worse. The worst feces of all, however, is galline feces. (Galline the adjective form used to describe chickens.) Our bus drove by a chicken farm, and on those hot days when bus windows were open, and the chicken farmers were dispensing of the feces, I could not even breathe. Also, feces can be both singular and plural.

the fence between the pool and the pasture so that any beach ball that went over there was instantly deflated.

He went swimming after loading hay, when there were hayseeds and hay dust in his arm hair. This always intrigued me. As did those red marks on his nose; as did the wrinkles in his ears. This pool was the epicenter of our summer.

Life was not always chores and wrinkles. There were times of mirth.

Brandy

Our dog Brandy, a Lab-German Shepard mix, was to be euthanized the week after I left for Boston. She had been in our family for nearly twelve years. Back in 1982, when we needed a new dog, Grandma and Grandpa drove my sister and I in the back of their pickup to meet and retrieve Brandy, who belonged to a co-worker of my aunt's. Today, if you drove two kids and their aunt in the back of a pickup, a parent would be in trouble. But in those days, it seemed to be encouraged.

Brandy was a revelation. She was kind, brilliant, sweet, angry when appropriate, ferociously loyal, astonishingly vulnerable. She loved having her tummy rubbed. She was independent yet devoted. She loved exploring. She was adept at catching woodchucks—which astonished us, her being a city dog and all. And we added the job of carcass removal to our weekly list of chores. I surreptitiously gave her bologna. And milk. And ham. But she always liked Grandpa the best. She was terrified of thunder, and it was during thunderstorms that the rule against letting her in the house was relaxed. She slept in the back landing during the winter. And she was there through my high school years; welcomed me home for all my college breaks; looked at me with incredulity and bewilderment when I smoked cigarettes behind the garage but accompanied me nonetheless.

When Dad sold the farm in the summer of 1992, she

accompanied us to our new home and it was there, in these new surroundings, that we realized the spring in her step was gone, and her demise was imminent. But she persevered; she took up residence in the laundry room. On October 1, 1993, Brandy ran around the house about four hundred times at lightning speed, faster than I had ever seen anything move. Then she ran off into the woods. Grandpa told us that she did this to find a suitable place to die.

A week later, a Friday, the Friday before I was to move to Boston, she returned. This amazed every one of us. Confused us, too. I was slated to move to Boston on Sunday morning. I slept with Brandy the night before. And the goodbye was like nothing I have experienced since. I owed Brandy an apology. The youthful devotion to her declined in direct proportion to the increase in chronic self-absorption wrought by adolescence. It must have been confusing for her when I didn't give her bologna anymore; to see the bologna treats wane and eventually dissipate, to see the cherub-faced sweet boy turn into a smoky-faced young man; to get older; to wonder if the man who gave you away was ever coming back.

Still I left her behind, and off we drove. All my stuff fit into the trunk and the backseat of a sedan. Having just said goodbye to Brandy for what I knew was the last time, I thought of the day we went to get Brandy in Grandpa and Grandma's truck; considering them now, the two trips seem eerily similar—both like no adventure I had ever had before. Both life-changing. And both taking on a mythological hue in light of the passing of the dramatis personae: Grandpa, Grandma, Aunt Karen, and Brandy. All gone now.

My parents euthanized Brandy when they drove back to rural upstate New York from Boston. They buried her in our backyard. Mom sent me her ID tag. I have used it as a key ring ever since. In a weird way, Brandy has been there when I met my wife, when my kids were born, and during law school graduation.

There's another photo of Grandpa where he is a little boy and he is holding a dog, and I think, "Of course he is holding a dog!" I picture them romping about Grandpa's boyhood farm and wonder what such romping might've looked like. Then I realize that at some point, Grandpa would have had to say goodbye to the dog, and I wonder what that goodbye might've looked like. I assume that he was sad saying goodbye to the dog, but I wonder if he was able to show that he was sad or if in those days boys could not show sadness at the loss of farm pets.

I think about how my dog Brandy always loved Grandpa more, and how it made me feel as though I was doing something wrong when Brandy would leave my side to go be with Grandpa. I think of the summer of 1983, following the death of our beagle J.D., whom we had for over a decade when our family was suddenly and jarringly dog-less. And when aunt Janet learned that her colleague was looking to find a new home for his three-year-old Shepard Lab mix, named Brandy. So Grandma and Grandpa and my sister and I drove in Grandpa's pickup truck to meet and retrieve Brandy. And I was astonished at how frightened Brandy was on the drive home when it was just me, as docile as could be, and Grandpa helped me get acquainted with her, taught me how to approach her, taught me the fundamentals of what dogs like that we had taken for granted in light of JD's omnipresence and acquiescence. We stopped at McDonald's and Grandpa secretly gave Brandy a hamburger and we got home really late and Dad unloaded the dog house and re-erected it against the back of the house and we kept Brandy on a chain for those first three days—to make certain she knew this was her home.

Cliff

There was nothing subversive about Grandpa. He gave every indication that he was perfectly okay with the status quo; perfectly okay with the momentum which carries things and people along; perfectly okay with the established institutions of which he was a part—the church, the town, the senior citizens groups of which he was a member. He bought his cars at the same place for decades; bought his farm machinery at the same place for decades; wore the same slate-blue Dickies workwear shirts and pants for decades.

Only twice, so far as I am aware, did he talk back to someone.

The first was to Cliff Meidenbauer, owner of the golf course and country club at the end of our road. Whether every town knows it or not, every small town has a Henry F. Potter, and he was ours. To be sure, there are degrees of and a continuum upon which Henry F. Potters are located, but every town has their own. Cliff owned the 500 acres or 1,000 acres (I'm not so good at estimating acreage) on which the golf course sat. Grandpa owned less than that.

Furthermore, Cliff was always expanding and building and improving his golf course. The mere presence of a golf course in Grandpa's hollow simultaneously irked and pleased him—the wealthy, pastel-wearing city-folk who came to his hollow to swing their clubs around and talk business and dividends and stocks surely annoyed him, but the notion of his hollow as a place of refuge and a destination to which the city-folk should aspire to go ultimately pleased him. So too his relationship with Cliff. He let Cliff use the driveways on land that Grandpa owned and that abutted the golf course. He tolerated the whizzing golf balls and inattentive golfers who drove their carts in the road.

One day, in the 1950s, Grandpa was driving a truckload of hay bales when Cliff pulled out in front of him in his convertible; Grandpa had to stop abruptly and swerved in order to avoid hitting him. As a result, the hay bales toppled onto the road. Grandpa returned home and asked my dad and my aunts to go help him reload the hay. When he returned, Cliff was picking up some of the hay bales himself and loading them onto his own truck.

When Grandpa would tell us this story he always stopped there, but with a gleam in his eye and a wry smile on his face, he would add, "And that's the end of the story." Grandma would typically pick up where he left off and let us know that Grandpa cursed him out to the point where Cliff got his men to stack the truck for Grandpa and then drove off.

The only other time was when Grandpa's father-in-law—the man from whom he bought his farm—was telling him what to do. His father-in-law, Bernard, ended a sentence with ". . . or else." And Grandpa stopped what he was doing and said, "Or else what?" Hearing no response from Bernard, he repeated, "Or else what?"

And that's the end of that story.

Except sometimes when I wonder if I am a sociopath—like when I am stuck in traffic and am so annoyed and need to know that my inconvenience is justified and I legitimately yearn to see carnage in the road up ahead and am sort of disappointed when the traffic jam clears and I drive by the source of the delay and see no decapitations but merely a fender bender or an old Chevy Citation overheating—and I tell myself that everyone, even Grandpa, falls apart now and again.

The Little Runt

Of all the stories in this book, my favorite is also probably the one Grandpa would be most embarrassed by if he knew I told.

I already knew that Grandpa was pious (see saying the rosary before and during my Bar exam). He was also irreverent. I liked him best when he was irreverent.

Irreverence manifested itself in different ways. At one

family party, he wore the terry cloth polo shirt with horizontal bulls and "BULLSHIRT" on it. He once stuck some green play slime up his nose. He was fun.

This best story, though, happened in the summer of 1984. Our family and Grandpa and Grandma and friends of theirs—we will call them Doris and Bertram—all went to Canandaigua, New York, for the New York Farm Show: a showcase of new farm machinery and technologies and framing trends. My mother and sister and I went to visit her college friend, Joan, who lived on Canandaigua Lake, one of the Finger Lakes. My dad and brother and Grandpa and Grandma and Doris and Bertram went to the Farm Show. They all agreed to meet at four p.m., then Grandpa and Grandma and Doris and Bertram would drive home, and Dad and my brother would drive to Joan's house to have dinner and then drive us home.

My siblings and I always had fun at Doris and Bertram's expense. They gave out apples and dimes to trick or treaters; she had enormous feet and wore white pumps; he was a smaller man. We never dared voice these opinions in the presence of Grandpa and Grandma because they were friends. When my dad and brother walked in to Joan's lakeside house, my brother caught my attention and mouthed the words "I have to tell you something." So we walked out to the dock, he looked around to make sure no one could hear us, and he told me this: that he, Dad, Grandpa, and Grandma had all met at the designated meeting place at four p.m. At four-fifteen, Doris and Bertram had still not arrived. My brother said Grandpa got really annoyed and asked, "Where is that little runt?"

This is what made Grandpa real for me. Like the time he cried.

That is what told me that he was a little bit different than the other farmers in the town.

This is what cemented Grandpa's genius for me.

And it was genius. It showed that he understood people's

214

foibles and idiosyncrasies and insecurities. And why people who don't have small penises don't care if people make fun of the size of their hands. He understood people. He knew how to be authentic; and how to really *emote*. Gone was the artifice and the poise and the courtesy to which his typical human interactions—at least the ones I saw—were tethered. As it turns out, Grandpa was neither perfect nor immune from the resentments I felt on a daily basis. Nor was he immune to anger. Furthermore, it doesn't get much worse than a man calling another man a "little runt." Say it out loud. It's terse and abrupt and filled with consonants. Additionally, a runt just doesn't connote a small size; it connotes weakness.

As kids, we frequently saw Doris working in the barn and carrying buckets and unloading hay whenever we drove past their house. They were farmers, too.[151] We always made fun of Doris and Bertram for as much, and—as it turns out—Grandpa saw it as well. I loved this. I loved that he and I saw the same thing when we saw an older woman carrying a large bucket of pig slop. Was it sexist and mean and misogynistic? Yes. But it was what we thought at the time. It was silly and funny and mean; but no one got hurt.

Lastly, I love the story because it takes back the term "runt" typically associated in farm stories like the one with the smallest animal of the litter; the pig who gets adopted by the girl and later gets messaging from the friendly spider; the dog on the verge of being tossed into the river in a bag filled with stones because he will never amount to much of a coon hound who gets saved and ultimately rescues the family from their burning home.

Grandpa was really fucking pissed at Bertram to say this in front of my brother.

And we all get pissed at people. They went on to enjoy another two decades of friendship. So this was a minor blip in

---

151 Obviously.

the course of their relationship.

My brother was unaware of what caused Doris and Bertram to be late. Nor did he know if they apologized when they finally did arrive.

Jibby Cars

Grandpa and Grandma always bought nice cars. Pontiac Bonnevilles and Pontiac Catalinas and Pontiac Grand Villes. Typically, they stuck with Pontiac, though I do recall them deviating and getting an Oldsmobile or a Chevrolet a couple times. They would have considered Cadillac to be too flashy. They bought a car every two years, as though it were black letter law. As though to not do so was uncivilized. I loved this about them. That amidst the humility and country goodness and harvesting their own vegetables there was an element of snobbery. Though *snobbery* is the wrong word. They weren't buying cars to ingratiate themselves with someone or attain some sort of distinction, one of the earmarks of snobbery. They were doing so because they liked reliability and craftsmanship and design and American pride.

They always washed the cars themselves. And they always washed them thoroughly. Outside polish and wax and debug; inside vacuum and dust and wash the floormats. They always put Grandpa's initials ("JFA") on the dashboard using these metal stickers. I recall a CB radio in one car; a compass with a suction cup to affix it to the windshield in another. They loved their cars. They loved buying their cars (and they always bought them from the same small local dealership, which I always found interesting since they would likely have gotten a better deal at a larger place) and they loved washing their cars and they loved calculating the miles per gallon that each car received. They loved tying a spare key to the bumper with dental floss in case they ever locked their keys in the car. Grandma must have

216

read about that in a juicy and provocative issue of *Good Housekeeping* or *Reader's Digest.*

For as long as I can remember, Grandpa would also keep an old car—one he would buy used that was typically rusty and while technically drivable, still needed some engine work. He called each his "jibby car" and would spend months hammering out dents, sanding out the rust, cleaning and polishing all the engine parts, stuffing and sewing the upholstery, painting and ultimately selling them. He loved doing this. And took such pride in each one. Before putting the "For Sale" sign in the windshield along with his phone number,[152] he would take us for a ride in his sparkling new jibby car. It smelled like new car; and it smelled like Grandpa. I recall a Mustang—from the 1960s—with blue leather interior and a bright white exterior that we drove to Beachy's, an ice cream shop in nearby Darien. Grandpa drove, I sat in the middle, Mom sat in the passenger seat, and my aunt Karen and brother and sister sat in back. No one used seat belts. It didn't have air conditioning, so we rolled all the windows down. I recall the shine of the window roller handle. It literally sparkled. As did Grandpa's eyes through his paint-splattered bifocals.

The Three-Wheeler

In 1983, Grandpa bought a Yamaha 200 three-wheeler.[153] It was bright yellow and like nothing we had ever seen before, with big balloon-like, knobby tires (three of them) and a plush seat and a big engine. On it, Grandpa's posture changed, his

---

[152] Their phone number was 535-7534; the area code was 716. But you didn't need to specify an area code back then.

[153] By the early 1980s, both Honda and Yamaha had introduced their own models of the sit-on, straddle-ridden, three-wheeled, all-terrain vehicle. These were designed purely for recreational use. It featured a full suspension, a 248-cc air-cooled two-stroke engine, a five-speed transmission with manual clutch, and a front disc brake.

demeanor changed, his attitude changed. He could now go anywhere, on any terrain, anytime he wanted to. And he did. He purchased the three-wheeler ostensibly to save money on gas since he would no longer have to drive his truck to and from the farm every day. But he really got it to have fun. To treat himself.

He bought another, nicer one a few years later. And rode it until he was ninety-three, when he couldn't anymore. But for the twenty-four intervening years, he was on his three-wheeler every day—no matter how cold it was or what the weather was like—zipping up and down the road. He stopped and talked to us while on his three-wheeler as we waited for the bus every morning. And every morning we would get on the bus and all the kids would be peering out the window and looking at Grandpa on his three-wheeler.

At his wake, our neighbor Wayne said to me with his characteristic perpetual giggle, "Gary, when you're ninety-three and driving around on your three-wheeler, you know you've lived a good life."

The Gray Lunch Box

When Grandma packed Grandpa's steel-gray lunch box, she would look at me and literally snicker and say, "Should we give Grandpa an extra Snickers bar today?" and I would smile and nod my head yes.

My dad never used a lunch box because he worked on the farm, right behind our house. We brought him hot dogs and bologna sandwiches. They were fresh, using only the best ingredients, and his sandwiches were never wrapped in foil or plastic bags. Kids were the ones who used lunch boxes to take their lunches to school, and as a result, the lunches fucking sucked. Shit got stale and runny and after an hour on the hot and sweaty bus and then three more hours in the hot and sweaty classroom, the carrots had a slimy residue on them and bread was soggy and the juice in the thermos always leaked all over.

After he left the farm, Grandpa got a job working for the Town Highway Department, paving roads and filling in potholes and digging ditches and plowing snow. It was odd to see: Grandpa, a man with a lunch box. In fairness, he did not have a *Little House on the Prairie* or *Bambi* lunch box. His was industrial steel gray. With big motherfucking steel clasps to keep the lid down. And a domed lid in which he put his thermos—filled with hot coffee instead of Hawaiian Punch.

Knowing what I know now of how men talk, I am certain that talk on the road-paving gang was peppered with talk of boobies and beer and doughnuts. Did Grandpa enjoy this? I always viewed his work with the town as something more ministerial; was it escape? Did it allow him to curse and to comment on women's breasts? Did they talk about how much they wanted to fuck the country women? Or brag about the size of their penises?

The Sunday Drive

Grandpa was always driving. To me, this is a drag. Why drive when you can fly.

That weekend in 2006 that I went to visit him in Rochester, we went to church on Sunday. After church, we just drove with no destination and no plan and no itinerary. He was giddy. He pointed out things he observed—oddly shaped trees, quirky mailboxes, lingering snow banks, old tractors, cool doors on old houses—and was positively delighted with each observation.

In today's nomenclature, we call that *being in the moment.* He was completely immersed and enjoying what he was doing. It was his functional equivalent of yoga. Like we do when we sit down to eat a bowl of ice cream or an ice cream cone. It is something for which we all yearn.

Nickels

Grandpa had a thing for two-dollar bills.[154] He gave me one so that I would never be broke. He gave me lots of them over the years for good report cards and birthdays. But the one he gave me so that I would never be broke is extra special.

He also gave me a bank for a birthday I do not remember—must've been my first or second or third birthday—that only accepted nickels.[155]

The bank was about the size of a car battery; it was all metal and very heavy—especially when it had $8.45 in nickels. It was shaped like a cash register, and it had a lever that you would pull every time you deposited a nickel at the top. The

---

[154] Today, there is a common misconception by the general public that the two-dollar bill is no longer in production. According to the Treasury, it "receives many letters asking why the two-dollar bill is no longer in circulation." In response, the Treasury states: "The two-dollar bill remains one of our circulating currency denominations . . . As of April 30, 2007, there were $1,549,052,714 worth of two-dollar bills in circulation worldwide." Over 4.3 million two-dollar bills are entered at the American currency-tracking Web site Where's George? Because two-dollar bills are uncommon in daily use, their use can make a particular group of spenders visible. A documented case of using two-dollar bills to send a message to a community is the case of Geneva Steel and the communities in surrounding Utah County. In 1989, Geneva Steel paid its employee bonuses in two-dollar bills. When the bills began to appear in different places, people recognized the importance of the company to the local economy.

[155] Interestingly and I am certain coincidentally, Thomas Jefferson appears on both the nickel and the two-dollar bill. The back of the two-dollar bill has a depiction of John Turnbull's *Declaration of Independence* oil painting that depicts the presentation of the draft of the Declaration of Independence to Congress. The painting shows forty-two of the fifty-six signers of the Declaration, including what appears to be Jefferson stepping on John Adams's foot.

amount in the bank was displayed on the front in an old font; not a curlicue antique-y font, but a very definitive, powerful, nearly art deco font. The bank was black and covered in paint that surely contained lead. And probably asbestos and carcinogenic tobacco juice, too. Opening the bank would result in its complete and irreversible destruction somehow—so you could only do so once.

As a result, I loved nickels and to this day believe that they are the best coin. They are bigger than they should be; heavier; they have Jefferson on them—Thomas Jefferson, who still maintains some relevance today. But the nickel's design also makes no sense—why is it bigger than the dime?

I opened the bank in high school. Took the $17.55 that was in it and went to a movie.

The Emperor of Ice-Cream

Part IV

Good

The Emperor of Ice-Cream

When I think of an emperor, I typically think of men who rule their kingdom with might and a scowl and an impervious certitude. In his poem, Stevens takes that archetype and turns it on its head by making this emperor's sole job to be overseeing the distribution of ice cream, a rather unimportant job. But at the same time, the ice cream is *so* important that it needs an emperor to oversee it. I think Stevens is trying to realign our priorities just a bit. The man learns that you can't cover up death. And as absurd as it is to keep rollicking in the life, with its coarse muscularity and crude hunger and greedy concupiscence, that is still going on in the kitchen in the lady's absence, you must.

Grandpa was not the emperor of anything. Not even really of his own home. And though he spent 97.8 percent of his entire life in one solitary rural valley—twenty-eight years on the farm on which he was born, twenty-eight years on the farm on which his wife was born, and then thirty-seven years in the prefabricated ranch house he built some 375 boy steps away from that farm—he never endeavored to rule it or even influence it.

This is what Grandpa did: he loved ice cream; he luxuriated in ice cream; he recognized its luxury in the wake of hardship; recognized the need to splurge every now and again— both financially and calorically; he recognized the shortness and immediacy and evanescence of life. Which is, of course, part of the poem's resonance too—everything is fleeting. Being an emperor of ice cream would surely be gratifying for an instant, but such gratification would surely be abbreviated.

It took a while for me to recognize that all Grandpa wanted to be was a good man; it was enough for him. I now find it astounding. And comforting. It's so rare.

224

Life since then has been an effort to find out how he did it. After trying to escape him for so long, the recoil that occurred following the acknowledgment that his was a life that was actually rather enviable jarred me. But it was comforting, too. It happened in lots of little ways. It started with the May 2010 depression, kicked into high gear following the 2013 Boston Marathon, and is now part of a daily assessment.

In this book, he is the emperor.

This hardworking, austere, ice-cream eating, good man— my Grandpa.

A Sun of Fuller Fire

"How to Live. What to Do."

Last evening the moon rose above this rock
Impure upon a world unpurged.
The man and his companion stopped
To rest before the heroic height.

Coldly the wind fell upon them
In many majesties of sound:
They that had left the flame-freaked sun
To seek a sun of fuller fire.

Instead there was this tufted rock
Massively rising high and bare
Beyond all trees, the ridges thrown
Like giant arms among the clouds.

There was neither voice nor crested image,
No chorister, nor priest. There was
Only the great height of the rock
And the two of them standing still to rest.

There was the cold wind and the sound
It made, away from the muck of the land
That they had left, heroic sound
Joyous and jubilant and sure.

—Wallace Stevens

Inexplicably, Grandpa always seemed eager to escape whenever he was able. From the time I can remember, he and Grandma would leave and drive around the country for four or five weeks about once a year. They loved exploring. They flourished as they scouted and traversed. To be certain, he

226

never complained about the un-extraordinary house to which he returned nightly. He never complained about the sofa, those lamps, or those chairs that were purchased in such a hurry. He never rushed through the holidays, was annoyed at the pace of life, or expressed any disenchantment with any task or dental appointment or duty. He never complained about the smallness of his world, the messes it sustained, the way he lived or the cadence with which he lived it. Taken individually, these qualities are rare; in the aggregate, they are even more so.

Grandpa never got to remake himself. He never got to diverge or deviate or mutate or overhaul. He never lived more than a mile from where he was born. He never got to be anonymous; to roam around a brand-new place while giving zero fucks about anything and with zero concern about accountability. He never got to hear all brand-new sounds; taste all brand-new foods; spend a year doing everything for the very first time; experience different climates; experience the new rhythms and cadence of a new place. I always thought he was okay with this. But then the more I learn about him, and the more I consider it, the more I realize he likely had a perpetual yearning to be elsewhere. As Aunt Janet said, one of their defining characteristics was the idea that they were both capable of so much more. Grandpa traveled to forty-eight states. He never made it to Hawaii or Rhode Island.[156] In those years when he was no longer farming and could drive without worrying about his eyesight and the other perils of driving while old, he and Grandma would drive around the country for weeks at a time. I think the word is wanderlust.

On one of those trips—perhaps the same one in which he stood at the quadripoint of Arizona, Utah, New Mexico, and

---

156 Really, Grandpa? Rhode Island? I don't think he was "anti-Rhode Island" nor do I think he purposefully avoided it. It just never happened.

Colorado—he and Grandma stopped at the London Bridge in Lake Havasu City, Arizona.[157] They bought a piece of the old London Bridge for Grandpa to keep as his "worry stone." "What's a worry stone?" I asked. Grandma told me that Grandpa feels very anxious sometimes, that he worries, that he has a habit of jingling the change in his pockets when he does so. So, in lieu of the change-jingling, they hoped that he could take his thumb and rub the small piece of marble from the London Bridge. The way this changed my thinking was seismic. Grandpa worried? Grandpa was anxious? About what? How can a person simultaneously be full of joy and full of anxiety?

Similarly, he had an odd disdain for cities. As mentioned, he definitely hated Boston. Now that I know that the opposite of love isn't hatred, it's apathy, I wonder what that disdain was all about. He had an aunt Margaret who married a "rich Italian from New York City." Grandpa couldn't remember his first name but knew his last name was "Scalia like the judge." I'm not sure how Margaret met Mr. Scalia, but she did, and they got married, and they moved to New York City. Every now and again, Margaret Scalia and her husband would come back to the farm to visit and would always do so in a "big fancy car."

In one photo, she is in the passenger seat of what you know is a very expensive car. There are a bunch of younger men standing alongside the expensive car and Grandpa is one of them. He showed it to me from what was apparently a secret stash of photos, photographs he never showed until I went to visit him after Grandma died. The woman—the escapee, as it were—is Grandpa's aunt Margaret. She married an Italian named Scalia and I wonder if that is that Scalia and I hope it's

---

[157] London Bridge in Lake Havasu City, Arizona, was built in the 1830s and formerly spanned the River Thames in London, England. It was dismantled in 1967 and relocated to Arizona.

not but I also sort of hope it is. When people got married in the old days, they drove away, and it was okay not to see them again. Margaret drove to White Plains with her husband Frank Scalia, and Grandpa said, "Frank had money," with a mix of reverence and disdain.

In the photo, she is wearing a scarf. Not to keep warm but to keep her hair in place, like Thelma and Louise did. On others, such a display would be deemed vain, but you know it is unlikely that Grandpa ever made such an assessment of his aunt. The photo is black and white. The photo makes me think of photos that Grandpa is not in. There is a photo in my friend Dave's parents' summerhouse: a panoramic photo of Yale University's class of 1928. It is about three feet long and a foot wide. There are eight rows of about forty men in tweed suits and vests and saddle shoes posing in front of a group of imposing brick buildings. Some men barely smile, but most look at the camera with authority. Grandpa is fourteen years old when this photo was taken—of these men on the cusp of adulthood and the Great Depression. Did they circumvent the ravages of the Great Depression? Or did they succumb to it? Did their lives remain gilded lives of a gilded era? There are no photos of Grandpa in such a setting. Though it's hard not to feel there should be. Grandpa would have simultaneously loathed and loved these men from Yale; loathed and envied their smugness; loathed and admired their non-calloused hands; loathed and loved the way they glided through life with nary a care in the world; loathed and begrudged the way they navigated the refined restaurants of New York and Paris.

When Aunt Janet is driving me back to the airport after a visit with Grandpa in 2006, she tells me that one of the primary reasons she always suspected Grandpa and Grandma were attracted to each other was because they understood the yearning to escape while being tethered to a homeland. The stories Grandpa and Grandma told now make more sense.

The Emperor of Ice-Cream

When people ask me where I am from, the script is always the same. I tell them, and they express disbelief. Which secretly pleases me: the suggestion is that I am too urbane and sophisticated to have such origins. Then they inevitably comment on the amount and scope of the snowfall and cold; then they will let me know—in varying degrees—how I am so lucky to have escaped such a conservative and constricting place. Neither of these sentiments is necessarily false, though neither convince me that the speaker has a nuanced understanding of the region. And how complicated my feelings are about home.

Reducing any part of the United States to generalities can be insensitive, reckless and, in some cases, discriminatory. That said, most regions have come to be defined by certain broad traits: New England is steeped in intellectualism and Puritanism punctuated by a phonologically distinct accent, the West celebrates the fact it was founded by and is still inhabited by pioneer-spirited renegades, the Southwest revels in its Native American traditions, and the South is constrained by its Confederate past. What to say about the Midwest? They are hard-working and nice? There is no defining accent or music or literature or shared history or origin.

The Midwest is undefinable in so many ways. Not even those born and raised in the area can provide a rational answer as to which states belong to or in the Midwest and which ones do not. Buffalo is not really a Midwest town, but it's definitely not a Northeastern or Mid-Atlantic city. The region is overwhelmingly white, though ethnically heterogeneous. Like other major Midwestern cities like Detroit, St. Louis and Chicago, early settlers came not only from surrounding regions, but also Germany, Scandinavia, Ireland, and Poland. Like other Midwestern cities, Buffalo has seen better days. But in the days when it flourished – when the Erie Canal and the Great Lakes were hubs of, indeed necessary, for interstate commerce – it really and thoroughly flourished. When Grandma told me that she worked for a wealthy family in Buffalo as a domestic helper, it was easy for me to believe that Buffalo once housed lots of wealthy families.

Due to the new importance of the "white working class" in politics, it's a region that people are yearning to know better. But how to examine Western New York's complexities? It's snowy but also has incomparably beautiful summers. They have shitty sports teams that only become more adored the shittier they get. It also seems to not really know itself.[158] Its urban

---

[158] Though not the sole factor, confusion about the Midwest results from its failure to arrive at wholly truthful or enduring cultural distinction. In a 1998 essay titled "The Heartland's Role in US Culture: It's Main Street," University of Kansas professor James R. Shortridge traces the region's relative undefinability, starting with the first geographical reference of the "Middle West" in the 1880s. At the time, the phrase referred only to Kansas and Nebraska, and by nature of its small scope, the cultural tropes and mannerisms associated with the region were more universal: the people there were kind and moral, idealists; they were pragmatic and hard-working, but also humble. It was very *Little House on the Prairie*, —happiness is a piece of maple candy, manual labor is an integral part of your character.

But by the turn of the century, "the Midwest was America," Shortridge writes, as multiple industries in the region (notably Detroit's automobile industry) were proof of industrialization's success, and immigrants were finding opportunities in states that were thought to know the meaning of hard work. However, it was this very industrialization that would cause the heart of the country to suffer its first crisis of identity. The urbanization of cities like Chicago and Detroit did not coincide with the area's reputation for Christian morality, pastoralism, and agriculture. And, at least colloquially, many people within the region attempted to disassociate themselves from what they saw as centers of depravity, which is reflected in what we today consider "Midwestern." As Mark Athitakis said, "We change both the borders and the definition of Midwest to accommodate the visions most close to religion and the nuclear family."

The Midwestern literature of the early twentieth century reflected the region's new uncomfortable duality. With *The Jungle* (1906), for example, muckraker Upton Sinclair sought to expose the harsh working conditions in Chicago's meatpacking industry and argue the benefits of socialism. On the other hand, there was Sinclair Lewis's satirical *Main Street* (1920), about a liberal-leaning woman who follows love to a small town in Minnesota where her close friend tells her that she "must live up to popular code if [she believes] in it; but if [she doesn't] believe in it, then [she]

231

---

must live up to it."

In other words, Middle America found itself stuck. As the East Coast asserted itself in both culture and material reality as a center of modernity, the Midwest could not grasp the same identity; it was left to associate itself more with Lewis's *Main Street* than Carl Sandburg's poem "Chicago." But the opposite of modernity is at best stagnation, and at worst backwardness. As such, it wasn't until the mid-1960s, a time when a collective nostalgia for the past settled over America, that there was once again value ascribed to the unpretentious people living in what Shortridge described as "America's collective hometown."

Shortridge ends his essay with the assertion that while the Midwest can't be considered the "keeper of the nation's values," it remains "a place where people can still leave their doors unlocked and in which governors will occasionally answer their own telephone."

If not always rural, the Midwest is nonetheless "indelibly marked by rural values," Athitakis writes in the intro to his book, The New Midwest. Historically, when these values have been threatened, the Midwest has disassociated itself from those areas experiencing the threat. In the 1960s, just as the Heartland began to reclaim its national esteem, it saw grand outbursts of racial and economic decline that devastated parts of the region, primarily the central cities of large metropolitan areas. In Chicago, business in the railroad stockyards sharply declined, and the meatpacking industry, which had been decentralizing since the turn of the century, barely maintained a presence in the city. Detroit, torn apart by deindustrialization, saw the peak of its racial conflict in the 1960s and 1970s; in the summer of 1967, instigated by policy brutality but also as a larger response to underlying issues like segregation, redlining, and unemployment, Detroit's infamous Race Riot broke out.

These tensions were at odds with Midwestern ideals. So, the public responded as they saw fit: to distance themselves from those cities like Cleveland and Detroit, turn Ohio and Michigan into "Rust Belt" states, and pick up Iowa, with its "utopian gleam," in their stead.

Interestingly, it wasn't until 1984 that the US Census Bureau officially adopted the term *Midwest*.

Over the past twenty years, Athitakis argues, a good handful of writers have sought to drill into the "hearty, churchy, white-bread vision" of the region that's been projected through literature popular culture. But a specific region or issue must first become newly relevant for it to merit such a meditation. Athitakis brings up Detroit, a city crippled by decades of white flight, falling home prices, and the collapse of the automobile industry, which left it in an exceptionally poor state after the Great Recession. In 2013, Detroit filed the largest municipal bankruptcy case in US history and quickly became the national media's favorite example of economic constituency is characteristically urbane. But you drive just a few miles and you are in a rural area that feels like an entirely different planet.

I love cities. I loathe nature. Were it up to me, I would blacktop the whole country, add subways and chaos and crime and fancy restaurants and an overarching malaise coupled with an overarching sophistication and that would be that. I love the anonymity of cities. The disarray. The possibility. The tumult. The access to things. I think Grandpa would have flourished in such an environment. But then I think he would have withered, too. Once I was sitting on a bench in New York City smoking a cigarette and I looked around me, and on every corner there was something sketchy happening. Something sketchy was always happening on the streets of New York City—couples fighting loudly, people pissing on the sidewalk or trying to make a buck. I loved it. I loved the chaos. I loved the opportunity. I loved the limitless opportunities to indulge, and indulge *bigly*. But loving it created a feeling of separateness from Grandpa and the world that I felt I was *supposed* to love.

But it was more than location. It was being able to live in abundance, as though imminent ruin was not right around the corner or chasing me relentlessly. It was okay to be decadent; okay to be festive; okay to be celebratory; okay to bask; okay to

---

collapse and urban struggle. It was only after this, Athitakis says, that people outside of the region were ready to read about the Motor City.

Last year, Angela Flournoy published to well-deserved acclaim her debut novel *The Turner House*, in which Detroit's houses are characters as much as the families who live in them during the 2008 recession. *Detroiters*, a television series about two best friends attempting to build a local advertising empire, premiered in February on Comedy Central. "Detroit has been in the spotlight lately ... and through [the highest highs and the lowest lows], it's been a vibrant city full of character and life," reads the subhead to a 2014 article on *The Daily Beast*, which goes on to suggest the books about the city that are most worth reading.

savor and wallow and carouse and maybe even gloat now and again. That, too, is what living in a place of plenty brought.

I delved into city life. A few things in particular stand out:

I had been teaching at private high school in Boston. My fiancée had been working at an academic press in Boston. What better way to test our mutual mettle than plying our collective skill sets in the Big Apple? I am neither too proud nor too immune to cliché to say that we thought that if we could make it there, we could make it anywhere, both professionally and domestically.

The years I taught at that private high school in Boston, I taught countless poems and short stories by white American authors to boys who would go to some Ivy League school, whether I was there or not. I wanted to teach at an authentic New York City public school, like in the movies. I wanted teaching to be a transformative endeavor—one that resulted in metamorphoses of those I taught.

The whole notion of moving, of having choices, of relocating in an effort to find yourself, the notion of there being a self to find—all this felt indulgent. Just like when I was a kid, I felt Grandpa obsessing and judging. He wasn't. But that's how you think when you think only of yourself.

So that summer, the summer of 1998, when the world feasted on Bill and Monica and people left their jobs in droves for dot-coms and wealth seemed possible just by walking out your front door, I delved into the works of black and Latino authors and prepared lessons therefrom. I was elated when I read Henry Louis Gates's essay "In The Kitchen," about the hair-straightening rituals he endured as a child, and I used it as the foundation of an entire unit I called "Assimilation." I couldn't wait to empower and lead and transform.

The first day of school was enlightening. The kids I taught were poor but resilient, newly emigrated and proud. It became evident very early that they regularly endured more than any kid

234

should. But they stayed kids. The students' reading levels made it apparent that they weren't ready for Henry Louis Gates. Nonetheless, I felt such triumph in being a teacher. It seemed easy to make a difference. I called students in the morning to make sure they were awake and going to school and they respected me for that. I patted them on the back when they walked into the classroom. They were rarely touched with any affection.

Surprisingly, at least to me, my students were more responsive when they could escape into a new world rather than examine their own. My seniors had never read *The Catcher in the Rye*, so I taught that and they loved it, far more than they had *I Know Why the Caged Bird Sings*. Stories of childhood trauma bored them, they said with the aura of anyone who has been there, done that. Stories of people frolicking in other lands intrigued them. My freshmen loved *Romeo & Juliet* far more than they had *The House on Mango Street*. Oddly, they related to kids fighting with their parents much more than they could Esperanza's dreams of escaping her impoverished neighborhood. It turns out that empowerment came as readily and authentically from conquering the canon as much as it can come from stories of survival written by your people.

Quite a different phenomenon happened with the kids' writing. They were eager to look inward and share intimate details about their lives. When I asked kids to write fictional narratives, I expected fancy sports cars and limousines, international trips and intrigue, but most of the time I got stories about gang bangers, abortion clinics, drug-addicted relatives, and abusive uncles.

So they were simultaneously yearning to tell their stories while eager to hear the stories of someone else. I could understand that. I was eager to hear more about their worlds, about which I had little insight. I was also learning to see the value in expanding their world, fostering navigability through the white canon, even if it meant sacrificing awareness of their own. My goal had always been to provide them with the feeling that they had a place in public discourse; that they could be effective in whatever profession they chose; and to erase some of the cynicism that made them feel they could not make a difference. I was discovering a different pathway to that goal.

In December, I was tasked with going to listen to a band that my fiancée and I were considering hiring to play at our wedding reception. The Groove Bus was playing a holiday gig at the Windows on the World restaurant atop the World Trade Center's north tower. December is a particularly rough month in NYC, especially for those who do not live in a department store window or a neighborhood resembling such. The kids I taught were in what I would come to know as their chronic December funk, common with urban youth, precipitated by the onslaught of Christmas images and ideals and commercials. I found it exhausting—physically and emotionally. That summer, I had read "Santa Claus is A White Man" by John Henrik Clarke, the story of a black boy who encounters a racist Santa on his way to buy Christmas presents. I was determined, despite my recent epiphany, to read it with my classes and had done so that day. With disappointing results. None of the kids seemed to "get it." "Maybe they don't like reading stories about their own oppression," I thought. "Maybe I am a shitty teacher," I also thought. So, I secretly welcomed the opportunity to head out by myself and wallow.

I took the subway to the WTC, got off on the 105th floor of the North Tower to several raucous holiday parties. I found Groove Bus and sat down at the bar. The Groove Bus played reception standards to which I listened disinterestedly, more intent on getting wasted than assessing their adeptness at replicating Kool and the Gang. I put my credit card on the bar and sat back to listen and watch the night's improprieties unfold. It was a spectacular display, on several fronts. Outside, New York was lit up like a Christmas tree. Inside, there were hedge fund managers in sleek suits and with sleek hair frolicking with submissive women in festive crushed velvet dresses and trying-too-hard-to-be-festive stockings. I thought it all too spectacularly cliché to be true: the office party, the secretaries, the acquiescence, the yearning, the commuter train, the lipstick on the collar, the scents, the fornicating, the New York-ness of it all. I, in my green sweater, blue jeans, and brown loafers, seemed to be the only one not in a monochromatic shirt and tie and black suit. I was a confident man; but I was learning that separateness can have a debilitating effect. I detected it with the haphazard and apathetic way the bartender made my drinks for me, the way girls seemed not to give me a second glance.

With regard to the economic disparity of the sort regularly playing itself out in New York, I fancied myself both an observer and a participant. My students were poor. They wrote about things that astounded me. They had both a strength and a defeatism that perplexed me. I walked home from school feeling like the luckiest guy in the world; but after the walk home in one of the wealthiest zip codes in America, I felt utterly despondent. So being here, amidst the excess, made me feel both disloyal and triumphant. At the very least, it was disorienting. For which world was I better suited?

Like a kid reading Shakespeare, there was an allure in the escape of the sort afforded by the WTC. In seeing how other people lived. In imagining their homes, their cars, their vacations, the shape of their swimming pools. Where nouns like *summer* double as verbs. But it also made me want to stand up and assert, "I am here too. Acknowledge me." Much like my kids did when they walked into a Gap and received no service.

After too much gin, I traced my steps back to the subway to wait for the 4-5-6. The next thing I recall, I was being woken up by a conductor simultaneously shaking me and kicking me off the train with a mix of disgust, burliness, and anger. My pants were wet; I had peed myself. I stumbled off the train. The cold and the wind sobered me up. I had clearly never been here before. I walked downstairs and saw from the sign on a produce that I was on West 167th Street. I had no Metro card and no money and decided that walking east was my best chance at finding an ATM.

It was late and there were no people. Anywhere. I walked past a few steel gated stores without seeing anyone, bumped into a few older men hanging out outside a bar another block east, and saw a single older woman across the street. This is what it feels to be vulnerable, I thought. This is how it feels to be scared.

After a couple more blocks, the urine on my jeans beginning to freeze, I heard someone say, "Mr. G," with both authority and confusion. It was Cesar, one of my students.

He was holding the door of a Laundromat open, gesturing me to come inside. His face evinced a look of sheer bewilderment. I followed him into the Laundromat and asked, probably slurred, "What are you doing here, Cesar?"

"I live here."

"No, in the Laundromat. It's almost two in the morning." Looking at my watch.

"I had to wash my mom's uniform. She didn't get home until about midnight and has to go to her other job in the morning and then right to her job after that, so needed a clean uniform. A better question is what are you doing up here, Mr. G?"

I replied with nothing but an empty, shame-filled stare. And a few tears. I even felt my lip quiver from cold and disgrace as Cesar looked at my wet jeans and got a sense of what was happening.

"Laundry's almost done. We can go back to my house and my uncle will drive you home."

We sat in silence, me hoping I didn't but knowing I did smell, and he nonchalantly finishing his math homework as though this sort of encounter happened all the time. The dryer buzzed a few minutes later. Cesar removed the light blue shirtdress and folded it expertly. It had "Broadway Commercial Cleaning" embroidered on the left chest, over a big sprawling cursive "B."

I walked with Cesar a few blocks back to his apartment, a six-story, brown brick building on 169th street, me in my piss-soaked jeans and sweater and barn jacket; Cesar in his jeans and white T-shirt and too-big black puffy coat. I waited in the vestibule as Cesar ran upstairs. The floor was littered with old mail, cigarette butts, dust balls. A few minutes later, Cesar and his uncle, a small man about my age, wearing Timberlands and a leather coat over a bathrobe, came outside. The uncle, extending his hand, introduced himself, "I'm Javier."

"Gary," I said, and shook Javier's hand, doing my best to convey some sort of authority, acting as though it wasn't nearly two a.m. and as though I wasn't his nephew's English teacher standing there in piss-soaked dungarees.

Javier looked at me with a friendly face that displayed no judgment. We walked about a block and stopped at a brown Monte Carlo, probably a late 1970s model, with a tiny Puerto Rican flag hanging from the rearview mirror. Cesar told me to get in front as he climbed in the back seat. We drove south; and we rode in silence. New York was still lit up like a Christmas tree, and the towers were visible in the distance. Presumably The Groove Bus was packing up their instruments. I asked, again as though the normal tenets of etiquette applied to the situation, what Javier did for a living.

"I am taking some classes at City College. In the meantime, just working for my uncle doing asbestos abatement."

"What kind of classes?"

"Working toward my degree in criminal justice. Hope to be a police officer and then work my way through law school."

It struck me that Javier was trying to impress me; me, the man who was sitting in piss-soaked dungarees in the passenger side of his car; the man who probably owed them his life; the man who seemed to know absolutely nothing about anything. The inherent absurdity and absurd unfairness of this struck me with some force, even then; even in that compromised state.

We crossed over one of the bridges onto Harlem River Drive. Javier asked where I lived and I mumbled, "East Eighty-sixth." I told Javier that the corner of York and Eighty-eighth just off the FDR was fine, but he said he'd be happy to take me home. For the first time, Cesar spoke, "Let him take you home, Mr. G."

I opened the large squeaky car door at the front of my building, turned around and shook Javier's and Cesar's hands, only later realizing that I had not washed my own since pissing myself. I thanked them and held the seat forward as Cesar climbed into the passenger seat. He put down a magazine over the wet spot I had left.

I took the elevator upstairs, took off my jeans, washed myself, put on my pajamas, and then went to the hallway, threw my jeans down the trash chute and then stealthily climbed into bed.

I was ready for work and out the door before my fiancée woke up. I walked the three blocks to school, checked my mailbox, made some photocopies (kids would be doing worksheets that day because I was hungover as fuck), then went to my classroom where I waited for the tumult of the day—and my demise—to begin.

Cesar nodded hello when he walked into class. No smile, no snicker, no indication that anything was amiss and certainly no indication that anyone else knew what had happened a few hours before. Because no one else did know what happened. Or ever would know what happened.

And I didn't say anything to Cesar.

Until the following week, on the last day of school before Christmas break. Cesar stayed after class to help me clean up.

We chatted about school stuff. He told me he wasn't looking forward to break because he was always alone. I stopped myself before I could thank him or provide any commentary on his neighborhood or strategies or coping mechanisms. I just let him talk.

This night is illustrative of how the lifelong dream of living in a big city can (and did) devolve into something I perceived as shameful.

The thing about having a grandpa who you see every day is that he stays with you for every day thereafter. Even in the midst of all the delinquency of the city. And when you have a propensity for shame, it makes you feel it doubly—the shame of knowing that your Grandpa would disapprove of such behavior, and the shame of knowing that you once thought your Grandpa was somehow lesser because he stayed in the country, when all you have done is move to the city and drink and be stupid.

The irony here, of course, was how, despite leaving the farm, life was still being measured in piss. The epiphany that much, if not all, of life can be, and typically is, measured in piss was jarring. On the farm, cow piss just becomes something with which you must deal—like a house fly or a runny nose or pollen. But it's piss. I don't think I ever got used to the way cows pissed—how they pissed in gallons; how they gave no warning before they pissed and sometimes the piss splashed on your legs and if you were wearing shorts you were getting splashed with real cow piss; how in the winter you could see the steam coming off of the piss. When I lived in New York City, on the city's Upper East Side, one of my favorite things to observe was when the wealthy ladies would walk—clearly on their way to a dinner party at Lee Radziwill's or David Rockefeller's house—and have to walk through piss to get there.[159] I loved the way the sophisticated coalesced with the repugnant. As a parent, so much of your existence is measured in piss – changing diapers and discourse about potty-training and secret judgments about the efficacy and timing of others' potty-training regimen and piss on the floor and piss on furniture.

So my "ascent" to urbanity was neither as profound nor as complete as I had thought. It was more like a circle from one epicenter of piss to the next. A circle of piss. Like a moat of piss around my house. Not really. But that did strike me that next morning. How much like a cow I was. Certainly, life in New York was less like the literary luminosity and sophistication for which I strived and more like the hopeless small-town depravity I was trying to escape.

It was an awful feeling: to yearn to be away from a place for your whole life, and then to be at the place for which you have yearned only to see and know that you are fucking it all up. I felt such shame.

I felt this for the first time in November 1994. One Sunday evening, I went to see Seal at the Orpheum with a girl I was dating—we will call her Lorraine—and a friend of Lorraine's from out of town—we will call her Shania. Before the concert, Lorraine and Shania were going to walk to my apartment; we were going to have a few drinks and then catch the Red Line from Davis Square to Downtown Crossing. Shania arrived very provocatively dressed. Lorraine explained to me that Shania likes to go to concerts and see if she can sleep with the performers.

We got wasted and went to the concert and yada yada

---

[159] To be sure, New York City piss was different than hometown, small town cow piss. It was blended with Madison Avenue water and sushi and Starbucks and the best bagels and the most interesting people and perfect pairings of red wines and steak.

yada Shania did not come home with us. Lorraine and I called into work on Monday—this being before the days of cell phones—to wait for word on if Shania was alive and, if so, where she was. At about ten a.m., a cab dropped Shania off at my apartment and yada yada yada Shania had fucked Seal.

I made drinks and the three of us talked all day about the events of the previous evening, the lovemaking positions Seal and Shania engaged in, Seal's penis, Seal's mouth, Seal's everything. At one point, I recall saying, "It's nearly two p.m. and we haven't even begun to talk about Seal's balls." It was fun.

I had just spoken to Grandpa, because I had just been to an exhibit at the Museum of Our National Heritage in Lexington the Sunday of the concert; an exhibit of items (old teddy bears, letters, half-drunk whiskey bottles, car keys, old photos, etc.) left at the Vietnam Veterans Memorial in Washington, D.C. I called Grandpa and Grandma to tell them about it. Talking to Grandpa and Grandma over the phone was always memorable because if we spent twenty minutes on the phone, fifteen of that would be spent talking about whose dime was being used for the call, how expensive the calls were, how if it were my dime I shouldn't be spending the dime on phone calls to them, I should be saving my dimes for a plane ticket home, etc. So Grandpa was on my mind.

Lorraine and Shania went back to Lorraine's apartment, and I, drunk and knowing that a horrific Tuesday was nigh, went to bed around eight o'clock. I remember lying in bed and feeling simultaneously proud of how I had moved out of my small town and was now hanging out with people who fucked Seal, but also really ashamed that I was not living a life of which Grandpa would be proud. Then I was all, "Who cares if Grandpa would be proud—it's my life?" but then: "But for some reason I do care. Even if I shouldn't, I do."

The Emperor of Ice-Cream

In many ways, my life is just one big giant episode of Aesop's "The Town Mouse and the Country Mouse." For two decades, I yearned to be in the city, and then I was, and I spent most of it sling-shotting myself toward self-destruction. City life fosters many things: empathy[160] and awareness; appreciation for and exposure to the arts; opportunities; independence; self-reliance. In me, it fostered all those things, plus an appreciation for the anonymity the city afforded. And the opportunities for malfeasance. The degree and intensity and shelf life of shame is directly proportional to how vigorously one takes advantage of the anonymity and opportunities for malfeasance. The shame that comes from having almost been decapitated while puking out of a cab while going down on your girlfriend; of passing out on the NYC subway and being discovered by one of your students; of passing out on the Boston T and being driven home from Alewife by strangers—people who can only be described as guardian angels. Several times. Smoking cigarettes through it all and thinking—not with every cigarette, but at least one time per twenty—how disappointed Grandpa would be in you if he saw you smoking.

So many nights—as I sat atop a milk crate outside the Dunkin' Donuts near my house, chain-smoking four to ten

---

160 In the days after the 2016 election, an article by David Wong on *Cracked* called "How Half of America Lost Its F**king Mind" went viral. It listed five reasons why the Donald Trump phenomenon was explicable not by red vs. blue but rural vs. urban, and it relied heavily on pop culture to make its case. "Every TV show is about L.A. or New York, maybe with some Chicago or Baltimore thrown in," he wrote from downstate Illinois. "When they did make a show about us, we were jokes—either wide-eyed, naive fluffballs (*Parks and Recreation*, and before that, *Newhart*) or filthy murderous mutants (*True Detective*, and before that, *Deliverance*). You could feel the arrogance from hundreds of miles away." That tension between city-dwellers and country-dwellers runs so high these days—and is so front and center in the political conversation— and informs and contributes to so much of what we do and think these days. *Empathy* is an oft-used term to describe this need for understanding.

cigarettes in a row—I thought he'd be ashamed of me. Grandpa never would have done any of this. And the shame sticks; and has stuck.

I make fun of the country life and their country ways. But they make casseroles for each other when they die; they see each other; they help each other with their cows and their hay and their corn and their barn building; they rollick in their Garth Brooks and Toby Keith and drink their shitty beer from beer trucks—there's a simplicity that is enviable. And a camaraderie, too.

I'm not that naïve to think that country living doesn't also foster its own brand of loneliness and isolation; of alcoholism and meth use and opioid addiction; of devastating poverty and hopelessness and other things people typically associate with city dwelling. And I often feel entitled to make fun of the obesity, the tattoos, the absurd devotion to Jesus, etc. because I grew up there. I am both a member of the coastal elite and a forest-dweller.

Again I find myself wondering if Grandpa was happy. Again, the myth is that he was always the happiest guy in any room he was ever in. He had a jovial laugh. He was always well-dressed—never abandoned hygiene or anything. Later, when he started drinking whiskey before doing anything to ostensibly stop his hands from shaking, I wondered if he was an alcoholic. (I don't think he was.) In so many ways living on a farm was enviable. In so many ways it is the perfect metaphor for life— you just do the best with what you have been given. Period. You rely on the rain and the sun and certain truths to be true; like when you plant a seed it will grow and if you work hard you will be rewarded. But you also have to be able to let go and hope that the truths hold true. When a catastrophe happens— and it likely will—you take a deep breath and you deal with it and you either restart or you move on. And whatever grows you enjoy. When you get a lot of corn you eat it and you drink the milk and the things you need for sustenance and when you see raspberries or blackberries and things that are sweet you better enjoy those also.[161]

One of my favorite stories to teach—indeed one of my favorite stories period—is "The Lesson" by Toni Cade Bambara. In it, a teacher named Miss Moore takes a group of around-ten-year-olds on a field trip from their Harlem neighborhood to F.A.O. Schwartz. Sylvia, the narrator, loathes Miss Moore and her preoccupation with making sure kids learn; more specifically, making sure kids learn about social and economic injustices. Sylvia's defiance and belligerence simultaneously mushrooms and erodes as they walk through F.A.O. Schwartz, examining sailboats and racecars and dolls that cost more than most of their families make in a year. Miss Moore leads them in a discussion of that question of whether where a person is determines who a person is.

It's a good question.

In some respects, yes: a person cannot escape the nomenclature, the attitudes, the limitations, of where they live. Grandpa used the N-word once. And while he was politically more advanced than most in the county, he still wanted the government off his land. (Though he did always wear his seatbelt—unlike my other Grandpa, who refused to wear a seatbelt once it became compulsory in New York State.[162])

But in others, no—Grandpa never succumbed to some of the other more nefarious characteristics of living in a small

---

[161] It's likely that every single occupation could serve as an appropriate metaphor for life. Firemen, cowboys, gastroenterologists, dentists, teachers, lawyers, pediatricians surely have their own metaphors for how they proceed through life.

[162] New York State passed the first law in the US mandating the use of seatbelts in 1984 under the leadership of John D. States, an orthopedic surgeon who dedicated his career to improving automotive safety. Seatbelt and airbag and general vehicle occupant restraint laws are now *de rigueur* in most states, but in 1984, it was a big deal.

town. He never chewed tobacco or thought it acceptable to leave rusty trucks in his front yard. He always brushed his teeth, and generally engaged in good personal hygiene.

So many things go into making who we are. Geography is only one part of it. You can despise something—a place, for instance—but it is still a part of you. *Where we are* is not necessarily all of *who we are*—but the *where* is absolutely a part of the *who*.

Just like every geographical area has its meteorological challenges, so too every way of life has to contend with challenges unique to it: the mangled limbs of farming; the infidelity of NYC. There is a certain amount of depravity and intolerance and danger and helplessness everywhere.[163]

But maybe the old proverb is right, the grass is just always greener on the other side of the fence.[164] We just yearn to be at an elsewhere.

---

[163] I've seen depravity in the law, too. I am at an age where many of my contemporaries have kids who are at an age where they get busted possessing marijuana. And I am in a position where many of those contemporaries meekly ask me to help them get their kids off. I have done this. I have done this for Caucasian friends. I have done this for a Caucasian friend who I later sat with at a meeting and listened while he excoriated the "urban youth" and called them "thugs."

[164] That reminds me that Grandpa and Grandma loved Erma Bombeck. They had her book, *The Grass is Always Greener Over the Septic Tank.*

The Boy in the Pernicious Penny Loafers

"The American Sublime"

How does one stand
To behold the sublime,
To confront the mockers,
The mickey mockers
And plated pairs?

When General Jackson
Posed for his statue
He knew how one feels.
Shall a man go barefoot
Blinking and blank?

But how does one feel?
One grows used to the weather,
The landscape and that;
And the sublime comes down
To the spirit itself,

The spirit and the space,
The empty space.
In vacant space.
What wine does one drink?
What bread does one eat?

— Wallace Stevens

Years from now, as I face the firing squad, I will remember that distant evening when my wife and I walked to the Upper West Side to observe the balloons. I will recall that one unseasonably warm November evening—Thanksgiving Eve, 1999, to be precise—when we headed out into the city from our apartment on East Eighty-first Street, walked through

248

Central Park to the Museum of Natural History, and observed the inflation of the balloons for the next day's Macy's Thanksgiving Day parade. We were newlyweds, married four months prior, and this was to be our first Thanksgiving in Manhattan. We found the entrance to the designated viewing path and along with about four zillion others intent on watching giant polyurethane Peanuts characters, the Honey Nut Cheerios Bee, Rocky and Bullwinkle, and Betty Boop get filled with helium.

There was a designated viewing path upon which spectators could perambulate and observe the balloons. Thousands of people, from every direction and with neuroses from every page of the DSM-IV, merged into the designated viewing path (hereafter "DVP") at its origin, like human tributaries toward a giant festive river of thanks; or like harvest vegetables falling out of a giant horn of plenty. Anyway, the DVP meandered through and among the helium inflation process for all of the balloons that were slated to float down Broadway the following day.

While in the DVP, meandering with my wife amid the autumnal reverie, I was kicked in the head by a boy riding atop his dad's shoulders. I saw him out of the corner of my eye. He didn't do it on purpose. It was just impossible to sit on top of your dad's shoulders and not have your feet head level with the person in front of you. I was soon kicked again and turned around to look the offenders in the eye. The boy was about three or four years old, a little too big to be riding atop his father's shoulders but in light of the circumstances, to wit, watching the Macy's Thanksgiving Day balloons being inflated, was not completely out of the realm of acceptable human behaviors. The boy was wearing penny loafers, argyle socks, brown cords, sweater, and puffy vest. The dad was dressed similarly, but with a shirt and tie and blazer. They both looked me in the eye and said nothing.

I turned back around. But with them on my radar screen I

began to listen to them. The boy's name was "Larken" and the dad would say it twice every time he said it. For example, "Look over there, Larken, it's Tommy Pickles from Rugrats, Larken," and, "Oh my gosh, Larken, it's the Cat in the Hat, Larken." These were all exclamations more than mere observations; as though each was being inflated exclusively for Larken's benefit and enjoyment.

After Larken kicked me in the head again, I turned around to confront him. The conversation went like so:

Me to Larken: "Larken, please stop kicking me in the head."

Larken's Dad (dumbfounded, as though no one had ever suggested Larken was anything but flawless in the history of Larken's short stupid life): "Larken isn't doing it on purpose."

Me to Dad: "Be that as it may, Larken still needs to stop."

Larken's Dad: "Be that as it may, I can't make his feet not touch you, buddy."

Me to Dad: "Yes, you can."

Dad to me: "I actually can't, buddy."

Me to Larken: "Quit it, Larken."

It was then that my brand-new wife pulled me forward and away from the conflict. I think she and the dad and probably Larken himself knew that I could have kicked Larken's fucking ass. I would have, too. Thanksgiving or no Thanksgiving; four years old or forty years old—I don't give a fuck. Anyway, we scurried through the DVP and away from Larken and his father. We probably missed the best balloons being inflated.

This event stays with me. I think about that fucking kid with greater frequency than is probably healthy. I don't do chin-ups while listening to Iron Maiden with the hope and expectation of one day exacting my revenge on Larken, but I do think about it nonetheless. Every Thanksgiving Eve in fact. (Along with the blessings and my children and the good lord above and the cornucopia and the blessings again and the joyfulness and the turkey.) Larken is about twenty-one years old today. Where is he? Does he go to an Ivy League school? Why is my second question, "Does he go to an Ivy League school?" Do I assume he is at an Ivy League school and, if so, why? Where does he live? Where did he live in November 1999? Did he and his mom take the train into the city to meet his dad after work? If so, from where? Connecticut? Pelham Manor? Larchmont? Manhasset? Some other gilded zip code?

Does he play sports? Lacrosse? Squash? Baseball? Does he still wear penny loafers? Do he and his family still visit the DVP on Thanksgiving Eve to watch the balloons being inflated? (And kick other unsuspecting patrons in the head, I'm sure.) I thought about him shortly after September 11, 2001. I guess he was still stewing in my brain two years later. Had he lost anyone he loved? If so, who? Was he scared? Ambivalent? What the hell kind of name is *Larken*, anyway? What would happen if I googled and researched and re-googled the fuck out of the scant information I have on Larken—would I be able to locate him? Do his parents love him? Does he have siblings? Is he loved? When did he lose his virginity? Is he gay? Straight? Bi? Out? Transgendered? Is he a birther? An anti-vaxxer? A vegan?

I am learning that I have a very low tolerance for people who were born on third base. I have zero tolerance for people who were born on third and think they hit a triple, but some tolerance for those merely born on third. I am assuming that Larken was born on third base; probably a safe assumption, in light of the fact he was wearing penny loafers and nice cords and a nice shirt and had a dad who was also similarly attired and who looked at me with eyes which registered nary a thought or a hint of analysis or a modicum of a possibility that he would ever apologize. How corrosive is this lack of tolerance? I am starting to wonder; particularly in light of recent events where we have seen some kids of a famous father who genuinely think that they are better (genetically, intellectually better) than other

251

people. And that really bothers me. More succinctly, it is an injustice. I was in New York teaching kids, many of them sons and daughters of undocumented workers, who took the subway over an hour each way to and from school, to go home and take care of their siblings, do their laundry, and cook their own meals while the parents worked. The third-base kids could not last a day doing that.

When we were little, we had a plaque of an old Native American proverb hanging on our kitchen wall. It said: "Grant that I may not criticize my neighbor until I have walked a mile in his moccasins." This hung near the heating register over which we stood on winter mornings to get warm, so it was the subject of a great deal of analysis. "Mom, if you walk a mile in the neighbor's moccasins, then do you have to walk back to give the moccasins back to the neighbor?" "What if you and your neighbor have different-sized feet?" "Who wears moccasins in Buffalo in January?" "What if it's raining and you ruin the neighbor's moccasins?" Later, whilst teaching English in the very city where Larken kicked me, I taught *To Kill a Mockingbird* and highlighted the passage, "You never really know a man until you understand things from his point of view, until you climb in his skin and walk around in it."

I don't hate Larken. I don't think I do, anyway. I don't know for certain that he is an asshole, but the warning signs were there in November 1999. It's not his fault his parents named him Larken, bought him penny loafers and a puffy vest for toddlers. Or neglected to tell him to stop kicking people in the head when he did so. But I have never walked a mile in his moccasins. Or his steel-toed penny loafers of torment, as it were. And while the Native American proverb is silent as to penny loafers, it would seem that it might be applicable. Luckily—for all of us—empathy is a learned skill.

There were a few painful lessons from that day. I learned that there are two types of people: people whose parents would defend them for kicking someone in the head with penny loafers; who would call anyone alleging their child was less than perfect "buddy"; people not afraid to be belligerent. And there were people whose parents would admonish them for kicking someone in the head with penny loafers; who taught their kids to apologize, and to not be entitled. I learned I was the latter.

I also learned that no matter how hard I tried, I would never be those people. They were bred to be superior. They knew they were superior. They knew they were entitled to things. They carried themselves differently. Something happened that night. When you realize that that for which you have aspired for decades is invariably and indubitably beyond reach, you change. Such epiphanies happen rarely. There was the one I had in 1985 when I was a sophomore in high school and realized that I would never be popular since I did not play football and did not drink. And there was that time on my 35th birthday when I realized I would never be POTUS. I understand that this sounds like self-pity. Maybe it is. I shouldn't complain. I'm a successful attorney. But still not the sort of attorney who paces back and forth in front of a jury box during a rousing closing argument; or one whose Porsche screeches to a halt at the courthouse steps with new evidence to stop the execution; or one who wears sassy red blazers to hold a news conference with Scott Peterson's mistress, Amber Fry.

The Lawyer in the Two-Thousand Dollar Coat

"The Snow Man"

One must have a mind of winter
To regard the frost and the boughs
Of the pine-trees crusted with snow;

And have been cold a long time
To behold the junipers shagged with ice,
The spruces rough in the distant glitter

Of the January sun; and not to think
Of any misery in the sound of the wind,
In the sound of a few leaves,

Which is the sound of the land
Full of the same wind
That is blowing in the same bare place

For the listener, who listens in the snow,
And, nothing himself, beholds
Nothing that is not there and the nothing that is.

—Wallace Stevens

In preparation for their eventual demise, Grandpa and Grandma started giving their things away decades before their actual demise. In their defense, it's true that you never know when your time is up, and therefore you can never start giving your things away too early.

Whenever something no longer fit Grandpa, they would ask my brother or me if we wanted it. Most of the time, we would take it and then give it away to Goodwill ourselves.

254

Occasionally, I would find a tie I would wear. There was one I wore throughout college—an art deco design, half gold and half brown—that looked great with a brown tweed blazer I had.

We were back in Buffalo for Christmas 2002. Grandpa came over and brought a long wool coat that no longer fit him. It was uncharacteristically formal. He, not Grandma, asked me if I wanted it. He said that, as a lawyer, I would probably need a fancy winter coat. I tried it on, and it fit. It was wool, a dark navy blue herringbone pattern. It was fully lined with silk and had these marbleized buttons. There was an abundance of pockets—both interior and exterior pockets—and all were lined and had their own button or zipper. I said to Grandpa, "This is a really nice coat, Grandpa, it must've cost you a fortune." He said, "It did." I asked him how much, and he replied, "In 1942, I paid a hundred dollars for this coat."

The story, as Grandpa told it, was that in the winter of 1942 he had to euthanize and bury an entire herd of cows due to some disease. It took him days of working nonstop, with no sleep, to put a gun to the head of each cow, kill it, and then bury it. He took out a loan to buy a new herd of cows. There was some money left, and with it, he bought this wool coat for $100. Hearing of this lavishness, this splurge of which he was unashamed, this indulgence, this excess, made me very happy.

I told him that $100 in 1942 was probably like $2,000 today.[165] He agreed and said, "I just really wanted the coat. I had been so cold taking care of the cows. I never wanted to be cold again."

I wondered later, upon learning of Grandpa's Aunt Margaret and how she married Frank Scalia and moved to New York City and came back at least one time in a fancy car, if this

---

[165] In fact, according to the American Institute for Economic Research's cost of living calculator, $100 in 1942 was the equivalent of $1,118.75 in 2002. It is the equivalent of $1,512.50 in 2017.

coat was a reaction to the Scalias. And a frustration with place. It might have been.[166]

Despite the fact that winters in Baltimore are relatively mild as compared to winters in Buffalo, I took the coat home. In December 2003, I interviewed with a Baltimore City Circuit Court judge for a 2004–2005 clerkship. It snowed the day before the interview. I said to myself, "If I wear Grandpa's coat to the interview, I am going to get the job." And I did. The coat is a little long; it's adorned in such a manner so as to make me feel like a sentry for George Washington's winter quarters at Valley Forge, or the singer in the video for Pet Shop Boys' "West End Girls" video.

The label says, "Executive Group" tailored in Rochester "Bond Clothiers." Bond Clothiers was a men's clothing retailer—the largest one in the United States in the 1930s and 1940s—which also had its manufacturing center in Rochester, NY.

Riding home on the bus from the circuit court interview, I imagined him driving to Rochester, the smell of gunpowder and dead cows still lingering in his nostrils; the sinking vulnerability that must have come with taking out a loan while having a pregnant wife at home; the chill of that winter still in his bones. I imagined him triumphantly walking into this Bond Clothiers store and feeling the feelings that come with triumphantly walking into a clothing store and buying a coat that will keep you warm for the rest of your life.

And then I tell myself again that he gave the coat to me.

---

[166] Someday I will splurge for an Ancestry.com account and find out about the Scalias. Aunt Margaret will likely have great-grandchildren my age. If she's related to Antonin Scalia I. Will. Lose. It.

Gary M. Almeter

The Farmer in the Tuxedo

"Man and Bottle"

The mind is the great poem of winter, the man,
Who, to find what will suffice,
Destroys romantic tenements
Of rose and ice

In the land of war. More than the man, it is
A man with the fury of a race of men,
A light at the center of many lights,
A man at the center of men.

It has to content the reason concerning war,
It has to persuade that war is part of itself,
A manner of thinking, a mode
Of destroying, as the mind destroys.

An aversion, as the world is averted
From an old delusion, an old affair with the sun,
An impossible aberration with the moon,
A grossness of peace.

It is not the snow that is the quill, the page.
The poem lashes more fiercely than the wind,
As the mind, to find what will suffice, destroys
Romantic tenements of rose and ice.

—Wallace Stevens

We found the photo while making preparations for my
parents' fortieth wedding anniversary.[167] It wasn't in their

---

[167] There is a version of this photo in my office. Once my assistant brought in some
very important papers for me to sign and while she stood by my desk and waited

257

wedding album and thus wasn't part of the wedding photo oeuvre with which we were familiar. That oeuvre was filled with bridesmaids and flowers and poses and streamers. This photo is square with a white border and the date printed in brown letters in a font that no one uses anymore. This photo was in a photo album of snapshots people gave them after their wedding—a photo album that my siblings and I had never seen. At this point, Grandpa was in a nursing home. He had been given last rites six months prior. When we visited him, we were never quite certain what he understood and how much of what was going on; we couldn't be sure if his laughter was an acknowledgment of something we had said, or just some sort of remnant of cognition.

In the photo, Grandpa stares directly at the camera. He is neither smiling nor is he serious. He is holding a sweaty beer bottle. He is holding it to his face and for the camera, as if to emphasize the notion that he is celebrating, is at a celebration. The amber bottle catches the lights from the fireman's hall and the lights dance on the glass.

It's one of those brown beer bottles, ubiquitous in the sixties and seventies but that disappeared for a while until recently, when it has returned with the onslaught of craft breweries. We do not know what kind of beer Grandpa is drinking because the bottle is turned so that the label is on the reverse side.[168] This does not appear to be intentional—like in

---

for me to thumb through all the pages where she had affixed those yellow and red "Sign Here" post-it tabs, she pointed to the photo and said, "Is that George Clooney?" I said, "Now, why the fuck would I have a framed picture of George Clooney in my office?" and she laughed because that is the sort of relationship we have, but I did think later that I need to be kinder to my assistant and maybe not curse so much. But this isn't about me. Then I told her about Grandpa.

(This is also the footnote where I realize that this book is all about me.)

168 Note to self, ask Mom and Dad what kind of beer they served at their wedding.

old TV shows when they couldn't advertise certain products, or like how in the Road Runner and Coyote cartoons everything the Coyote ordered was from a store called Acme, this before the day when product placement became so profitable. And how now James Bond drives BMWs. And E.T. ate Reese's Pieces.

In the photo, Grandpa is wearing a tuxedo. One of the rare times he did. It's a classic tuxedo like the kind you see men wear at the Oscars. The only time I personally witnessed him wearing a tuxedo in person was when his daughter, my Aunt Karen, got married in 1976.[169] His tux was brown, and he had a ruffled shirt with brown trim on all the ruffles. In this picture, the tux is black and his tie is tied flawlessly, and he is wearing cufflinks and a carnation boutonniere. If I close my eyes and am silent for a minute, I can hear Grandma telling him the right way to tie a bowtie and insert cufflinks and attach a boutonniere. I wonder if the bowtie is pre-tied, and I really hope it's not; one of those signs of sophistication he must have simultaneously eschewed and revered. I just want to know that he tied the tie himself, because I can picture Grandpa's face when he successfully tied the bowtie; but also because I know I've made fun of pre-tied bowties before, and I don't want to feel guilty for doing that anymore. His hair is gelled (though in those days, they surely called it something else—pomaded or greased). And the part is perfect; somewhere between a center part and a side part. His expression indicates something between joy and pride.

---

169 That wedding was fun. My cousins and I hung out on the dance floor and watched Cousin Cheryl and my sister Kris twirl around in their dresses. Two days before that wedding, I flipped my bike while riding it to Grandpa and Grandma's and got a cut on my forehead that required three stitches and a huge bandage. I felt like a rock star at the wedding with a huge bandage on my forehead. And my brother and I wore matching blue suits with big light blue buttons over flap closures. We wore shiny polyester shirts—mine was brown and his was red—with an intricate pattern of race cars and curvy roads all over them.

He's not wearing glasses, and this makes him look different. He wore the same pair of glasses—gold frames and square lenses with a slight brown tint and profound demarcations of varying degrees of magnification. Without his glasses, he looks younger and slightly less affable. He doesn't look drunk. I never asked him about drinking.

In the photo, he is young. I cannot see the meandering veins in his hands or the network of wrinkles in his earlobes that I thought were so beguiling and so beautiful when I was a kid. Grandpa was fifty-four years old in the photo. I have friends who are on the cusp of fifty-four now, and I wonder how they would be as Grandpas. The notion is laughable. They do not have the same gravitas and wit and wisdom and confidence and adeptness and self-deprecation. It is unlikely this will be so. This is not to disparage my friends, who are lovely people; it's just that my Grandpa was particularly good at grandfathering and did the sort of grandfathering that I associate with excellence. I suspect that men develop their own blends—with varying degrees and proportions of affability and humor and kindness and tolerance and selflessness.

The photo makes me think of my parents' wedding. What it must have been like; who got drunk; who danced with who; what sort of music they played. I know my parents' first dance was "More" by Andy Williams. We used to tease Mom and Dad because in photos of the wedding, it looks like they had a potluck dinner at their reception; an unfathomable idea and yet one to which no one of that era would have objected. It's practical. It's communal. In the photos, there is myriad Tupperware serving dishes in various colors with lots of three-bean salads[170] and Jell-O salads and fruits encased in Jell-O and chicken à la king and dips made from Lipton onion soup and then stuffed into celery and the who-the-fuck-knows-what-else.

---

[170] Why the three-bean salads? Because again, five-bean salads would have been far too decadent for these country folk—even at a wedding.

A potluck wedding is just the sort of thing that a country village like the one in which your parents got married would have. Though they deny that they required guests to bring a dish to pass at their wedding, we have photographic evidence of people so doing.

Before my parents' fortieth anniversary party, we took the photo to Kinko's. They blew it up to a poster size and affixed it to white foam board. We set this gargantuan version of the photo atop the table with the boxes of wine and the brown bottles of beer like the one in the photo. It was as though Grandpa was there instead of the nursing home. It was nice, this oversized remembrance of a man with an oversized personality; a reminder of a day and a man and how happy everyone was.

It's what happiness looks like.

Do we struggle through the world as it is? Or do we choose our own lives? The answer is both—to varying and impermanent and arbitrary degrees.

Echomimetic[171]

"Phosphor Reading By His Own Light"

It is difficult to read. The page is dark.
Yet he knows what it is that he expects.

The page is blank or a frame without a glass
Or a glass that is empty when he looks.

The greenness of night lies on the page and goes
Down deeply in the empty glass ...

Look, realist, not knowing what you expect.
The green falls on you as you look,

Falls on and makes and gives, even a speech.
And you think that that is what you expect,

That elemental parent, the green night,
Teaching a fusky alphabet.

—Wallace Stevens

I have this other photo of Grandpa, one of the last ever

---

[171] *Echomimetic* is an adjective that is best explained in English by the term "onomatopoeia," which is used in philology and literature and in the explanation of the origin of words in dictionaries. Onomatopoeia is a word that phonetically imitates, resembles, or suggests the sound that it describes. In modern Greek lexicography, the term onomatopoeia is virtually nonexistent, and the words of which the etymology it describes are almost always designated as echomimetic. The "echo" of echomimetic comes from Greek ἦχος which means "sound." Mimetic comes from Greek μιμητικός, meaning "imitating." Examples of echomimetic words in English are "bow wow," "buzz," "squeak," and "squeal."

taken of him, where he is reading a book about animals to my eighteen-month-old son.

In the photo, Grandpa is looking downward to read the animal book, so I can see that his hair is full and flowy and white with a metallic, silvery hue. I always thought I would have hair like that because whenever I went to the barber, the barber would almost always exclaim how thick and full my hair was, and I was so proud of that, and then in my forties I am realizing that I'm losing my hair at such a rate as to make the sort of hair Grandpa had an impossibility.

My son is looking at his great-grandpa with a mix of fear and wonder. And curiosity. As though looking for his own reflection, a reflection more overt than he knows. Grandpa is wearing a thick flannel shirt under a thick wool cardigan, and one must wonder how a person could be so cold indoors. Grandpa is reading with gusto. And pride. His lips are in a shape that human lips only make when they are endeavoring to replicate an animal noise. It could be the hoot of an owl, or it could be a generic "ooooh" as a general statement of astonishment, but it is most likely a moo. Frankly, I hope it's a moo.

Two of my kids would meet two of their great-grandpas. They call one "the Great Grandpa who kills animals" because that great-grandpa gave my son a pair of deer antlers for Christmas one year. They call the great-grandpa in this photo "the Great Grandpa who was in the nursing home," because that is where and how they knew him; I want them to know he is more than that. I drive them by the farmhouse in which I grew up to show them the pool that Grandpa built and the barn that held the cows and the garage and the house with the kitchen where Grandpa installed the tile floor with the yellow stripe around the perimeter at Grandma's behest—but then I find the house is dilapidated, the pool has crumbled and is brimming with mud and thorny shrubs and muck, the trees under which we drank beer and lemonade and under which

The Emperor of Ice-Cream

Grandpa opened a nettlesome fortune cookie are either dead or no longer there. It's barely a house at all. My kids see someone in the kitchen window looking at us. They scream and say the man in the window wants to eat us. He probably does. But only after he slathers us all with rancid ketchup. So I drive away.

In the photo, it is apparent that somebody set my son in his great-grandpa's lap and that was probably me, because it is very important that they know him. When my dad gives me things from Grandpa's house and I can smell Grandpa, I quickly put the thing under my kids' noses and invite them to sniff so that they can smell it too. Just so they know what I am talking about when I talk about this smell.

It's still astonishing to me how that smell lingers—a blend of mothballs and antiseptic salves and chlorine and hay and beer and those soaps with names that once evoked toughness and notes of grease and mildew and exhaust from a big-ass Pontiac Bonneville and special dirts from places out west and lace crocheted by hand and kept in a cedar chest and lavender and ice cream and instant coffee and pickled cauliflower and bushel baskets stained by strawberries picked by hand and Listerine and cow and work and all the dampness shaken off wet plastic rain bonnets. All of it still lingers.

Gary M. Almeter

Acknowledgments

Big booming thanks to the crew at Unsolicited Press, Rubie Grayson, Summer Stewart and my incredible editor Chandler S. White. Forgive the semi-colon; but you guys literally make dreams come true. Thundering thanks to Andrew Almeter for cover design and Rachel Rock Palermo for photo.

Ear-splitting thanks to the astounding group of Baltimore writers and creators who helped in so many ways, Rafael Alvarez, Matthew Norman, Kathy Flann, Jennifer Grow, Reese Cassard, John Benam, Jessica Myles Henkin, and John Waire.

Clangorous gratitude to Daniel Ford and Josh Mohr and Kirby Gann and Matt Burgess and Jerry Gabriel and Christopher Monks and Brian Agler and James Folta and Jason Rekulak and Marty Dundics and lots of people who, in the ordinary course of business, provided vast and necessary encouragement. They probably didn't even realize they were doing so.

Deafening thanks and a standing ovation to my teachers, Joe McShane and Paula Donnelly[172] and Richard Blake for being so exceptional.

A painted wooden sign with glued-on shells that says "Thanks" to the cousins, Tim, Cheryl, Lisa, and Darren for being so sassy. Resounding thanks to all the aunts for sharing

---

[172] One day, in a fifth-grade classroom in 1980, Paula Donnelly was grading papers while we, her students, did seat work. Suddenly, Mrs. Donnelly stopped what she was doing, got everyone's attention, and declared, "I have a question for Gary." Then she asked, "Gary are there times when you sit down with a pen in your hand and feel like you just **have to** write something?" I replied in the affirmative. Then she said, "Well it shows. Listen to this sentence class." And then she read my sentence for everyone. It was about Lewis and Clark. And I have never ever forgotten that moment. I don't think I ever said thank you to Mrs. Donnelly. She was always doing stuff like that.

their dad and their stories with us. Doug Supernaw-sized thanks to Jeff, Kris and Benjamin Lukens for conceptualizing and executing and sharing all the adventures.

A blare of trumpets and a chorus of angels singing "Thank you" to the tune of Handel's Hallelujah Chorus to Dan and Kathy for being good and kind and generous and selfless and creative and encouraging and forgiving and patient and authentic and loving and fun and funny and likable.

Exuberant, carved into cedar or mahogany sort of thanks to Elliott for asking me what my goals were and for not laughing when my answer was insufficient and then for helping me identify new ones. Hearty thanks to all the Sturtevants for housing and helping me.

Colossal thanks to the Malgosza, Ho Chi Minh, Deborah Chantel, Moshkan Bedoya, and Beastie for doing all their wonderful stuff that will be the wonderful memories of tomorrow. They are all in my field of vision while I write this. Ho Chi and Deborah are arguing about whose turn it is to unload the dishes. Malgosza is complaining about the smell of dog pee in the living room. Moshkan is wheeling a toy shopping cart up the stairs. Beastie is sniffing for that certain wayward Cheerio under the dining room table. It's chaos. It's beautiful. It really does smell like pee. But it's home. And it's a miracle.

About the Author

Gary M. Almeter grew up on a small dairy farm in Western New York, about 300 child-sized steps from his Grandpa's house, where ice cream - usually Maple Walnut or Butter Pecan - was always available. He is now an attorney whose short stories, essays and humor pieces have appeared in McSweeney's Internet Tendency, 1966, Splitsider, Verdad, and Writer's Bone. In addition to winning his 8th grade spelling bee, he has been awarded numerous awards for his non-fiction, including the Maryland Writers Association's Best Essay award in 2015. Gary has a B.A. in English from Le Moyne College; an M.Ed. in Secondary Education from Boston College; and a J.D. from the University of Maryland. He currently lives in Baltimore, MD, about 300 adult-sized steps from the best ice cream shop in Baltimore, with his wife, three children, beagle, and numerous deferred domestic projects.

About the Press

Unsolicited Press was founded in 2012 and is based in Portland, Oregon. The press produces stellar fiction, nonfiction, and poetry from award-winning writers. Learn more at www.unsolicitedpress.com.

9 781947 021822